MATTHEW MATTERS

The Didsbury Lectures
Series Preface

The Didsbury Lectures, delivered annually at Nazarene Theological College, Manchester, are now a well-established feature on the theological calendar in Britain. The lectures are planned primarily for the academic and church community in Manchester but through their publication have reached a global readership.

The name "Didsbury Lectures" was chosen for its double significance. Didsbury is the location of Nazarene Theological College, but it was also the location of Didsbury College (sometimes known as Didsbury Wesleyan College), established in 1842 for training Wesleyan Methodist ministers.

The Didsbury Lectures were inaugurated in 1979 by Professor F. F. Bruce. He was followed annually by highly regarded scholars who established the series' standard. All have been notable for making high calibre scholarship accessible to interested and informed listeners.

The lectures give a platform for leading thinkers within the historic Christian faith to address topics of current relevance. While each lecturer is given freedom in choice of topic, the series is intended to address topics that traditionally would fall into the category of "Divinity." Beyond that, the college does not set parameters. Didsbury lecturers, in turn, have relished the privilege of engaging in the dialogue between church and academy.

Most Didsbury lecturers have been well-known scholars in the United Kingdom. From the start, the college envisaged the series as a means by which it could contribute to theological discourse between the church and the academic community more widely in Britain and abroad. The publication is an important part of fulfilling that goal. It remains the hope and prayer of the College that each volume will have a lasting and positive impact on the life of the church, and in the service of the gospel of Christ.

1979	Professor F. F. Bruce†	*Men and Movements in the Primitive Church*
1980	The Revd Professor I. Howard Marshall†	*Last Supper and Lord's Supper*
1981	The Revd Professor James Atkinson†	*Martin Luther: Prophet to the Church Catholic*
1982	The Very Revd Professor T. F. Torrance†	*The Mediation of Christ*
1983	The Revd Professor C. K. Barrett†	*Church, Ministry and Sacraments in the New Testament*
1984	The Revd Dr A. R. G. Deasley	*The Shape of Qumran Theology*
1985	Dr Donald P. Guthrie†	*The Relevance of John's Apocalypse*
1986	Professor A. F. Walls	*The Nineteenth-Century Missionary Movement***
1987	The Revd Dr A. Skevington Wood†	*Reason and Revelation*
1988	The Revd Professor Morna D. Hooker	*Not Ashamed of the Gospel: New Testament Interpretations of the Death of Christ*

1989	The Revd Professor Ronald E. Clements	*Wisdom in Theology*
1990	The Revd Professor Colin E. Gunton†	*Christ and Creation*
1991	The Revd Professor J. D. G. Dunn†	*Christian Liberty: A New Testament Perspective*
1992	The Revd Dr P. M. Bassett	*The Spanish Inquisition***
1993	Professor David J. A. Clines	*The Bible in the Modern World*
1994	The Revd Professor James B. Torrance†	*Worship, Community, and the Triune God of Grace*
1995	The Revd Dr R. T. France†	*Women in the Church's Ministry*
1996	Professor Richard Bauckham	*God Crucified: Monotheism and Christology in the New Testament*
1997	Professor H. G. M. Williamson	*Variations on a Theme: King, Messiah and Servant in the Book of Isaiah*
1998	Professor David Bebbington	*Holiness in Nineteenth Century England*
1999	Professor L. W. Hurtado†	*At the Origins of Christian Worship*
2000	Professor Clark Pinnock†	*The Most Moved Mover: A Theology of God's Openness*
2001	Professor Robert P. Gordon	*Holy Land, Holy City: Sacred Geography and the Interpretation of the Bible*
2002	The Revd Dr Herbert McGonigle†	*John Wesley***
2003	Professor David F. Wright†	*What Has Infant Baptism Done to Baptism? An Enquiry at the End of Christendom*
2004	The Very Revd Dr Stephen S. Smalley	*Hope for Ever: The Christian View of Life and Death*
2005	The Rt Revd Professor N. T. Wright	*Surprised by Hope*
2006	Professor Alan P. F. Sell†	*Nonconformist Theology in the Twentieth Century*
2007	Dr Elaine Storkey	*Sin and Social Relations***
2008	Dr Kent E. Brower	*Living as God's Holy People: Holiness and Community in Paul*
2009	Professor Alan Torrance	*Religion, Naturalism, and the Triune God: Confronting Scylla and Charybdis***
2010	Professor George Brooke	*The Dead Sea Scrolls and Christians Today***
2011	Professor Nigel Biggar	*Between Kin and Cosmopolis: An Ethic of the Nation*
2012	Dr Thomas A. Noble	*Holy Trinity: Holy People: The Theology of Christian Perfecting*
2013	Professor Gordon Wenham	*Rethinking Genesis 1–11*
2014	Professor Frances Young	*Construing the Cross: Type, Sign, Symbol, Word, Action*
2015	Professor Elaine Graham	*Apologetics without Apology*
2016	Professor Michael J. Gorman	*Missional Theosis in the Gospel of John*
2017	Professor Philip Alexander & Professor Loveday Alexander	*Priesthood and Sacrifice in the Epistle to the Hebrews*
2018	Professor Markus Bockmuehl	
2019	Professor Michael Lodahl	*Matthew Matters: The Yoke of Wisdom and the Church of Tomorrow*
2020	Professor John Swinton	*Moving beyond the Empire of Illusion: What Do We Do about the Problem of Evil?*
2021	Professor John M. G. Barclay	

*** unpublished*

Matthew Matters

The Yoke of Wisdom and the Church of Tomorrow

THE DIDSBURY LECTURES

MICHAEL LODAHL

CASCADE *Books* • Eugene, Oregon

MATTHEW MATTERS
The Yoke of Wisdom and the Church of Tomorrow

Didsbury Lectures Series

Copyright © 2021 Michael Lodahl. All rights reserved. Except for brief quotations in critical publications or reviews, no part of this book may be reproduced in any manner without prior written permission from the publisher. Write: Permissions, Wipf and Stock Publishers, 199 W. 8th Ave., Suite 3, Eugene, OR 97401.

Cascade Books
An Imprint of Wipf and Stock Publishers
199 W. 8th Ave., Suite 3
Eugene, OR 97401

www.wipfandstock.com

PAPERBACK ISBN: 978-1-7252-6114-3
HARDCOVER ISBN: 978-1-7252-6113-6
EBOOK ISBN: 978-1-7252-6115-0

Cataloging-in-Publication data:

Names: Lodahl, Michael E., 1955–, author

Title: Matthew matters : the yoke of wisdom and the church of tomorrow / Michael Lodahl.

Description: Eugene, OR : Cascade Books, 2021 | Series: Didsbury Lectures | Includes bibliographical references and index.

Identifiers: ISBN 978-1-7252-6114-3 (paperback) | ISBN 978-1-7252-6113-6 (hardcover) | ISBN 978-1-7252-6115-0 (ebook)

Subjects: LCSH: Bible.—Matthew—Criticism, interpretation, etc. | Wisdom (Biblical personification). | Wisdom—Biblical teaching.

Classification: LCC BS2575.5 L63 2021 (print) | LCC BS2575.5 (ebook)

For Reuben Welch:
"Have you understood all this?"
They answered,
"Yes."

And he said to them,
"Therefore every scribe who has been trained
for the kingdom of heaven
is like the master of a household
who brings out of his treasure
what is new and what is old."
(*Matthew 13:51–52*)

Table of Contents

Preface xi

1. Wisdom's Invitation 1
2. Wisdom's Desire 17
3. Wisdom's Commands 33
4. Wisdom's Love for All 50
5. Wisdom and Foolishness 66
6. Upon This Rock (Wisdom's Risk) 81
7. Wisdom's Presence 97
8. Hardened Hearts (Wisdom's Concession) 113
9: Wisdom's Commission 128
10: Wisdom's Community 146

Bibliography 161
Name/Subject Index 165
Scripture Index 168

Preface

THE FACT THAT MATTHEW matters took me by surprise.

Back in the ancient days before we stored documents and sermons and other such things electronically on our computers or flash drives or somewhere in a cloud, I—like pretty much everyone else—kept everything in manila folders. Perhaps you can still picture them. After preaching a sermon—those written both during times when I served as a pastor preaching weekly (almost all of the 1980s) and when I was either an interim pastor or doing pulpit supply (all the rest of the time!)—I would stuff my sermon notes into folders designated by biblical book. I had, for example, a Genesis file, an Exodus file, a Lamentations file, and a Habakkuk file. (In my early years of ministry, I preached a sermon series each on Lamentations and Habakkuk—in case entire files on these books require any explanation.) Not surprisingly, my New Testament files were more fully stuffed: Romans, 1 Corinthians, 2 Corinthians, John, Hebrews, and so on. Because in my tradition our general practice does not include following the lectionary, I was blissfully free from such constraints (or such accountability).

But it was quite a few years into my life as a preacher that I eventually noticed, one day, just how fat my file of Matthew sermon notes had become. I hadn't intended it to be that way, certainly. But there it was, a well-worn and bulging manila file, tattered at the edges and fairly bursting at its seam with Matthean proclamation. That may have been the first moment that I said to myself, "I guess Matthew *matters*."

In the decades that have followed this discovery, my conviction that Matthew matters has only grown more fervent and determined. I have preached abundantly in many churches from Matthew's Gospel, and in those churches I have promised that one day there would be a book entitled

PREFACE

Matthew Matters—and that, further, I would acknowledge my gratitude to those churches for allowing me the honor of preaching to them on these Matthean matters. I am grateful that, finally, I can make good on that promise! So I offer my heartfelt gratitude first to the faithful farmers (and their friends) of Franklin Community Church of Nampa, Idaho; then to San Diego area Nazarene congregations in Spring Valley, Linda Vista, and El Cajon; then to Hemet Church of the Nazarene up there in the desert lands east of Los Angeles; and finally also to St. Timothy Lutheran Church in San Diego, where I have been privileged to serve as part-time teaching pastor for the past seven years. For all of you good folks, faithfully following Jesus, I am thankful.

I should add, however, that the following chapters are not sermons, though of course some matters about which I have preached are included. Nor is this book a commentary. Rather, it is an argument that Matthew matters because of some of the important teachings of Jesus (and *about* Jesus) that are unique to Matthew's Gospel. There is material encountered only in Matthew for which, were it not in our Bibles, we would experience significant impoverishment of our faith. Further, at least some of this material unique to Matthew deserves fresh attention precisely because it hasn't been getting much. I hope this book will help to address this lack because, as I hint in this volume's subtitle, the future shape, life, and health of the *ekklesia*—the Greek term for "church" found only in Matthew, of all of our Gospels—may well depend on it.

Because this is not a commentary, there is plenty in Matthew that I do not address here. This is a selective endeavor. I have chosen ten passages/themes that, in addition to being unique to Matthew's Gospel, are the most critical to a contemporary interpretation of Christian faith and practice. My choice of ten themes (and thus ten chapters) is an intentional homage to Matthew's creative arrangement of Jesus's teachings into five substantial blocks of teaching material (chapters 5–7, 10, 13, 18, 24–25). New Testament scholars generally agree in suggesting that Matthew's five teaching passages were crafted to mirror the five books of the Torah—in itself, of course, a recognizably Jewish move. In composing ten chapters I have doubled those five as a mirror of the Ten Commandments issued through Moses to the people of Israel (Exod 20:1–17). Since the commandments—whether we mean the Ten given at Sinai or the 613 the rabbinic tradition tabulated in the Torah—are given with human obedience in mind, we return to the deep concern of both Judaism and Christianity (especially

Preface

as framed by Matthew) that *concrete, everyday human action in the world is of critical importance.*

★ ★ ★

In addition to stuffing that manila folder with so many sermons from Matthew, I have taught from Matthew's Gospel repeatedly for pastoral continuing education events at Point Loma Nazarene University in San Diego, where I am privileged to serve as a professor of theology. I have also told *them*—pastors and pastoral staff members from across the Southwest and beyond—that a book called *Matthew Matters* would someday be forthcoming, and at least a couple of them never fail to remind me of this. Among these pastors, to whom I owe a great debt for their kindness, friendship, and support, I mention particularly Mark Lehman, Sonya Brown, Gary Reynolds, Vanessa Hernandez, Scott Pryor, Chris Archer, Laura Duckworth, Loretta Huff-Herrera, Eloisa Rudeen, Trevor Cartwright, David Edwards, Karla Sanchez-Renfro, M'Lynn Martin, Hank and Maria Allyn, Tim and Shawna Songer Gaines, and Jeff and Angela Compton Nelson.

Most importantly, the occasion that finally provided me the impetus to write this book was the invitation to deliver the 2019 Didsbury Lectures at Nazarene Theological College, a vibrant theological community affiliated with the University of Manchester. NTC hosted me and my spouse Janice during the autumn semester of 2019, during which I was on sabbatical from Point Loma, and we loved our months in Manchester. My thanks go especially to students Denis Haywood, Sandro Oliviera, and Jorge Garcia Salazar; to professors Dwight Swanson, Steve Wright, Svetlana Khobnya, Geordan Hammond, Samuel Hildebrandt, Mi Ja Wi, Julie Dunn, and Thomas Noble; and to Didsbury Lecture Series organizer Kent Brower, academic dean Peter Rae, and school principal Deirdre Brower Latz. Cheers, mates! A couple of weeks prior, I shared some of why Matthew matters with the delightful students of Ukraine Evangelical Theological Seminary in Kiev, during which week of lectures I was co-hosted by the seminary and European Nazarene College. Warm gratitude to UETS President Ivan Rusyn and Dean Denys Kondiuk, and most especially to EUNC faculty and dear friends Sylvia Cortez, Volodymyr Masyuk, and Andrei Khobnya.

My lectures in Ukraine also engaged the issues of Muslim-Christian relations and conversation. This is not a coincidence. I am persuaded that Matthew is a particularly crucial gospel testimony about Jesus, his works and his words, for us today and certainly for the church of tomorrow. One might even say that my hope for the future church is that it shall find creative ways to become more "Jewish," and I intend in this volume to explain the character of this perhaps peculiar hope. I believe Matthew has still-untapped potential as a springboard for serious Jewish-Christian theological conversation. Further, given that at least in some ways Islam represents something like a return to something not unlike what Israel's prophets proclaimed, turning to Matthew as a kind of middle-ground gospel may reap interesting rewards. The Christian-Muslim theological conversation (which inevitably must also include Judaism) has been a driving concern of mine for two decades[1] and shall continue to be a critical site for Christian theological reflection in the decades and, undoubtedly, the centuries to come. While there are other scriptural resources that have proven helpful in thinking about Jesus alongside our Muslim friends and colleagues,[2] I am confident, or at least hopeful, that Matthew can matter greatly in such endeavors. While this book is not directly about the Muslim-Christian conversation, I will direct attention toward it at appropriate moments.

The fact that Jesus' great commission provides the conclusion of Matthew's Gospel is also noteworthy, for if we are to engage in theological reflection regarding Christian mission in our world of many "nations" or peoples or ethnicities (to say nothing of many religious traditions), surely the great commission occupies an important place—and it will in this volume, particularly in chapter 9.

* * *

Once we returned from sabbatical and I neared the book's completion, two pastors whose lives and preaching have deeply influenced me, and many

---

1. See Michael Lodahl, *Claiming Abraham: Reading the Bible and the Qur'an Side-by-Side* (Grand Rapids: Brazos Press, 2010); "The (Brief) Openness Debate in Islamic Theology: And Why That Debate Should be Different among Contemporary Christians," in *Creation Made Free: Open Theology Engaging Science*, edited by Thomas Jay Oord, 53–68 (Eugene, OR: Pickwick, 2009); "Reading Paul on Idolatry (Romans 1:18–32) alongside the Qur'an: A Theology of Divine Signs," in *Reading the Bible in Islamic Context: Qur'anic Conversations*, edited by Daniel J. Crowther, Shirin Shafaie, Ida Glaser, and Shabbir Akhtar, 224–38 (London: Routledge, 2018).

2. A stunning example is Daniel A. Madigan, S.J., "The Gospel of John as a Structure for Muslim-Christian Understanding," in *Reading the Bible in Islamic Context: Qur'anic Conversations*, edited by Daniel J. Crowther, Shirin Shafaie, Ida Glaser, and Shabbir Akhtar, 253–70 (London: Routledge, 2018).

Preface

others, read drafts and offered invaluable feedback. Thank you to my pastor, Rev. Dee Kelley of San Diego First Church of the Nazarene, for such kind and encouraging responses to these chapters. I have loved our discussions and sharing of life together over breakfasts these many years. And a similar word of gratitude to Rev. Robert Fuesler, pastor at St. Paul's United Methodist Church in Coronado, for your friendship, your theological camaraderie, your insightful responses to *Matthew Matters*, and for giving me the privilege of serving as Theologian-in-Residence for your warm and loving congregation. Despite the challenges of COVID-19, it's been a blast!

One final name remains. Reuben Welch taught religion courses and served as university chaplain for Pasadena College/Point Loma Nazarene University (the school moved from Pasadena to San Diego in the early 1970s) for several decades. He was—and in his mid-90s, still is!—a beloved Bible teacher for hosts of college students and, now, adult Sunday School students at San Diego First Church of the Nazarene. It has been a privilege and joy to participate in his Sojourners Sunday School class, as opportunity allows, since moving to San Diego in 1999. Reuben is my very favorite Bible teacher in the world, and having sojourned with his class through the Gospel of Matthew sometime back around the turn of the millennium, I am quite certain that I have "borrowed" material from his classes far more often that I could possibly know or acknowledge. So my deepest thanks and heartfelt admiration to you, Reuben.

I

Wisdom's Invitation

ONE OF THE REASONS why Matthew matters is that only Matthew includes this perennially beloved invitation of Jesus:

> Come to me,
> all you that are weary and are carrying heavy burdens,
> and I will give you rest.
> Take my yoke upon you, and learn from me;
> for I am gentle and humble in heart,
> and you will find rest for your souls.
> For my yoke is easy, and my burden is light.
> (Matt 11:28–30)

This text provided inspiration for the justly famous statue of Jesus as "Christus" that adorns the apse of the National (Lutheran) Cathedral of Denmark. Celebrated Danish sculptor Bertel Thorvaldsen was commissioned to create iconic sculptures of Jesus and his twelve apostles as part of the rebuilding of the cathedral after its destruction in 1807 by the British Royal Navy during the Napoleonic Wars. These inviting words from Matthew's Gospel are inscribed on the base of this imposing icon, which portrays the figure of Jesus with arms outspread, hands open: he stands in regal invitation. This is the church that Søren Kierkegaard most often attended, and it is not difficult to imagine Kierkegaard finding inspiration in this sculpture as he wrote the opening chapters of his classic text *Practice in Christianity*.

In those opening chapters, Kierkegaard offers an extended meditation on this Matthean invitation; repeatedly in those pages the Melancholy

Dane, in response to the passage, simply exclaims "Amazing!" For example, "The helper is the help. Amazing! . . . Ordinarily a physician must divide himself among his many patients, . . . [b]ut when the helper is the help, he must remain with the patient all day long, or the patient with him—how amazing, then, that this helper is the very one who invites all!"[1]

In another striking line, Kierkegaard writes, "In order to invite them to come to one in this way, one must oneself live in the very same manner, poor of the poorest, poorly regarded as the lowly man among the people, experienced in life's sorrow and anguish, sharing the very same condition as those one invites to come to one, those who labor and are burdened."[2] Lovely as this may sound, and as inviting—and even true!—as Kierkegaard's words may feel to our contemporary Christological sensitivities, one may wonder if they match very well Matthew's portrait of Jesus. Perhaps only a closer examination can tell. Certainly we can agree with Kierkegaard on one thing: "Amazing!"

The Nazarene and the Baptist

But of course this amazing invitation has a context. These are the concluding words of Matthew 11, a chapter that opens with Jesus proclaiming his good news from town to town and John the Baptist stuck in a prison cell. Then those haunting words: "When John heard in prison what the Messiah was doing [lit., "the deeds" or "works" of the Messiah, or "messianic deeds"], he sent word by his disciples to ask him, 'Are you the Coming One, or should we look for another?'" (11:2). The poignancy of this question should not elude us. Matthew had depicted Jesus's baptism as having occurred without a doubt from John, other than whether or not their roles should have been reversed: "I need to be baptized by you, and do you come to me?" (3:14). It is difficult to determine whether, for Matthew, Jesus's ensuing baptismal experience was more than a private one. While it is true that "suddenly the heavens were opened *to him* and *he saw* the Spirit of God descending like a dove and alighting on him" (3:16), perhaps implying a solitary experience, Matthew then reports "a voice from heaven" (3:17) that affirmed Jesus's divine sonship. Was this a voice that John would have heard? It seems that the text fairly demands it on two counts: 1) the words "This is my Son, the Beloved, with whom I am well pleased" (3:17) sound more like a public

---

1. Kierkegaard, *Practice in Christianity*, 15–16.
2. Kierkegaard, *Practice in Christianity*, 13.

announcement than like reassuring words addressed directly and privately to Jesus; and 2) there already existed in Jewish tradition the notion of the *bat kol*, the "heavenly voice," that was believed to have been audible, and to more than just one person, from time to time. Indeed, the general idea with the *bat kol* is the public expression of the divine will in a social setting. The point is that Matthew very likely implies that John was party to at least some of the extraordinary phenomena that the Gospels associate with Jesus's baptism. This, to be sure, makes his question from Herod's dungeon all that more spiritually poignant.

We may add to the baptismal scene the manner in which Matthew summarizes the preaching of both John and Jesus. In 3:2 we read that John's message was, "Repent, for the kingdom of heaven has come near." After Jesus's baptism, we read that "Jesus began to proclaim, 'Repent, for the kingdom of heaven has come near'" (4:17). The Greek is identical, and this is likely no accident. It would seem that Matthew wants his readership to appreciate that, by all early appearances, John and Jesus were on the same page. They are proclaiming the imminence of God's reign. John has witnessed something powerful at the Jordan River, a divine voice from the heavens confirming Jesus's unique status. Yet, these months later, as John awaits his fate in chains, he sends his disciples to ask Jesus the questions of an agonized heart: Are you really the One? God's *Coming One*? Or should we be looking for somebody else?

We should note how carefully Matthew stipulates what it was, exactly, that raised these questions for John: it was when he "heard what the Messiah (*ho Xristos*) was doing," or, more literally, "when he heard of the deeds of the Messiah" (11:2). The obvious implication is that Jesus was doing things that John did not expect of a messiah, of God's "coming one" (Gr., *ho erkomenos*). This in turn suggests that even though the preaching of both could be characterized as "Repent, for the kingdom of heaven has come near," they may have had radically differing notions about that approaching kingdom. Perhaps John expected by now to see the ax not only lying at the root of the trees (3:10), but chopping them down with great verve? Perhaps he wondered why the winnowing fork was not already in Jesus's hand, clearing the threshing floor, gathering his wheat into the granary, and burning the chaff with unquenchable fire (3:12)? It is likely that these were the sorts of deeds John expected of the Coming One. Where was the long-anticipated fire? Thus, "when John heard in prison the deeds of the Messiah" (11:2), it appears he was airing his doubts. *Good for John.*

Jesus, rarely interested in answering this sort of question directly, replies with his *deeds*—the very deeds, we should presume, that raised the question for John in the first place! "Go and tell John what you hear and see: the blind receive their sight, the lame walk, the lepers are cleansed, the deaf hear, the dead are raised, and the poor have the good news preached to them" (11:5). And given that Jesus replies with the very deeds that have prompted John's pained query, it seems unavoidable that Jesus's brief postscript is intended particularly for his questioner—"and blessed is anyone who takes no offense at me" (11:6).

There is something deeply existential about this interchange. We know that John's questions are not concerned with casual Christological conundrums; they arise from a heart of unmet expectations, of unfulfilled dreams, of pained experience. This is the grist for good theology. He is asking honest questions, and so ought we. But Jesus is an existentialist here as well: he answers by his deeds, the very deeds that have prompted the painful question, and thus in a sense he seems to be rubbing salt in John's spiritual wounds. "And happy," Jesus adds, "is the person who does not stumble over me." (*Ouch.*) There is not much consolation there, but there is correction. John, Jesus implies, must think differently about God's Coming One, which means that John must think differently about God's *coming*, which very likely means he must think differently about *God*. Ultimately at stake here, we shall see, is the very nature of divine Wisdom—and the wisdom of the divine nature.

Even so, Jesus proceeds to acknowledge John's role as a prophet, indeed as "Elijah who is to come" (11:14).[3] In material shared by Matthew and Luke (7:31–35), Jesus then contrasts the nature of their ministries—"John came neither eating nor drinking," while Jesus "came eating and drinking"—but in neither case have they found a welcoming audience (11:18–19). Then we encounter in Matthew a most fascinating summary statement: "Yet wisdom is vindicated by her deeds" (11:19).

While this may strike us as an unusual saying, we should first acknowledge the use of the word "deeds" (*erga*) here as an echo of "the deeds of the Messiah" which had prompted John's question from prison. Now Jesus announces that divine Wisdom's "deeds" or doings provide their own justification or validation. It appears that Jesus is characterizing himself and

---

3. Interestingly, the identification of John the Baptist with Elijah is summarily denied by the Baptist himself in John 1:21. Apparently, John the Baptist, or more precisely the author of the Gospel of John, did not have "ears to hear" this (Matt 11:15). Luke's silence (7:26) suggests he lacked the ears as well—or at least the nerve.

Wisdom's Invitation

his ministry as embodying divine Wisdom herself ("*her* deeds"), and very likely that John needs some schooling in this wisdom; hence, "the least in the kingdom of heaven is greater than he" (11:11). Would John accept such schooling? Only if he were to choose not to take offense at, or stumble over, this Coming One. It should give us pause that none of our gospels offers a triumphalist postscript to this poignant interchange; we are not informed that John accepted this reply with gladness, or for that matter whether or not he received it at all before losing his head.

If Matthew implies that Jesus the Messiah's deeds are the very deeds of Wisdom divine, Luke seems to understand the matter differently. Luke has Jesus saying that "wisdom is vindicated by all her children" (7:35) rather than "by her deeds." Given the context, it appears that Luke includes John with Jesus as the "children of wisdom," such that while the general populace could find reasons for ignoring their ministries, divine Wisdom is nevertheless vindicated or validated by them both despite their differences from one another (cf. Prov. 8:32). Jack Suggs, in his *Wisdom, Christology and Law in Matthew's Gospel*, suggests that, for Luke, Jesus and John the Baptist belong to the long line of Wisdom's prophets, yet occupy unique places of honor as "the eschatological envoys of Wisdom" who "stand at the turn of the ages."[4] Matthew's shift from "wisdom's children" (i.e., John and Jesus) to Wisdom's "deeds" (i.e., Jesus's deeds) very possibly signals a dramatic movement toward a Wisdom Christology in which Jesus *speaks* and *acts* as Sophia incarnate.

To establish this possibility further, we may observe a comparable shift when juxtaposing Luke 11:49-51 with Matthew 23:34-36. In Luke, Jesus is reported as having said to a gathering of offended Torah experts, "Therefore also the wisdom of God said, 'I will send them prophets and apostles, some of whom they will kill and persecute'" (11:49). Suggs believes that Jesus is most likely citing a lost Jewish wisdom source, a kind of oracle in which Wisdom is speaking.[5] In essentially the same narrative scene in Matthew, Jesus scolds "scribes and Pharisees" with a similarly scalding judgment: "Therefore *I* send you prophets, sages, and scribes, some of whom you will kill and crucify" (23:34). Here, Jesus does not quote the voice of Wisdom but speaks *as* the voice of Wisdom. Thus, it is arguable that Matthew effectively identifies Jesus himself as "the Wisdom of God" who is speaking in his gospel, and who sends prophets, sages and scribes—quite possibly

---

4. Suggs, *Wisdom, Christology and Law in Matthew's Gospel*, 45.
5. Suggs, *Wisdom, Christology and Law in Matthew's Gospel*, 16ff.

the Matthean community itself?—into the world (and more specifically, to Israel) where they are met with violent resistance. For Matthew, then, Jesus is divine Wisdom speaking, sending, and doing in the world. Accordingly, Jesus's community is to be a wisdom people.

Indeed, we may even find strong hints of this theme in Jesus's prayer that soon ensues: "I thank you, Father, Lord of heaven and earth, because you have hidden these things from the wise and the intelligent and have revealed them to infants" (11:25–26). Think of the description of Wisdom in Proverbs 8, where she "was there when [God] established the heavens" and "marked out the foundations of the earth" (Prov 8:27, 29), "rejoicing before [God] always, . . . and delighting in the human race" (Prov 8:30, 31). "You that are simple, turn in here!" Wisdom cries (Prov 9:4), and to those "without sense" she calls, "Come, eat of my bread and drink of the wine I have mixed. Lay aside immaturity, and live, and walk in the way of insight" (Prov 9:5–6). It is this very Wisdom who pleads, "And now, my children, listen to me"; do these "children" perhaps become the "infants" of Matthew 11:26? The "scoffer" and the "wicked" of Proverbs, however—are they perhaps "the wise and intelligent" of Matthew 11:26 from whom Wisdom's treasures are hidden? Similarly, since "I was there" from the beginning, "beside [God] like a little child; and I was daily [God's] delight" (Prov 8:27, 30)—and Jesus is this very Wisdom of God incarnate in the world that God has created—might Proverbs 8 provide a kind of textual and theological backdrop for Jesus's claim in 11:27 that "no one knows the Son except the Father, and no one knows the Father except the Son"? "For," as the Wisdom of Solomon adds, "she is an initiate in the knowledge of God" (8:4) and is more than willing to share with those who long to learn from her (8:7–8).

The eminent Roman Catholic scholar Daniel Harrington certainly thought so. In his commentary *The Gospel of Matthew* he wrote,

> [In] the background of the Father-Son saying in Matt 11:27 is the Jewish (and early Christian) debate about what and where wisdom is [a debate with which is it obvious the Matthean community was familiar and in which it was involved]. The tradition of wisdom as a (female) person had been well established since Proverbs 8. The question at issue was, What is wisdom, and where is she to be found? . . . Matthew 11:27 presents Jesus as divine wisdom incarnate. Those who know him know the Father—which is after all the ultimate in wisdom.[6]

---

6. Harrington, *The Gospel of Matthew*, 169–70.

Wisdom's Invitation

All of these preceding considerations, of course, have led us back to the opening of this chapter, that "amazing" invitation with which Matthew 11 concludes. In this lovely and compelling passage unique to Matthew, Jesus speaks as the very embodiment of Wisdom divine. Consider it once more:

> Come to me,
> all you that are weary and are carrying heavy burdens,
> and I will give you rest.
> Take my yoke upon you, and learn from me;
> for I am gentle and humble in heart,
> and you will find rest for your souls.
> For my yoke is easy, and my burden is light.
> (Matt 11:28–30)

The Figure of Wisdom and Jesus

While biblical scholars may debate the extent to which this invitation draws from earlier formulations in Jewish wisdom literature, I am convinced that for Matthew and his *ekklesia*-community this interpretation of Jesus as Sophia incarnate is indispensable: Jesus is the fulfillment of centuries' worth of Jewish longing for the presence and instruction of God's own Wisdom. In his *Jesus and Community*, Gerhard Lohfink, among many others, cites Sirach 24:22–25 and 51:23–27 as especially pertinent. In the first passage, Wisdom, who "came forth from the mouth of the Most High" (Sir 24:5) and traversed all creation before making her "dwelling in Jacob" (24:8), issues the invitation, "Come to me, you who desire me, and eat your fill of my fruits" (24:19). Not long thereafter, this Wisdom is associated closely with the Torah, "the book of the covenant of the Most High God, the law that Moses commanded us" (24:23), such that, in Lohfink's words, "in Jesus's day the 'wisdom' which comes from God and illuminates human beings had long . . . been identified with the Torah."[7]

The second passage from Sirach (51:13–30) is a kind of autobiographical acrostic appendix, much of which, written in Hebrew, was found among the Dead Sea Scrolls. This concluding poem ostensibly heralds the author Jesus ben Sirach's own lifelong journey in search of divine Wisdom: "While I was still young, before I went on my travels, I sought wisdom openly in

---

7. Lohfink, *Jesus and Community*, 61.

my prayer" (51:13). Near the end of his acrostic, the author seems almost to stand in for the figure of Wisdom: "Draw near to me, you who are uneducated, and lodge in the house of instruction" (51:23). Yet the instruction this Jesus offers is telling, certainly appearing to anticipate the Matthean invitation: "Put your neck under her yoke, and let your souls receive instruction; it is to be found close by" (51:26). Thus, to put the point most simply, the Jewish wisdom tradition had not only personified divine Wisdom as a female figure, but further had come essentially to identify this Wisdom with the Torah, God's covenantal binding with the people Israel. Later, the Gospel of Matthew (to a greater extent than the other Synoptic Gospels) further merges this Wisdom-Torah complex into the very person, words, and deeds of Jesus the Nazarene. As divine Wisdom incarnate, Jesus calls into existence a *school* or social-pedagogical movement—Matthew calls it *ekklesia*, perhaps to distinguish it from *synagogue*—into which we, by virtue of hearing his amazing invitation, are invited to become participants. This is a school of wisdom, of wise, godly living. In Suggs's words,

> The invitation which Jesus offers is the old invitation of Wisdom and the yoke which is offered is the yoke of Wisdom, the yoke of the Torah. . . . We should be very clear that in the Matthean setting what is offered by Jesus is *not* an alternative to the yoke of the Torah. Jesus speaks *as* Sophia, and . . . [this means that Jesus speaks] *as* Torah as well.[8]

Graham Stanton, however, has raised doubts about Suggs's influential reading of Matthew on this point. His first objection is that Jesus's self-characterization as "gentle and humble in heart" (Stanton uses the KJV "meek and lowly") does not square well with the way in which Sophia is generally inscribed in the Jewish wisdom tradition. "At Sirach 24:1, which introduces the so-called Sophia myth," Stanton writes, "Sophia speaks with *pride*."[9] He finds evidence of the same in Proverbs, where Wisdom regularly lifts her voice: "She stands by the gate and calls aloud in a rather arrogant manner."[10] Nothing particularly "meek and lowly" here! Stanton believes that Jesus's self-description as gentle and humble "may well be Matthew's own addition to his source" since, while it "is out of character with the portrait of Sophia

---

8. Suggs, *Wisdom, Christology and Law in Matthew's Gospel*, 106.
9. Stanton, *A Gospel for a New People*, 369.
10. Stanton, *A Gospel for a New People*, 369.

in the Wisdom writings, [it is] very much in line with Matthew's portrait of Jesus."[11]

But is this not precisely the point? There is a rich theological possibility looming here. We might profitably link it to John the Baptist's query considered earlier. If Matthew's Jesus "will not wrangle or cry aloud, nor will anyone hear his voice in the streets" (Matt 12:19), then indeed he may be quite *unlike* Sophia—that is, *Sophia as she was generally characterized in the Jewish traditions preceding Jesus.* But Jesus is not simply a personification or symbol of divine Wisdom, as we take Sophia to be; he is *the actual embodying* of divine Wisdom. Jesus as Wisdom incarnate reconfigures the notion of divine Wisdom—perhaps even transforms it—and surely divine Wisdom is not at all other than the divine nature. Thus, the issue at stake, ultimately, is *what God is like*. Stanton certainly is right that "we can see, in all probability, the evangelist's own hand"[12] at work in this reconfiguration, but that does not necessitate the conclusion that Matthew did not present Jesus as Sophia incarnate. It is the evangelist's own hand, wisely and gently guided by the Spirit of Wisdom, we trust, that offers us this radical reshaping of the nature of divine Wisdom—indeed, once again, of the divine nature itself—as gentle, humble, quiet, unobtrusive, and yet (or better, *therefore*) as always inviting.

But Stanton has another objection. "I find it difficult," he remarks tellingly, "to see how either Matthew or his readers could make the jump from v. 27 where Jesus is presented as 'the Son' to v. 28, where, it is alleged, Jesus is Sophia/Wisdom."[13] Granted, this can seem problematic or even a little awkward. Feminist theologians have sometimes raised the same objection, though from the other side of the coin, so to speak. What happens to this regal, powerful presence and voice of Woman Wisdom if she becomes absorbed by the Jewish male Jesus of Nazareth? Is she gone, dissipated, disappearing? Sublimated into the male? Silenced by the Word that has become flesh as a first-century Jewish man? Such questions should not be dismissed.

But for the moment, back to Stanton, who elaborates, "In the Wisdom tradition Sophia is always portrayed in strongly female terms. Those who search and seek after her are always men: sexual imagery lies just beneath the surface in many passages."[14] Hence, again, for Stanton, this figure of

---

11. Stanton, *A Gospel for a New People*, 370.
12. Stanton, *A Gospel for a New People*, 369.
13. Stanton, *A Gospel for a New People*, 370.
14. Stanton, *A Gospel for a New People*, 370.

Woman Wisdom is entirely incommensurate with Jesus the Jewish male; such incongruity would have been as obvious "to ancient Jewish sensibilities as it is to ours."[15] Such comments merit careful deconstruction. It is correct that Sophia is very often, if not always, "portrayed in strongly female terms." To add that those who seek for her are always men, however, seems only to observe, but not interrogate, the patriarchal system of thought, practice, and writing at work within this tradition. And why would we assume that Wisdom's call was extended only to men, or even that only men could give her heed? There is certainly nothing in these texts to restrict the company of hearers to males. Even if the male scholars who wrote this material had only themselves in mind as the audience of Wisdom's wooings, it is an odd claim to make that those who seek divine Wisdom are always men. Further, none of this changes if we agree with Stanton that "sexual imagery lies just beneath the surface in many passages." To acknowledge the erotic element in the desire for Wisdom is not to dismiss it from Judaism, Christianity, or, in this case particularly, our Christologies. Surely we are cognizant of the sexual imagery that lies just beneath the surface of much medieval Christology (and not only there!), to say nothing of many biblical passages.[16]

It seems to me that to worry about whether or not a first-century Jewish male could be imagined to be the embodiment, or perhaps stronger, the incarnation of Sophia—that is, of divine Wisdom personified as a woman—is to think in overly bifurcated ways about gender. I would argue that there is little in the Gospel testimonies regarding Jesus to suggest that he would have been terribly troubled by the notion. His lament over Jerusalem as a mother hen comes to mind (Matt 23:37), for just one example. Beyond this, the Gospels' stories of his being touched by women, being anointed with perfume by a woman, having his feet washed by the tears and long flowing hair of a woman, or for that matter washing his disciples' feet—all of this bespeaks, I think, a man who did not feel constrained by cultural bifurcations and expectations regarding gender performance.

If we wonder whether it would have been likely, or even possible, for Matthew to have imagined Jesus to be Sophia incarnate—and this seems to be the heart of Stanton's objection—I find the earlier observation offered, regarding the term "deeds" that connects the Messiah (11:2) with a female

15. Stanton, *A Gospel for a New People*, 370. Here, Stanton is citing M. D. Johnson's "Reflections on a Wisdom Approach to Matthew's Gospel," *Catholic Biblical Quarterly* 36 (1974) 61f.

16. See Jantzen, *Power, Gender and Christian Mysticism*; Jantzen, *Becoming Divine*; Coakley, *God, Sexuality, and the Self*.

Wisdom ("her deeds," 11:19), to be compelling. Granted, it is an interpretive decision to read this dual usage as hermeneutically significant; perhaps one could just as readily read it as coincidental. I believe, though, that both context and Matthew's generally acknowledged literary deftness can tip this argument: the deeds Jesus was performing as the Messiah, while at least initially unexpected and perhaps even troubling to John, were precisely the deeds of Woman Wisdom. In the words of Elizabeth A. Johnson, "His parables, healings, exorcisms, and inclusive table community are Wisdom's deeds, revealing her renewing and friend-making power at work to establish the right order of creation."[17]

Who Are the Weary?

If this is the case, then at least in Matthew's Gospel it is the very voice of *God*—as Woman Wisdom—who calls out to us, "Come to me." More precisely, this invitation is offered to "all you who are weary and are carrying heavy burdens." Who are these people, exactly, and what is the burden from which Jesus promises to give "rest"? Not surprisingly, this issue is not settled either! The most typical interpretation is that Jesus is offering release and rest to those "weary and heavy laden" by Pharisaic interpretation and application of the Torah. Stanton acknowledges that "this approach is attractive, . . . but that there are grounds for caution" even if "an anti-Pharisaic thrust cannot be ruled out at the end of chapter 11."[18] But he presses a reading in which Jesus is speaking to his own disciples, the "infants" to whom the Son has revealed the Father (11:25), as those who are weary and carrying heavy burdens. He concludes that the weariness in question is "the costly and demanding nature of discipleship," fraught with opposition and rejection, such that the invitation becomes "a word of encouragement to hard-pressed disciples."[19]

However, in this case it seems a *non sequitur* for Jesus to encourage his disciples to "take my yoke upon you, and learn from me" (11:28). In Stanton's reading, it is precisely because they *have* taken Jesus's yoke upon them, and learned from him—precisely because they *are* faithful disciples—that they are experiencing hardship, "weary and carrying heavy burdens." This is not to deny that such an invitation would have functioned in the way that

---

17. Johnson, "Wisdom Was Made Flesh and Pitched Her Tent among Us," 107.
18. Stanton, *A Gospel for a New People*, 373, 375.
19. Stanton, *A Gospel for a New People*, 342.

Stanton describes for the Matthean community in the latter years of the first century. But again, if "the 'yoke of Jesus' is the yoke of discipleship,"[20] as Stanton contends, it would seem odd for Jesus to invite those who are his disciples, already suffering for his name's sake, to take on the yoke of discipleship. Of course, the call to become Jesus's followers is always an ongoing, dynamic journey, so there is an inevitable element of truth in this reading. Nonetheless, something else must be going on here.

Perhaps the most novel suggestion has been offered by Warren Carter in his important 2000 work, *Matthew and the Margins*. He first acknowledges that the invitation "echoes wisdom's call,"[21] but against Stanton does not hear this as a call to those who already follow Jesus; noting the inclusive nature of "all" (*pantes*), Carter interprets this as an open invitation, "especially [to] the harassed and helpless crowds (9:36)," to become his disciples.[22] What, then, is the rest that Jesus offers the weary ones? Carter points out that the term *pephortismenoi*, "heavy laden" or "carrying heavy burdens," is rare; he appeals to Sirach's usage—"hard work was created for everyone, and a heavy yoke is laid on the children of Adam" (Sir 40:1)—to suggest that it means simply the exertion of living in a world of hardship, struggle, and strife. Life is hard—for everyone. But it is harder, often much harder, for the oppressed. Further, Carter appeals to the Septuagint's usage to shed light on Matthew's use of "weary" (*kopiōntes*). There, writes Carter, it "refers . . . to beatings, weariness, physical tiredness from work or heat or battle. It often identifies the afflicted, trouble, 'oppressive labor and sorrow,' the human lot from which only God can save."[23] At this point, however, Carter makes a sizable interpretive leap:

> [The "weary,"] then, are not those "oppressed" by the law, as some argue, but those who are burdened by life under Roman imperial control and its unjust political and socioeconomic structures. They are afflicted by disease and demons (4:23-24), by hard labor, by payment of taxes, tolls, and debts to the political, economic, and religious elite. . . . Jesus saves from the punishment of Roman rule (21:41; 22:7; 1:21) in establishing God's empire, now in part and at his return in full (4:17; 24:27-31).

---

20. Stanton, *A Gospel for a New People*, 375.
21. Carter, *Matthew and the Margins*, 259.
22. Carter, *Matthew and the Margins*, 259.
23. Carter, *Matthew and the Margins*, 259.

Wisdom's Invitation

I find this attractive but unlikely. Certainly, Jesus taught his disciples to live together as *ekklesia* in a way that was not to mimic the hierarchical power structures of the world, and the Romans would be at the top of that list. But Carter's "sociopolitical and religious reading" seems to move us beyond this observation toward an image of Jesus as Zealot, and there simply is insufficient textual support from the Gospels to follow this reading. The implication of Carter's interpretation would be that "God's empire" operates in direct competition with the Roman empire, such that in fact Jesus would be intent on establishing a kingdom *not* "not of this world." This ought not at all imply for us that God's rule is only an ethereal, otherworldly realm; to the contrary, the reign of God does indeed take root, in and through Jesus, in the real soil of this world. God's reign, however, is meant to blossom in the community of discipleship that Jesus's invitation, rather than divine force, makes possible. It is an alternative to the power structures of this world (ideally!), but it is not their replacement; indeed, to replace those structures by force would only be to perpetuate their violence. Carter's claim that "Jesus saves from the punishment of Roman rule" requires a long stretching of the Matthean text.

Again, there is no question that Jesus offers to those who respond to his invitation the possibility of a communal existence radically different from Roman rule. Matthew bears witness to this alternative later in his gospel when we read that Jesus gathered his bickering disciples around himself and said, "You know that the rulers of the Gentiles lord it over them; and their great ones are tyrants over them. It will not be so among you; but whoever wishes to be great among you must be your servant" (Matt 20:25–26). Certainly, then, Carter has a point: gentile rulers who operate as tyrants, lording their authority over their underlings, provide no "rest for the weary." They just make things a whole lot worse. Jesus calls his disciples to a very different sort of social arrangement, characterized by humility and servanthood. Given such a community, the one who is "gentle and humble in heart" is its perfect founder, leader, and exemplar.

What is truly remarkable is that if indeed Jesus speaks as divine Wisdom incarnate, and describes himself as "gentle and humble in heart," this is not simply (or even primarily) a description of the personality traits of Jesus of Nazareth; it is divine Wisdom, i.e., *God*, who is gentle and humble. What are the implications of such a Christology, in which divine Wisdom is "humble" and "gentle" rather than boastful and bullying? Lohfink comments, "It is said of this teaching of Jesus . . . that it is a yoke which does not oppress, a *light burden*. Why? Because Jesus is gentle and humble of heart."[24] Indeed, it is crucial to note that Jesus's invitation to undertake his yoke, to learn from him, is predicated precisely on this particular rationale: "for I am gentle and humble in heart." Divine Wisdom incarnate presents himself, recommends himself, to us as our teacher precisely on that basis.

There is no question that the phrases "take my yoke upon you" and "learn from me" are essentially equivalent. Jesus invites us to become his learners, his students. It is time to revive this image of Jesus as our teacher, and of ourselves as his learners, his disciples. The church of tomorrow will (and must), I believe, become more deeply invested in this imagery and its implications. Further, it seems unavoidable that one of the most important lessons Sophia incarnate desires to teach us is to become, likewise, "gentle and humble in heart." What sort of churches will we have, if we become, as Jesus's learners, communities of gentleness and humility? Are we willing to shoulder this yoke of Jesus?

What of the "Rest"?

Finally, then, such questions lead us again to consider this "rest" that Jesus offers to all who are weary and heavy-laden. This is not about Jesus replacing the Torah *per se*, but about Jesus embodying the Torah in the way of divine Wisdom. Thus, the issue also is not about Christianity versus Judaism, as though the problems of legalism and abuse of power have been solved by the church, or as though Judaism got it all wrong. This becomes clear in Matthew 23, where Jesus teaches the sort of thing one can only imagine reading in this gospel: "Jesus said to the crowds [of Jewish people] and to his disciples [*his own* community of learners!], 'The scribes and the Pharisees sit on Moses' seat; therefore, do whatever they teach you and follow it" (23:2–3a). Let us pause for a moment. Jesus here instructs his Jewish audience, including his *ekklesia*, to observe carefully the Pharisaic—and, one could argue, the subsequent rabbinic—interpretations of the Torah, because they instantiate the authority of Moses. It is self-evident that these words of Jesus have not gained a substantial or appreciative hearing in the annals of Christendom. And it is probably too late to turn back that clock. However, might not the church of tomorrow do much better at trying to learn not only from Jesus, but in the spirit of gentleness and humility to be

---

24. Lohfink, *The Theology of the Gospel of Matthew*, 61.

open to learning from the deep wisdom of the Jewish tradition? Matthew matters because it encourages us in that direction.[25]

In this passage, then, the critique is not directed toward the Pharisees' *teaching* but toward their *behaviors*. So, "do whatever they teach you and follow it; but do not do as they do, for they do not practice what they teach. They tie up heavy burdens, hard to bear, and lay them on the shoulders of others; but they themselves are unwilling to lift a finger to move them" (23:3–4). The connections to our passage in Matthew 11 seem undeniable. For Matthew, the distinction between Jesus and the Pharisees is much less about teaching and much more about character. One sort of character gives "rest" to learners; another sort lays heaven burdens on the learners' shoulders, and lifts nary a finger to help. How does Jesus characterize those who impose heavy burdens?

> They do all their deeds to be seen by others; for they make their phylacteries broad and their fringes long. They love to have the place of honor at banquets and the best seats in the synagogues, and to be greeted with respect in the marketplaces, and to have people call them rabbi. (23:5–7)

We ought to appreciate that the issue here is not phylacteries or fringes or synagogues or rabbis. This is not simply a Jewish problem that Jesus addresses; it is a human problem. Thus, it turns out to be just as much a Christian problem. Not phylacteries but status; not fringes but degrees, and from which institutions; not synagogues but churches and their membership numbers; not rabbi but reverend doctor. The drive for power, prestige, and status is oppressive of others, destructive of relationships, and harmful to a community's psyche. It is, essentially, emotional and even spiritual bullying. There is no "rest" in an atmosphere of such competitiveness, oppression, and paranoia. This is not the way of Wisdom divine.

Thus, just as Jesus teaches his disciples in regards to Roman practices of hierarchical power "lording it over" the underlings, so also he instructs us in regards to religious abuses of power closer to home: "The greatest

---

25. Two theologians who have been profound influences upon me were pioneers in exploring this direction. Roman Catholic scholar Bernard Lee did so especially in his two-volume series *Conversations on the Road Not Taken* (vol. 1, *The Galilean Jewishness of Jesus: Retrieving the Jewish Origins of Christianity*; vol. 2, *Jesus and the Metaphors of God: The Christs of the New Testament*). Episcopalian theologian Paul van Buren did so especially in his masterful three-volume work *A Theology of the Jewish-Christian Reality* (vol. 1, *Discerning the Way*; vol. 2, *A Christian Theology of the People Israel*; vol. 3, *Christ in Context*).

among you will be your servant. All who exalt themselves will be humbled, and all who humble themselves will be exalted" (Matt 23:12). These words would be incoherent if not spoken by Wisdom incarnate, whom we have come to believe is "gentle and humble in heart." The one who is humble has earned the right to invite us to share in the honor of his humility, in the greatness of his gentleness (cf. Heb. 5:8–9). In his presence there is rest for our souls—and so, we trust, rest for our community of learners together following Jesus. It is precisely because Sophia is, in reality, gentle and humble that Jesus's yoke is "kind" or "good."[26] This yoke fits because it is fashioned in the wisdom of our Maker. It is a yoke in which we may share.

To return, then, to Kierkegaard's adjective: if indeed the Power that calls forth and molds the seemingly infinite galaxies is "gentle and humble in heart," then such a Maker truly is *amazing*. I suspect we are still trying to learn this. In the invitation of Matthew 11:28–30, Kierkegaard argues, we are encountered by an incomprehensibly profound

> [d]ivine compassion, . . . [an] unlimited *recklessness* in concerning oneself only with the suffering [of others], not in the least with oneself, and of unconditionally recklessly concerning oneself with *each* sufferer—people can interpret this only as a kind of madness over which we are not sure whether we should laugh or cry.[27]

And yet, Kierkegaard adds, "the inviter was indeed this divine compassion."[28] It is left to us to imagine an *ekklesia*, a communion of disciples, who take upon themselves the inviter's yoke and learn from him. What will such faith communities look like, and how shall they behave? This, I believe and hope, shall be the church of tomorrow.

There is one last consideration in our attempt better to comprehend this amazing invitation of Jesus. Immediately after this passage, at the outset of chapter 12, Matthew introduces a story with the temporal phrase "At that time . . ." While this is admittedly an interpretive move, it is arguable that the phrase serves to alert us readers that we ought to understand Jesus's invitation in the light of this story that immediately follows it, and vice versa. And this indeed we shall do at the turn of this page.

---

26. The adjective "easy" is a regrettable translation. See Mitchell, "The Yoke is Easy, but What of Its Meaning?"

27. Kierkegaard, *Practice*, 58.

28. Kierkegaard, *Practice*, 60.

2

Wisdom's Desire

I desire mercy, and not sacrifice.

"At that time"—during that very stretch of time during which he extended his amazing invitation, Matthew is telling us—"Jesus went through the grainfields on the Sabbath" (Matt 12:1). This temporal indicator, "at that time," signals the critical importance, I believe, of reading this narrative of Sabbath controversy in the direct light of Jesus's description of himself as gentle and humble, of his yoke as kind, and of his burden as light. In other words, the story we are about to encounter is an instantiation of his claims in Matthew 11:28–30.

This story is common to the Synoptic Gospels, so in and of itself it is not a reason why Matthew matters. But in Matthew, there is literally more to the story. Only in Matthew does Jesus, in his debate with his critics, cite the words of the prophet Hosea, "I desire mercy and not sacrifice" (12:7; Hos 6:6). While interesting, that might conceivably be overlooked were it not for the fact that this passage marks the second time that Jesus—again, only in Matthew's Gospel—has appealed to this line from Hosea. The prior instance occurs in the controversy regarding Jesus's table fellowship with "tax collectors and sinners" (9:11), also a narrative common to all three Synoptic Gospels. The fact that in both stories only Matthew features Jesus's appeal to Hosea suggests the critical importance of this prophetic line for his gospel. "I desire mercy, and not sacrifice" becomes, for Matthew, a kind of programmatic or platform statement for properly interpreting Jesus's ministry—and, accordingly, for learning from divine Wisdom. Put differently, Jesus's amazing invitation is sandwiched between these stories that instantiate God's desire for human flourishing. Thus, these stories, while familiar, merit closer attention.

Jesus and Tax-Collectors

In the earlier passage, we read of Jesus calling "a man named Matthew sitting at the tax collector's booth" to become his follower (9:9). Daniel Harrington comments, "In the Roman empire contracts for collecting taxes and tolls were often put out to bid. The highest bidder in turn hired local people to collect the fees,"[1] usually at toll booths where fees were collected on goods (such as fish caught in the Sea of Galilee) as they were transported out of the region. Of course, the bidder and his hires handed on these taxes to the empire, but there were opportunities aplenty to increase one's personal profit by assessing higher rates of taxation. "Even if they were not skimming off the top, they were suspected of doing so," adds Harrington. "In Judea of Jesus's time they [very likely were] . . . looked upon as collaborators with the Roman [occupation] and therefore as disloyal,"[2] betraying their own people. Further, the nature of this work necessitated constant contact with both Roman coinage (with its potentially idolatrous connotations) and Roman officials.

Not only were tax collectors ritually unclean, then, they were also often considered cheats and, even worse, traitors, generally barred from synagogue participation.[3] It was scandalous enough that Jesus would call one of them to become his disciple; even worse was the scenario of Jesus reclining for dinner in Matthew's house, where "many tax collectors and sinners came and were reclining with him and his disciples" (9:10). Table fellowship with such undesirables as these would be unconscionable. Jesus risks being characterized as a sympathizer, if not a collaborator, with Roman occupation. "It was one thing for Jesus to show his mercy to outsiders," George Montague observes. "It was quite another, and supreme exposure of vulnerability, for him to call and welcome a tax collector as one of his own.

---

1. Harrington, *The Gospel of Matthew*, 127–28.
2. Harrington, *The Gospel of Matthew*, 128.
3. Montague, *Companion God*, 130.

But Jesus is making a community of the most unlikely, and that will have its challenges."[4]

It can be no surprise, then, that for most Pharisees Jesus's actions were mystifying at best. I would encourage a deeper sympathy for their distress. The Pharisees had a noble mission that, for our purposes, might be summarized briefly as the restoration of the people of Israel to true holiness. Granting the existence of real differences among their various schools, the Pharisees were essentially a lay movement dedicated to appropriating for themselves the high standards of ritual holiness associated with the Jerusalem temple and its priestly practices, and attempting to legislate those standards (as thoroughly and consistently as possible) for Jewish home and social life. This was a holiness movement! They took very seriously the Deuteronomic theology of blessings and curses (cf. Deut 28); thus, the Roman occupation was the judgment of God upon the nation. The Pharisaic mission, then, was to teach the people to "obey the LORD your God, by diligently observing all his commandments" so that "blessings shall come upon you and overtake you" (Deut 28:1, 2). The future of their people was at stake.

To be for God "a priestly kingdom and a holy nation" (Exod 19:6) required that Israel be a people set apart from sin and impurity. To mingle with tax collectors and other non-observant Jews ("sinners") was clearly not behavior that priests could engage in and remain ritually pure for temple service; the Pharisees, accordingly, would not engage in such behaviors nor encourage others to do so. We might wonder, though, why they cared so much about what Jesus was saying and doing. Certainly it is possible that some acted out of envy, but more likely his critics were concerned that his growing popularity held dangerous potential for leading the people of Israel astray. Indeed, a recurring description of Jesus in the rabbinic writings of subsequent centuries, the Talmud, is that he was "a sorcerer who led Israel astray."[5] This was already a lively suspicion during Jesus's own lifetime. Thus the question: "Why does your teacher eat with tax collectors and sinners?" Why does he set such a horrid example?

Jesus's reply appeals to the reality of human need: "It is not the healthy who need a doctor, but the sick." A generous reading of this text will at least leave open the possibility that Jesus perceived the Pharisees—or at least some of the Pharisees—to be "the healthy." In any case, he proceeds

---

4. Montague, *Companion God*, 132.
5. See Schafer, *Jesus in the Talmud*.

to challenge his critics with a homework assignment in language typical of rabbinic instruction, "But go and learn what this means: 'I desire mercy, not sacrifice'" (9:12–13). "Sacrifice" evokes the whole web of meanings associated with the temple in Jerusalem: altars, animals' spilled blood, priests, ritual purity requirements. All of it bespeaks what Marcus Borg has called "the politics of holiness": set apart space, people, animals, all kept ritually pure in order to be part of a sacrifice acceptable to the Holy One.[6]

Of course, the struggle between priestly and prophetic strands in Israelite worship and practice was nothing new or rare; Jesus could easily have offered any number of quotations from the prophets in their stinging critiques against the presumption of people who sometimes seemed to think that all God needed was another bull on the altar—that offering sacrifices was a way to buy off God, to do a kind of "religious" duty that bore little to no relation to their actual everyday lives and relationships, especially to the poor. This contrast can, admittedly, be overstated; biblical scholarship is agreed that the prophets of Israel assumed the validity and efficacy of the temple sacrificial system. It was the *misuse* of that system that troubled them. It is a perennial temptation to assume that "God" is all about religious matters like worship and prayer and proper sacrifices. In this way, God can be restricted to a narrow and largely irrelevant corner, presumably having been bought off by the required sacrificial rites. Even in the Psalms we join with David in prayer, "For you have no delight in sacrifice; if I were to give a burnt offering, you would not be pleased. The sacrifice acceptable to God is a broken spirit; a broken and contrite heart, O God, you will not despise" (Ps 51:16–17).

Recall that only in Matthew do we read that Jesus cited the words of Hosea, who in turn "it seems certain . . . has in mind the oracle of Samuel in 1 Samuel 15:22–23,

> Does Yahweh delight in offerings and sacrifices
> As much as in obedience to the voice of Yahweh?
> Obedience is better than sacrifice,
> Paying attention is better than rams' fat. . . .
> Just as you [Saul] rejected Yahweh's word,
> So Yahweh rejects you from being king.[7]

6.. See Borg's insightful contrasts between the "politics of holiness" and the "politics of compassion" in *Jesus: A New Vision*, 86–93, 131–42.

7. Translation from Andersen and Freedman, *Hosea*, 431.

Wisdom's Desire

Assuming that it is indeed the case that Hosea has in mind his prophetic predecessor Samuel's word of judgment against King Saul, it seems all the more critical that in Hosea the point has shifted from obedience to God, as perhaps a general principle of sorts, to a specific (yet universal) divine desire: mercy or steadfast love (Heb. *hesed*). Earlier Hosea had already indicted the people of Israel on the charge of "no faithfulness or loyalty [*hesed*], and no knowledge of God in the land. Swearing, lying, and murder, and stealing and adultery break out; bloodshed follows bloodshed" such that even the land itself was in mourning, along with all of its living creatures—humans, animals, "birds of the air" and even "the fish of the sea" (Hos 4:1–3). Thus, even if all of Israel were to come "with their flocks and herds . . . to seek the LORD," they would not find the Holy One (Hos 5:6). God had withdrawn from Israel, Hosea proclaimed, because God's desire is for *hesed* rather than bloodshed.

Here the story of King Saul and the prophet Samuel rears its bloody head. Through the prophet, the king had been instructed by God to wreak vengeance upon the Amalekites "for what they did in opposing the Israelites when they came up out of Egypt" (1 Sam 15:2). Saul's instructions were to "utterly destroy all that [the Amalekites] have, . . . man and woman, child and infant, ox and sheep, camel and donkey" (15:3). Saul did so—almost. "He took King Agag of the Amalekites alive" and kept the best of the sheep and cattle, but "utterly destroyed all the people with the edge of the sword" (15:8–9). We read that, because of Saul's selective obedience, God spoke to the prophet: "I regret that I made Saul king, for he has turned back from following me, and has not carried out my commands" (15:10). We read further that "Samuel was angry, and he cried out to the LORD all night" (15:11). When Samuel tracked down Saul, the king informed the prophet that the best sheep and cattle had been spared "to sacrifice to the LORD your God" (15:15). "Stop!" the prophet interjected. "Has the LORD as great delight in burnt offerings and sacrifices, as in obedience to the voice of the LORD? Surely, to obey is better than sacrifice" (15:16, 22). To ensure that there was no mistaking what obedience to God entailed in this particular matter, Samuel took up a sword and "hewed Agag in pieces before the LORD" (15:33).

Intense!—and perhaps in tension with Hosea's rendition of what God desires? But I shall tread carefully here. It may in fact be that there is no necessary tension between the Samuel story and Hosea's insistence upon *hesed*. I will grant that the bloodshed that Hosea decries (Hos 4:2) is the blood of Israel's poor on the hands of Israel's rich and powerful, and especially the priests (4:4–9). Perhaps Hosea would not have been much bothered by the story of Agag's dismemberment. But is the quality of mercy strained? Is God not the God of the gentiles also (Rom 3:29)? Certainly when it comes to Matthew's good news about Jesus, the words "I desire mercy, and not sacrifice" have taken on such universal significance as to call for a love that includes even one's enemies—which in Jesus's own time could not but apply first and foremost to the Roman occupiers. In the light of Jesus and his reading of Hosea, obedience to divine command can never again be construed to include hacking someone, evil king or otherwise, into pieces. If in Samuel God's desire is that humans obey whatever it is that God commands them, in the teaching of incarnate Wisdom—drawing upon Hosea—we find that God's desire is *mercy toward all others, a compassion rooted and grounded in steadfast love.* This compassion is extended first toward people most in need ("the sick"), the people on the margins (the stranger), the people most vulnerable (the "little ones"), but again, even also to enemies (Matt 5:44)—presumably enemies even such as Agag. Living compassionately is what God desires of human beings because this is in fact God's very nature. God is *hesed.* I believe the church of tomorrow must, and shall, become a people deeply invested in celebrating God's great, compassionate love—and not simply of celebrating this love, but of becoming a people who reflect this love in all directions, to all of God's beloved creatures.

A couple of other interesting theological implications suggest themselves. We note first that Jesus, quoting Hosea, says that God *desires* mercy. However, the fact that Jesus is quoting this to people who, as far as Jesus is concerned, do not exemplify such mercy, but instead a kind of hardhearted superiority, already means that what God *desires* is not what God is *getting.* Jesus is demonstrating mercy toward tax-collecting traitors and other assorted sordid sinners, but apparently he is in rare company. God desires mercy and not sacrifice, but mostly God was getting—and more than likely, still is getting—ritual sacrifices (perhaps in the form of "praise and worship"?) rather than mercy toward the vulnerable needy. From a biblical standpoint, it seems inevitable that God's desires go unfulfilled on a regular basis. God's will can be frustrated; indeed, Hosea's own emotional turmoil reflects God's pains over Israel: "My heart recoils within me; my compassion grows warm and tender" (11:8). Thus, Israel's prophets could even come to share in the divine pathos over the suffering of creation's marginalized and forgotten poor.[8] If God desires mercy, one quick glance at the world should assure us that God does not necessarily get what God desires. Further, this should be a sobering consideration for our churches, which all too often invest themselves heavily in the sacrifice of praise as though this is what satisfies God's desire. Yet the words of divine Wisdom echo down through the centuries to the church of tomorrow: "I desire mercy, and not sacrifice."

A second consideration, like unto the first, is that Jesus calls upon his critics, and upon us, to "go and learn what this means"—to study, to wrestle with the holy Scriptures, to *learn* what kind of human beings God desires to people creation. Whatever the nature of God's mysterious work in the world, it is not magic. God in Christ calls upon us all to "go and learn"—and learning can be very hard labor. Learning what God desires can stretch and pull us in directions we'd rather not go. Wisely, God shall not force us into mercy toward others. If humans cannot manipulate God with just the right ritual sacrifices, God likewise shall not manipulate humans, to whom God has entrusted response-ability, into living lives of compassion. The result, after all, would not be compassion but automation! This would not be the way of *hesed*. We, then, like the Pharisees, are called upon to "go and learn what this means." Study, thought, reflection are required. Of course we do need the divine physician's touch in order to live the implications that we learn, but a physician is neither a magician nor a warlord. Instant results are not guaranteed. This physician carefully and lovingly labors with us, not in spite of us, toward our and creation's healing. To this end, Wisdom divine calls unto us to "go and learn."

Jesus and the Hungry Ones

In that spirit, let us now "go and learn" from Matthew 12 and the second story, that of Jesus and his disciples walking through the grainfields one Sabbath day. As they do, the disciples begin to "pluck heads of grain and to eat" (12:1). Not at all coincidentally, Matthew is the only gospel writer who assures his readers that Jesus's disciples were hungry (12:1). Importantly for Matthew, our most Jewish of the evangelists, the disciples were not simply idling their way through the fields, mindlessly plucking grain out of boredom as they trudged along. "The disciples were hungry," so there is a legitimate and perhaps even pressing human need at issue here. Jewish legal

---

8. Heschel, *The Prophets*, 233.

reasoning regarding Sabbath behavior, probably already by Jesus's time, made allowances for doing whatever necessary to save a human life: "A case of risk of life supersedes the Sabbath" (*Yoma* 8.6, Talmud). In the case of this story, however, we can safely assume that no one was about to starve to death! Nonetheless, Matthew is careful to assure us that human hunger, the need that we feel in empty stomachs, was at the heart of this controversy.

We should note, too, that the problem was not that they were picking grain that was not theirs. The Torah made allowance for just such an act of hunger relief. In Deuteronomy 23:25 we read, "When you go into your neighbor's standing grain, you may pluck the ears with your hand, but you shall not put a sickle to your neighbor's standing grain." Harrington comments, "Such humanitarian legislation was intended to sustain the needy without giving them permission to pile up supplies. There is, however, no mention of the Sabbath in these cases."[9] It was, of course, precisely this concern for upholding Sabbath observance that motivated the Pharisees' observation: "Look, your disciples are doing what is not lawful to do on the Sabbath" (Matt 12:2). After all, the people of Israel were expressly commanded by God to do no labor—none whatsoever, and no exceptions—on the Sabbath day. If the Pharisees were ever going to succeed in getting the people to live faithfully in accordance with God's covenant, Sabbath observance would be a likely place to begin, since much of it could be publicly observed and regulated.

In this second passage of Matthew, we read that Jesus responded to his critics, "If only you had known what this means, 'I desire mercy and not sacrifice'" (12:7). This "if only" is fascinating, a perfectly fitting postscript to the earlier assignment, "Go and learn". I suggest that this "if only" reveals a divine yearning, perhaps Heschel's divine pathos—a longing of God for the world to be different, to be a place where compassion flows toward human suffering and need, where the hungry have plenty to eat and the sick receive adequate attention and care. Carter writes, "Mercy is not pity but doing God's justice, which challenges the restrictive practices and structures of the status quo and seeks to establish a life-giving community of shared resources and sustaining relationships."[10] If only we would so live! This "if only" of Jesus is essentially the same pathos he will annunciate later in this gospel when he cries out in the voice of Sophia incarnate, "Jerusalem, Jerusalem, you who kill the prophets and stone those sent to it, how often

---

9. Harrington, *The Gospel of Matthew*, 172.
10. Carter, *Matthew and the Margins*, 206.

did I wish to gather together your children, as a bird gathers her fledglings under wings, and you were not willing!" (23:37). Matthew's Jesus calls us to take seriously, indeed to feel, this divine pathos in the world, a divine desire for mercy that flows forth from the very heart of God the Merciful, the Compassionate—and then to act, to live, accordingly. The church of tomorrow, insofar as it is shaped by Matthew's Gospel, will undertake the yoke of learning what these words mean, "I desire mercy, and not sacrifice," and will put them into practice.

Jesus and the Pharisees

Not surprisingly, it is Jesus who leads the way in this practice. All three Synoptic Gospels follow up the grainfield controversy with the story of Jesus's healing of the man with a withered hand on the Sabbath, and in a synagogue. Indeed, Matthew insists that we see the two stories as intertwined; Jesus "left that place [i.e., the grainfield] and entered their synagogue" (12:9). Thus, it is not only the Sabbath, but now the controversy unfolds in a very public Jewish space. Now the problem of Jesus as a potential misleader of the people is intensified; a man of such charisma who plays fast-and-loose with the Sabbath is a dangerous figure, to say the least. Let us recall: if Roman political/military occupation is divine judgment upon wayward Israel; if only Israel's wholehearted return to faithful covenantal obedience can secure God's deliverance and blessings; if the Sabbath is one of the most publicly observable arenas of obedience to God's Torah; if Jesus seems quite willing to reject the Pharisees' understandably strict enforcement of Sabbath observance; and if Jesus's charisma as a teacher and healer continues to grow in recognition and influence among the Jewish people—then this man is a threat to the well-being and future viability of the people of Israel. Perhaps one cannot readily blame the Pharisees for being too careful.

But Jesus clearly has no interest in backing down from this fight. If Jesus had been more like many of us, perhaps he would have pulled aside the man with the withered hand and whispered to him back in the corner of the synagogue, "Say, friend, I'm really sorry about your hand and all. And I am quite happy to heal you—but let's wait till the sun goes down. I have these guys tracking my every move and just looking for an opportunity to accuse me yet another time. I don't want to give them any more ammo for a while. So how about we meet right outside by the synagogue after the sun goes down, and I'll heal your hand! Sound good?"

Of course we cannot imagine Jesus operating like that. But it's only a withered hand! He's not about to die from it. Were his condition more serious, to the point of life-threatening, the Pharisees (at least the more "liberal" schools) would have quickly agreed that one must act always to save a life. Life-saving labor is allowed, indeed virtually mandated, on the Sabbath. But this man was not in such danger. Nonetheless, human well-being is at stake. The Gospel of Mark makes this point even more clearly by telling us that Jesus insisted that "the Sabbath was made for the sake of human beings, rather than human beings for the sake of the Sabbath" (Mark 2:17, my trans.). Indeed, the sense of conflict is heightened in Mark by his adding that in the synagogue, Jesus "looked around" at his critics "with anger; he was grieved at their hardness of heart" (Mark 3:5). It is remarkable that both Jesus's anger and the Pharisees' perceived "hardness of heart" are swirling around something so simple as one hand not in working order. It truly can seem like a small matter; again, if the issue is that it's the Sabbath day, it would be a matter of hours and this would be a non-issue.

But Jesus will not wait those few hours. And he is angered and grieved at the hardened hearts of his critics—hearts closed off against human suffering and need, even (perhaps especially?) relatively slight suffering and manageable need. Let us repeat: this man was not on his deathbed, nor anywhere near it—no more than any of the disciples was starving in the grain fields (even if we can imagine one of them whining, "I'm starving!"). But Jesus would not wait. Instead, he forces the issue: What is the nature and purpose of the Sabbath day? Is it really intended by God to be a day on which one does nothing? (But see Exod 20:8–10!) Or is it a day on which to do good, to extend mercy, to care for even the most simple of human needs? We remember Hosea's prophetic words attributed to the Holy One, "I desire mercy, and not sacrifice"—and also that the Sabbath is the day set apart from the rest of the week, like the priests are set apart from the rest of the people, like kosher foods are set apart from the unclean, like the temple is set apart from other places and spaces. The Sabbath is a part of the priestly logic of holiness-as-separation, the logic that inspired the Pharasaic mission. So at the heart of this controversy is a disagreement about the nature of the Sabbath, to be sure; but even more profoundly, it is a disagreement regarding the nature of *God*, who gave the Sabbath. On this matter, Jesus would not compromise. "Stretch out your hand."

The Synoptic Gospels report that this synagogue encounter marked the beginning of the end for Jesus; in Matthew's words, "The Pharisees went out and conspired against him, how to destroy him" (12:14). Let us keep this in mind, for it is a point to which we will return.

Matthew's double use of Hosea's prophecy, "I desire mercy, and not sacrifice," is noteworthy on many counts, not the least of which is the degree to which Christian interpretations of the doctrine of the atonement have generally ignored this prophetic sentiment, gravitating often toward the very language of sacrifice. But might the words of Hosea, so critical to Matthew's good news about Jesus, be considered pertinent and applicable to Christianity's doctrine of the atonement? Asked otherwise, if God does not desire sacrifice, if God "takes no delight in sacrifice" (Ps 51:16) but delights rather in mercy or compassion toward others, is it possible that speaking of Jesus's crucifixion as a sacrifice offered to God on our behalf is misleading, perhaps even inappropriate? On the other hand, given the history of Christian teaching, can we talk about the atoning work of Jesus apart from the language of sacrifice and its attendant metaphors? Should we? Need we?

Jesus's Execution in Matthew

Let us begin with the relatively humble claim that Matthew's Gospel does not appeal, at least directly, to the language-world of sacrifice to understand Jesus's ministry or execution. Consider Jesus's Parable of the Wicked Tenants, found in all three Synoptic Gospels (Matt 21:33–41; Mark 12:1–12; Luke 20:9–19), in which the landowner (God) plants a vineyard (Israel) and leases it to tenants ("the chief priests and Pharisees" [Matt 21:45]). The landowner subsequently sends slaves (the prophets) to "collect his produce" (21:34), but these slaves meet with violent ends at the hands of the tenants. "Finally," though, "he sent his son to them, saying, 'They will respect my son'" (21:37). But the landowner is tragically mistaken, for "when the tenants saw the son, they said to themselves, 'This is the heir; come, let us kill him and get his inheritance.' So they seized him, threw him out of the vineyard, and killed him" (21:39).

Granted, this is "just a parable," and one should be wary of trying to load too much theology into any one biblical passage, especially any one of Jesus's elusively slippery parables as variously reported by our Gospels. *But*—we can at least say that Matthew expected his readers to understand this parable as a quick sketch of the history of Israel up to and including the ministry of Jesus. Certainly in this parable the murder of the landowner's son is in no way portrayed as a sacrifice desired, let alone required, by the landowner; indeed, it is a travesty. Interestingly, in all three Synoptics the landowner expresses at least the hope, if not the confident expectation, that the tenants will respect his son. Had this hope—God's own hope?—been fulfilled, the son would not have been murdered but respected and welcomed. In this regard, the landowner's hope mirrors, once again, Jesus's own lament over Jerusalem: "How often have I desired to gather your children together . . . and you were not willing" (23:37). Similarly, the landowner had sent both servants and son to the vineyard to "collect his produce" (23:34), "which," in John P. Meier's words, "naturally means the complete doing of God's will."[11] If Meier's suggestion is correct, I would add that for Matthew this doing of God's will is, most fundamentally, *doing mercy* (and, of course, not sacrifice). Obviously, these wicked tenants show anything but mercy to the landowner's slaves and, finally, to his son. These who "seized [the son], threw him out of the vineyard, and killed him" (21:39) are precisely those who had not come to know "what this means, 'I desire mercy and not sacrifice.'" Accordingly, soon after this parable, Jesus, embodying the voice of divine Wisdom, pronounces a powerful word of judgment upon the religious leaders of Israel: "Therefore I send you prophets, sages, and scribes, some of whom you will kill and crucify, and some you will flog in your synagogues and pursue from town to town, so that upon you may come all the righteous blood shed on earth, from the blood of righteous Abel to the blood of Zechariah" (23:34–35)—the blood of the righteous from A down to Z! Surely Matthew intends his readers to include the blood of the righteous Jesus within this list. "Wisdom's gracious care is rejected as Jesus is executed," writes Elizabeth A. Johnson, "preeminent in a long line of her murdered prophets."[12] If this bloodshed be considered a sacrifice, surely it is not a sacrifice that God desires, let alone requires.

Following Matthew's chronology, only a few days later Jesus reclined with his disciples for a final meal on Passover. He lifted the cup, gave thanks to God, and said to them, "Drink from it, all of you; for this is my blood-of-the-covenant, which is poured out for many for the forgiveness of sins" (26:27–28). The language is reminiscent of that same prophet Zechariah, who had written, "Rejoice greatly, O daughter Zion! Shout aloud, O daughter Jerusalem! . . . because of my blood of the covenant with you, I will set your prisoners free from the waterless pit" (Zech 9:9, 11). It is crucial

---

11. Meier, *The Vision of Matthew*, 151.
12. Johnson, "Wisdom Was Made Flesh," 107.

to appreciate that the blood-of-the-covenant is not the blood of sacrifice, at least not if sacrifice is associated with divine appeasement. The classic text is Exodus 24:3–8, in which Moses instructs the people Israel regarding "all the words of the Lord and all the ordinances" (Exod 24:3) and the people respond with a collective vow of obedience, after which Moses splatters both the altar and the people with the blood of oxen: "See the blood of the covenant that the Lord has made with you in accordance with all these words" (24:8). Granted, the oxen are "sacrificed . . . as offerings of well-being to the Lord" (24:5), or a "peace offering," but the sacrifice is not intended to procure divine forgiveness. In the case of Exodus 24, the blood ratifies or seals the covenant between God and Israel. "Likewise," Carter writes, "Jesus's death seals a covenant marked by God's release from sins and obedience to God's will manifested in Jesus's teaching. A new exodus . . . is underway. God's liberating work continues."[13] It is the sign of a covenant that runs so deep as to be written in blood, we might say. But what actually matters is the kind of living signified and required by this covenantal bond, rather than the ritual shedding of blood, in the view of Hosea (and other prophets)—a view taken up wholeheartedly in Matthew's portrayal of Jesus. So, once more, "obedience to God's will manifested in Jesus's teaching" might arguably be compressed into Hosea's description of what God desires.

None of this is to deny the presence of sacrificial language in the New Testament as a way to interpret the significance of Jesus's crucifixion. But it is to question the degree to which such language has been overly determinative of Christian theological reflection, especially in the West, and even more especially in the past several centuries. As Ernst Kasemann lamented fifty years ago, "Now there exists a Protestantism which, although it is not specially interested in cultic things, hangs grimly on to the doctrine of the sacrificial death." This would not be objectionable, he continued, "if it were regarded, as it is in the New Testament, as one among several interpretations of the cross. But here an attempt is made to tie us down to one single formula and style of preaching; and that is going too far."[14] Very typically this dominance is uncritically attributed to St. Anselm of Canterbury (1033–1109) and his classic text *Cur Deus Homo* ("Why God Became Human"). I would like to close this chapter by countering this assumption about Anselm's theology.

13. Carter, *Matthew and the Margins*, 506.
14. Kasemann, *Jesus Means Freedom*, 112.

Jesus and Anselm

Anselm's theory of the atonement is typically described as a "satisfaction" theory, and so it is. But already we must tread carefully. The idea of satisfaction in much Christian preaching of the atonement seems to veer toward the notion that it is God's demand for justice that is satisfied, or perhaps even simply God who is "satisfied"—almost, we might say, emotionally—by the death of Jesus such that it is his death that makes God's forgiveness of our sins possible.

But for Anselm, what is satisfied is a debt, the collective debt that human beings owe to God. "What is the debt which we owe to God?" Anselm asks through his student and dialogical partner Boso. The teacher's reply: "All the will of a rational creature ought to be subject to the will of God."[15] We know the rest of the argument: the collective debt of human obedience to God's will has not been satisfied; indeed, the debt has grown to unfathomable proportions through the passage of human history. It is a debt that humanity owes, but it is a debt so crushing that only God could possibly pay it. Thus, Anselm argued, God became human in order to satisfy the massive, collective human debt to God.

But here is the critical point: the debt is not satisfied by Jesus's (or anyone else's) death *per se*, but by the *faithful obedience* of the God-Human to the will of God. Remember that what is owed, according to Anselm, is "all the will of a rational creature." In this regard, Anselm is not far from Irenaeus's recapitulation theory, grounded in Romans 5: "just as by one man's disobedience the many were made sinners, so by the one man's *obedience* the many will be made righteous" (Rom 5:19). Indeed, he insists in Book I, chapter 9 that Boso is "not drawing a proper distinction . . . between, on the one hand, what Christ did because of the demands of his obedience and, on the other, the suffering inflicted upon him because he maintained his obedience, which [suffering] he underwent even though his obedience did not demand it."[16] *Jesus endured the suffering that was inflicted upon him because he faithfully maintained his obedience to God—even though his obedience to God's will did not demand, indeed did not include, that he suffer and die.* This, I dare say, is a point oft overlooked in the reading of Anselm. Jesus satisfies the human indebtedness to God not through suffering or a sacrificial death, but by faithfully maintaining his obedience in the face of religious

---

15. Davies and Evans, eds., *Anselm of Canterbury*, 283.
16. Davies and Evans, eds., *Anselm of Canterbury*, 276.

and political opposition. This suffering may not be terribly surprising, but it is not a matter of necessity—for it is not what God desires, let alone that in which God takes delight. Anselm makes the point repeatedly: Jesus was persecuted to the point of execution because "he had maintained truth and righteousness unflinchingly in his way of life and in what he said," which, Anselm adds, "is what God demands from every rational creature, and [is what] every creature owes . . . to God as a matter of obedience."[17]

"God, therefore, did not force Christ to die," Anselm reasons, a claim that flies directly in the face of much of Western atonement teaching that too often assumes itself to be Anselmian. "Rather," the embattled Archbishop of Canterbury adds, "he underwent death of his own accord, not out of an obedience consisting in the abandonment of his life, but out of an obedience consisting in his upholding of righteousness so bravely and pertinaciously that as a result he incurred death."[18] With these words, Anselm encourages us to return to Matthew's Jesus in the grainfields, and then in the synagogue, one Sabbath day. There, Jesus upheld righteousness so bravely as to insist, against all opposition and accusation, that the God he was obeying "desires mercy, and not sacrifice." He insisted that such obedience demanded acts of compassion toward his hungry disciples and the man with the withered hand. He would not back down from this vision of divine righteousness, such that "the Pharisees went out and conspired against him, how to destroy him" (Matt 12:14). Or, once more in Anselm's words, his faithful obedience consisted in "his upholding of [divine] righteousness so bravely . . . that as a result he incurred death."

Thus for Anselm Jesus's death is not a sacrifice offered to God; rather, the divine Son's faithful *life* is offered to God as a satisfaction of the collective, universal human debt. This faithful life consists precisely in mercy, in compassion, in actively seeking the well-being of each neighbor he encountered. Of course, it is no great surprise that such a life would end violently and early. However, even at this point it is noteworthy that Anselm does not conclude that since the debt has been satisfied by the God who became human, we are now all off the hook. In Book II, chapter 18, Anselm returns to this crucial theme: "When Christ endured with kindly patience the sufferings—injuries and insults and death on the cross along with robbers—which were inflicted on him because of the righteousness which, as we have said earlier, he was obediently maintaining, he set an example to mankind

17. Davies and Evans, eds., *Anselm of Canterbury*, 276.
18. Davies and Evans, eds., *Anselm of Canterbury*, 277.

...."[19] Jesus's faithful obedience even in the face of great opposition and suffering, Anselm insists, exemplifies the fact "that people should not turn aside ... from the righteousness which they owe to God."[20] The church of tomorrow, as it takes upon itself the yoke of Jesus, will likewise understand and practice the truth that Jesus's faithful obedience does not replace ours, as though his life cancels human action and responsibility. Jesus is not our substitute; he is our representative and our example to follow.

Even so, we are probably not as enamored over the language of debt and its satisfaction as Anselm was. God is not a business keeper scrutinizing the ledger. But as we draw this chapter to a close, it may be helpful to recall the words of Paul, "Owe no one anything, except to love one another; for the one who loves another has fulfilled the law" (Rom 13:8). Here Paul gestures toward a theological anthropology rooted in mutual indebtedness; God has created us such that what we owe one another is love. Notice that it is not so much what we owe to God as what we owe to one another; in this regard Paul's dictum parallels Hosea's insistence that what God desires is not sacrifices offered toward the heavens, but compassion extended toward our fellow creatures. "Love does no wrong to a neighbor," Paul continues; "therefore, love is the fulfilling of the law" (13:10). To do no wrong to the neighbor—and, conversely, to do what is good and right to the neighbor—fulfills the divine law because it is the essence of Wisdom's desire for human beings: "mercy, and not sacrifice." We shall contemplate the implications of such a command in the following chapter, but surely it takes little reflection to realize that this is virtually an infinite debt. It may force us to ask humbly, and tremblingly, as it was asked long ago, "Who is my neighbor?" If indeed the category of "neighbor" ultimately excludes no one, then the burden of loving my neighbor as one like unto my very self is a debt that shall never be satisfied. Nor is it a debt with which Jesus does away.

---

19. Davies and Evans, eds., *Anselm of Canterbury*, 349.
20. Davies and Evans, eds., *Anselm of Canterbury*, 349.

3

Wisdom's Commands

> *You shall love the Lord your God with all your heart,*
> *and with all your soul, and with all your might.*
> *You shall love your neighbor as yourself.*

THE CITATION OF THE Mosaic commandments to love God with all of one's being, and to love one's neighbors as one's very own self, is of course not unique to the Gospel of Matthew. All three Synoptic Gospels present scenarios in which these two great commandments are cited (and we shall very soon cast a glance in their direction). Thus, the appearance of these commandments, in and of itself, is not why Matthew matters. It is in small editorial embellishments on these commandments that Matthew is unique—and, as we shall soon discover, one of those embellishments would make a world of difference, three centuries later, to St. Augustine in his attempt to develop a Christian rule of biblical interpretation.

The Dual Command in the Synoptic Gospels

In Matthew, as in Mark its predecessor, the dual commandments of love are cited in a context of confrontation and controversy. The passage about love for God and neighbor (Matt 22:34–40) is situated after challenges about paying taxes to Rome (22:15–22) and the resurrection of the dead

(22:23–33) and just before Jesus's counter-question regarding the identity of the Messiah (22:41–46). Correspondingly, these passages of controversy typically end with descriptions of Jesus's superiority in theological debate: the response to Jesus's reply about Caesar's image on the Roman coin was amazement and retreat (22:22); the response to his interpretation of the words from the burning bush was astonishment (22:33); finally, when Jesus asks the gathered Pharisees about what it means for David to call the son of David "Lord," Matthew testifies that "no one was able to give him an answer, nor from that day did anyone dare to ask him any more questions" (22:46). Controversies controverted.

Interestingly, in Mark's rendition of the dual commandment story the sense of conflict is less pronounced. A scribe overhears Jesus debating with the Sadducees about the resurrection "and seeing that [Jesus] answered them well, he asked him, 'Which commandment is the first of all?'" (Mark 12:28). Jesus replies with the *Shema* from Deuteronomy (Deut 6:4–6) and then adds the second, from Leviticus (Lev 19:18), commenting, "There is no greater commandment than these" (Mark 12:31). The scribe replies enthusiastically that Jesus ("Teacher") is right in this dual reply, that love for God and neighbor is "much more important than all whole burnt offerings and sacrifices" (12:33). Jesus in turn recognizes the wisdom in the scribe's reply, responding with somewhat muted praise, "You are not far from the kingdom of God" (12:34).

Luke's Gospel may be the most fascinating insofar as in its case, the dual command is not on Jesus's lips but on his interlocutor's.[1] When a Torah legal expert asks Jesus, "Teacher, what must I do the inherit eternal life?" Jesus places the ball back in his questioner's court. "What is written in the law? What do you read there?" (Luke 10:25–26).[2] His questioner then replies with the commands of love for God and neighbor from the Torah. Jesus responds, "You have given the right answer; do this, and you will live" (10:28). Intriguingly, Luke informs us that the questioner wanted to justify

---

1. In this, Luke reflects what we know to have been the case during the era of Jesus, that Hellenistic Jewish writing could identify the dual command of love as the core or heart of the Torah; in Rudolf Schnackenburg's words, "[N]ot a few scholars think that the condensation of the many commandments into the first and second commandments of love stems only from the Hellenistic Jewish-Christian community since this view appears in Hellenistic Judaism" (*The Gospel of Matthew*, 222). Schnackenburg then cites as evidence *Testament of Issachar* 5:2, 7:6; *Testament of Daniel* 5:3; Philo, *On Special Laws* 2:63.

2. I have written more extensively on this tremendous passage in the essay, "And He Felt Compassion: Holiness beyond the Bounds of Community."

himself, and so asked, "And who is my neighbor?" (10:29). We can surmise that the justification desired had to do with his disinterest in defining "neighbor" very broadly or inclusively. In any case, it is a great and enduring question and it provided the immediate impetus for Jesus's provocative parable about a compassionate Samaritan. But far too often overlooked is the way in which Jesus transforms the question; whereas he is asked "And who is my neighbor?" in the end Jesus turns the question inside-out by asking, "Which of these three, do you think, *was a neighbor* to the man who fell into the hands of the robbers?" (10:36, italics mine). Thus the question no longer is whether or not someone is my neighbor, but whether or not I will *be* or *become a neighbor* to those I encounter, and in particular to those who suffer or are vulnerable. If I venture to *become* the neighbor, then in fact there is no one who is not my neighbor, for my very stance in life shall be consistently to take the initiative of drawing nigh to every person. "Go and do likewise," Jesus adds (10:37).

By turning the category of "neighbor" inside-out in this Lukan passage, Jesus transcends the language of Leviticus, which, as it turns out, is considerably radical already. When the Torah expert asked the question, "Who is my neighbor?" it is unlikely that he was entirely without an opinion on the matter. The words of Leviticus 19 were addressed "to the congregation of the people of Israel," calling them to "be holy, for I the LORD your God am holy" (Lev 19:2). It is this people as God's community here being addressed; hence, "your kin" (19:17) and "your people" (19:18) are interchangeable with "your neighbor" (19:18). So at least the easiest and most obvious answer to the question would be, "My neighbor is my fellow Jew." However, the Torah expert undoubtedly knew that even Leviticus did not stop there; later in the same chapter we read, "When an alien resides with you in your land, you shall not oppress the alien. The alien who resides with you shall be to you as the citizen among you; you shall love the alien as yourself, for you were aliens in the land of Egypt: I am the LORD your God" (19:33–34). The category of "neighbor" has just been uncomfortably extended to "alien" or "stranger"—just as Jesus adopted the figure of the despised Samaritan and made him the model of what it means to become the neighbor to others. In the very telling of this story, Jesus was enacting love for "the stranger," or even, sociologically speaking, "the enemy"—since that is what Samaritans were to most Jews in first-century Israel.

To Love an Other

But what does it mean to love one's neighbor, let alone the stranger, as oneself? We hear it so often, yet ponder its implications so rarely. With this question, for over four decades I have labored happily under the influence of Martin Buber, who wrote in *Between Man and Man*, "The neighbor is to be loved 'as one like myself' (not 'as I love myself'; in the last reality one does not love oneself, but one should rather learn to love oneself through love of one's neighbor), to whom, then, I should show love as I wish it may be shown to me."[3] In other words, let us not interpret this as a subtle commandment first to love ourselves, followed by the pop psychology rationale that unless I love myself I cannot love others. Without denying the grain of truth there,[4] it is far more critical to recognize with Scripture that such a hard line cannot be drawn between one's neighbors and one's self; surely we grasp that "one's own welfare is intertwined with that of the other."[5] It is not so much that I am to love the neighbor as or to the degree that I love myself, but that I am to love the neighbor *as one like unto myself*, as one who is like me—and thus as one who is with me and with whom I am. Indeed, I am to love the neighbor as though the neighbor were my very self. This requires me to see this other one as being something, indeed someone, very much like me—a person with consciousness, with feelings, with longings, with a stomach; with dreams, desires, loves, needs, hopes, hurts, disappointments, and yearnings. Mine will not always be identical with my neighbor's, but there will be much recognizably in common. As I hunger, my neighbor feels its pangs. As I need clean water and air, so also my neighbor needs. As I love, my neighbor loves. As I fear, my neighbor fears. And even the holiness text of Leviticus called the Israelite community beyond the neighbor to include the stranger in the same calculations. By recognizing myself—or at least one very much like unto myself—in the neighbor and even the stranger, there exists the soil in which true and deep empathy begins to take root and flourish.

---

3. Buber, *Between Man and Man*, 73.

4. Loving oneself, writes Muslim philosopher Shabbir Akhtar, "comes naturally to sane healthy individuals.... The person who loves himself is not misguided so long as he loves the true self, rather than worships the false self. That latter attitude constitutes the sin of narcissism. The true or higher self is worth knowing and nourishing. Indeed, it brings us to God as we stare at our own true image" (*The New Testament in Muslim Eyes*, 190).

5. Carter, *Matthew and the Margins*, 445.

Similarly, we note that in Leviticus the divine command to love the stranger as one's very self is not presented simply as an authoritative demand; rather, it is rooted in God's appeal to the Israelites' own historical experience: "for you yourselves once were strangers in the land of Egypt" (19:34). Such an appeal depends upon our capacities to perceive "the stranger" as one who is like ourselves, not entirely foreign to our own personal and collective experience. The Israelites knew, even if only through stories of their ancestors' enslavement in Egypt, what it "feels like" to be the stranger, the dehumanized, the oppressed, the marginalized. God's calling to Israel was to imaginatively extend that experience to those they encountered who were "strangers" to them. Empathy, then, is feeling with and for this one who is other but not at all entirely other from me.

We recall that in Luke the Torah expert asked the question "Who is my neighbor?" because he wanted to justify himself. This should not surprise. For to see the neighbor as one who is fundamentally like me, and then to act accordingly, is a terribly tall order. Surely there is something in this command that calls us to walk (or stumble!) ever onward, to plunge ever deeper, to become ever more liberal in our applications. Again, Leviticus broadened this call to include the "stranger" and Jesus in Matthew and Luke extended it even to "enemies" (Matt 5:43–48; Luke 6:27–36). We can never be done with this commandment. We will never, certainly in this life, be able to claim to have fulfilled it. It may be that we shall never cease growing in its dynamic possibilities even in the age to come. When shall I love all neighbors (and "strangers!") as though each was my very own self? And what would such love require? When shall I be willing to see my self in these others, and to see these others in me? When and how am I able to become the neighbor to all of these others? What would it take? How would I then live? How could we ever "finish" such a calling as this?

To Love the Other That Is God

Notably, the Torah expert in his desire to justify himself did not ask "And how am I to love God with all my heart, soul, and might?" (Deut 6:5)—but surely he could have. For this command likewise exceeds the depths of our capacities. What would it take to love God with all of our being and all of our energies? And in every moment of our lives? How can we come to love God "whom no one has ever seen" (John 1:18; 1 John 4:12) in this way? Perhaps he asked about the neighbor because it is the more empirical of the categories; at least "loving God" might seem the more internal, less observable, less testable of the two loves. But again, what does it mean to love God like this? There is a considerable tendency in current church talk to speak of "falling in love with God" in a way that, in my judgment, trivializes love for God. Too many of our contemporary worship songs make this love sound like a syrupy romantic infatuation—as though this is what God desires or needs. Not that our emotions are to be left out of the equation, to be sure—for we are called to love God with all of our being, all of the time. But surely this love cannot be reduced to emotional highs, chills down the spine, or giddy palpitations of the heart.

If we follow the lead of Deuteronomy, in which we find the *Sh'ma*, we would likely conclude that loving God entails "observ[ing God's commandments] diligently, . . . keep[ing] these words that I am commanding you today in your heart" (Deut 6:3, 6). But, on the other extreme, does this reduce love of God to following commands? Shall we reduce love to moralism? Yet what other sort of love could be commanded, or demanded of us, anyway? What sort of love is it that can be commanded? Perhaps it was due to such questions that John Wesley preferred not to interpret the commands to love God and neighbor simply as commandments, but as *promises* of God to God's people: not so much that we *must* love God and neighbor, but that, by the grace of God through Jesus Christ in the empowering fullness of the Spirit, we *shall* love God and all neighbors. As what Wesley called "covered promises," God shall see to it. (Of course Wesley would never expect that God shall see to it entirely apart from our divinely given and empowered volition and participation!) It is quite possible that we in the Wesleyan-holiness tradition have been far too quick to presume that the promise has already been fulfilled in many of our lives. But there is an eternal, illimitable dynamic to such love as this; there are no limits to such love as this. I trust that the church of tomorrow, especially congregations within the Wesleyan stream, will continue to interpret the substance of the holy life as John Wesley did—utter love for God with our entire being, and love for all people ("neighbors," "strangers," and yes even "enemies") as our very selves. But the church of tomorrow will recognize that this is a calling that is never fully achieved, for there are depths and breadths of love that can never be entirely fathomed (let alone attained) "under the conditions of existence" (to use Tillich's favored phrase). I believe the church of tomorrow will understand itself, more profoundly than we have in the past, to be a people on the move toward "Love Divine, All Loves Excelling,"[6] to be an alternative community striving to march ever more faithfully to the beat of God's everlasting, long-suffering love for all creation. Certainly many of our churches, and individual lives, today settle for far less.

Matthew Matters?

With such rich material about this dual commandment in both Mark and Luke, one might wonder whether Matthew matters on this score. What does Matthew add to the mix? What is unique to Matthew on this matter? Let us undertake a careful exegesis of the passage in question.

We read that a Pharisee with particular expertise in the Torah ("a lawyer") "asked him a question to test him: Teacher, which commandment in the law is the greatest?" (Matt 22:34–35). The description of this encounter as a "test" creates an adversarial setting. The test, in this case, probably involved the question whether or not any commandment could be deemed by human beings to be greater or more important than any other. There were Jewish scribes who would have argued that, since God is the source of all commands in the law, they are all of equal import. It is not up to humans to decide their importance or arrange them according to their notions of value. A divine command is just that, a divine command. Subsequent attempts especially by Christian interpreters to distinguish between ceremonial laws and moral laws would find no sympathy from these quarters.

Other Jewish legal experts, however, sought a logic or grounding for divine commandments. We have mentioned already that some Hellenistic Jewish texts contemporary with Jesus, and even prior to Jesus, had identified the dual command of love for God and neighbor as the heart and ground of the Torah. But it is critical to mention that this would never have been understood as a rationale for devaluing, let alone eliminating, any of the other commandments. In David Sim's words, "The principle of summarizing the entire law under a fundamental statement is thoroughly Jewish, [but] is never presented . . . as a replacement for the Mosaic code."[7] Undoubtedly the best-known example of such a summary comes to us in the Talmudic story of two of the greatest early rabbis, Shammai and Hillel. As the story goes, a gentile visited the homes of each of these great teachers

---

6. To cite the title of one of Charles Wesley's great hymns. It should be noted that this phrase (and title) is actually designating God.

7. Sim, *The Gospel of Matthew and Christian Judaism*, 127.

in turn, offering in jest to convert to Judaism if the rabbi could teach him the Torah during the time that he, the would-be student, could remain standing on one foot. (The obvious implication is that he would want it in brief compass!) The first, Shammai, known to have been the stricter of the two in regard to legal interpretation, was so infuriated by the request that he chased the *goy* from his door with a measuring stick in hand. The second, Hillel, accepted the challenge; presumably in the time that his visitor could keep one leg raised, Hillel simply said, "What is hateful to you do not do to your neighbor; this is the whole Torah; the rest is commentary. Go and learn it" (*Shabbat* 31a). The gentile smart-aleck was so impressed by this reply, so the story goes, that he did indeed become a Jewish convert.

It is not at all difficult to assume that Jesus had heard this story, and probably often, since Hillel lived in the decades preceding Jesus's birth and died in Jerusalem when Jesus was a boy. Did Hillel's famed reply influence what we read in the Sermon on the Mount, "In everything do to others as you would have them do to you; for this is the law and the prophets" (Matt 7:12)? It seems difficult to avoid this likelihood, and in any case there is no reason to do so. Further, we are challenged to reflect on the difference between the two formulations: *not* doing to others what I find hateful or even disagreeable to myself is certainly praiseworthy, but is a negative principle that only forbids certain actions. I am left with/in a certain passivity.[8] But to *do* to others what I would have them do to me requires that I act, that I undertake the initiative, that I seek the other's well-being—and to do so "in everything"! We are once again confronted with a commandment that cannot possibly ever be fully accomplished—and this, while a perennially challenging thing, is also a very good thing.

In any event, to the question "Which commandment in the law is the greatest?" Jesus gave an unsurprising answer. The *Sh'ma* (Hebrew, meaning "hear" or "listen") was, and remains, the heart of Jewish piety and daily prayer:

> Hear, O Israel: the LORD is our God, the LORD alone.
> You shall love the LORD your God with all your heart, and with all your soul, and with all your might.
> Keep these words that I am commanding you today in your heart.
> (Deut 6:4–6)

---

8. This is not a Christianity versus Jewish phenomenon. After all, the apostle Paul offered a similar negative formulation: "Love does no wrong to a neighbor; therefore, love is the fulfilling of the law" (Rom 13:10).

Wisdom's Commands

This passage provides the basis for Jewish practices such as wearing *tefillin* or phylacteries ("bind them as a sign on your head, fix them as an emblem on your forehead," 6:8) and the affixing of *mezuzot* to doorposts ("write them on the doorposts of your house," 6:9). Indeed, the *Sh'ma* itself is always an important portion of the biblical text that is rolled up and placed inside the mezuzah. This passage is so germane to Jewish practice, prayer, and identity that its status as the greatest commandment would generally go unchallenged, except by those who would fastidiously reject any ordering of the divine commands.

We should note that, by reciting the *Sh'ma*, Jesus had satisfied the question, "Which is the greatest commandment?" Like many professors, however, he proceeded to over-answer the question! But of course it is not really a matter of over-answering; rather, Jesus is pointing out that these two commandments are inextricably bound. Indeed, this is made most clear by the first of editorial comments unique to Matthew: "And a second is like it" (Matt 22:39). We presume the second is like the first because they both involve the calling, the command, to love. We note, too, that Jesus does not collapse the two commandments into one; he certainly does not say that loving God is nothing other than loving the neighbor. Buber long ago was careful to stress that while "the neighbor is to be loved 'as one like myself'... God is to be loved with all my soul and all my might."[9] Buber continues beautifully:

> By connecting the two Jesus brings to light the Old Testament truth that God and man are not rivals. Exclusive love to God ("with *all* your heart") is, *because he is God*, inclusive love, ready to accept and include all love.... [God] limits himself in all his limitlessness, he makes room for the creatures, and so, in love to[ward] him, he makes room for love to[ward] the creatures.... We are created along with one another and directed to a life with one another.... A God in whom only the parallel lines of single approaches intersect is more akin to the "God of the philosophers" than to the "God of Abraham and Isaac and Jacob."... For [the real God] is the creator, and all beings stand before him in relation to one another in his creation, becoming useful in living with one another for [God's] creative purpose.[10]

---

9. Buber, *Between Man and Man*, 73.

10. Buber, *Between Man and Man*, 73, 74. Few passages in theological writing have had as deep or as long-lasting an impact upon me as this.

So now Jesus has listed two commandments, and one might expect that, given time and opportunity, Jesus could keep on ranking the commandments from #3 all the way down to #613. But that of course is not the logic of his reply. Jesus is not offering the #1 and #2 hits on a Top 40 Survey of the Commandments. He is digging much deeper, offering the very ground and rationale for *any* and *all* commandments in the Torah. And so we encounter this second editorial flourish, unique to Matthew's Gospel, providing us another reason why Matthew matters: "On these two commandments hang all the law—and the prophets" (22:40). Jack Dean Kingsbury comments, accordingly, that "keeping the injunctions of the law, or doing the will of God, is always, in essence, an exercise in love."[11]

Like two pegs driven into a wall upon which to hang the family's outer garments, the Mosaic commands to love God wholeheartedly and one's neighbor as one's very self are presented as the stakes that support and bolster everything else Moses wrote—and then, significantly, Jesus adds to it the writings, the demands, the preachments, of all the prophets of Israel. (And so he over-answers again!) The very fabric of the Jewish tradition, Jesus insists, is this sort of everlastingly demanding love toward God and toward each and every fellow human being. This is the law and the prophets. John Meier acknowledges the point made earlier, that "the joining together of love of God and of neighbor can also be found in Hellenistic-Jewish writings of the time," but then adds that "there is no real parallel to this concise expression of the double command as the presupposition, substance, and basis of all written revelation."[12]

It is this very idea that "the double command [is] the presupposition, substance, and basis of all written revelation"—or, in the simpler and more picturesque words of Matthew, that "on these two commandments hang all the law and the prophets"—that was to influence St. Augustine (354–430) so profoundly several centuries later. With a confident hope that the church of tomorrow may richly benefit from Augustine on the matter of biblical interpretation, let us now turn to a close reading of his argument in Book XII of his *Confessions*.

---

11. Kingsbury, *Matthew*, 90.

12. Meier, *The Vision of Matthew*, 158. Sim suggests, "The conflict which Matthew introduces to this passage is a certain indicator that the correct method of interpreting the law was a major bone of contention between his own community and the leadership of formative Judaism" (*The Gospel of Matthew and Christian Judaism*, 128).

St. Augustine on Reading Scripture

The sainted bishop of Hippo has just been rehearsing variant readings of the very opening of Holy Writ, "In the beginning God made heaven and earth."[13] It is noteworthy that he can quickly list four competing interpretations *of just the opening phrase of the Bible* alongside his own. This might seem remarkable, but seven centuries later the great French rabbi Rashi (1040–1105) would write of the Bible's opening, "This verse cries out, 'Interpret me!'" Of course, every verse (and every person and thing, for that matter) cries out the same, but Rashi was reinforcing the particular difficulty of Genesis's genesis, helping us to appreciate, hopefully, how and why considerable controversy could be swirling through the church of Augustine's world—simply on the matter of how best to interpret that opening phrase. For it is clear that Augustine is confessing his own ongoing frustrations with people who disagree with him on precisely this matter. "Having heard and pondered all this, I have no wish to 'contend in words; that is no good for anything except undermining its hearers'" (2 Tim 2:14).[14]

Augustine reminds us that Genesis is part of the Torah, the law, and that "the law good for upbuilding, . . ." because "its purpose is 'love that proceeds from a pure heart'" (1 Tim 1:5). This already anticipates where his argument will lead him, and us. He continues, "I know on which commandments, according to our Teacher, 'hang all the Law and the prophets'" (Matt 22:40).[15] Give ear, then, to Augustine's prayer:

"What hindrance is it to me, my God, light that lightens my eyes in secret,[16] . . . that these words [of Genesis 1:1] may be understood in such diverse senses, seeing as they are none the less true for it? What if I take them to mean something other than Moses took them to mean?"[17] Augustine invites the plurality of interpretations of the text in the confidence that divine light and communication offer a surplus of meaning(s) to creaturely intellects, even meanings differing from the author himself. Augustine here is refreshingly postmodern—or, far more appropriately and correctly,

---

13. Augustine, *Confessions* (trans. Burton), 302. I will rely on this translation throughout, but for exceptions that will be noted.

14. Augustine, *Confessions*, 303. The careful reader will note that I am altering Burton's format slightly, but not his text.

15. Augustine, *Confessions*, 303.

16. Given that the discussion is inspired by interpretations of Genesis 1, this is very likely an allusion to God's creative invitation to "let there be light" (Gen 1:3).

17. Augustine, *Confessions*, 303–4.

pre-modern—in his approach to issues of interpretation and questions about authorial intent.

"All of us who read him are striving to hunt down and comprehend his meaning, and, believing him to speak truly, we dare not suppose him to have said anything that we know or think is false."[18] We note how Augustine begins to shift us toward the notion of a community of interpretation—"all of us who read him"—that strives hard together to read Scripture faithfully and coherently. It should strike us as significant that Augustine suggests that we ought not to interpret Scripture in ways that controvert "anything that we know or think is false." Not to over-read his counsel, but here are wise words for an interpretive community (the church) that still experiences controversy regarding the reading of Genesis 1, though now the argument swirls around young earth creationism/evolutionary descriptions. Augustine does offer us wisdom as communities of interpretation. "What harm," then, "does it do if someone takes [the text] to mean something that you, light of all true-speaking minds, show him is true—even if this was not the meaning of the writer whom he is reading, seeing as Moses too meant something that is true, even though it was not the same thing?"[19] Dare we trust the light of God to enlighten our fellow readers—even if our resulting interpretations clash? And are we sufficiently humble to acknowledge that all readings, including our own, are indeed interpretations of a text whose author's mind finally remains a stranger to us?

Augustine then canvases, again, conflicts of interpretation over the opening verses of Genesis in which he has been embroiled. He prays, "Behold, my God, how confidently I, your servant, who have vowed to offer the sacrifice of confession to you in these writings, . . . say that through your immutable Word you made all things, both visible and invisible. Would I say with the same confidence that this was what Moses had in mind when he wrote 'in the beginning God made heaven and earth'?"[20] Augustine makes a distinction between a theologically contoured confession of faith, that God creates all things through the Logos that became flesh and dwelled among us as the human being Jesus of Nazareth (John 1:1–14), and the burden of interpretation involved in laboring over the opening lines of the Bible. The first is a hermeneutical presupposition with which a Christian might begin the work of interpretation; the second involves the process of

---

18. Augustine, *Confessions*, 304.
19. Augustine, *Confessions*, 304.
20. Augustine, *Confessions*, 309.

trying to work through the niceties of the text in ways that are faithful to that presupposition.

A little later Augustine takes off his gloves:

> "Let no one make any more trouble for me" (Gal. 6:17), saying: "Moses did not mean what you say he meant; he meant what I say." ... O God, life of the poor, in whose breast there is no contradiction, rain down your tender influences on my heart, and let me endure with patience such people ... [who] are proud and know not Moses's meaning, but love their own—not because it is true but because it is theirs.[21]

Remember that Augustine is not claiming that these people bugging him are necessarily wrong in their interpretations, for he has already opened up the possibility of a plurality of readings, "all of which may yet true."[22] For Augustine the problem is a proprietary and thus privatized approach to the issues of text, interpretation, and truth. Augustine has already admitted that *everyone* "know[s] not Moses's meaning"—an admission that would naturally lead to humility *vis a vis* other readings. I can, and should, certainly believe that my interpretation is a faithful one, true to the dual command of love (an idea soon to be developed), and perhaps even the very best one available—if I do not believe that, it is probably time to seek another interpretation! But I can also hold this conviction lightly, and humbly, ready to be challenged and instructed by fellow readers in the community of interpretation in which we share. In such an interpretive community, Augustine's pests "would love the other['s] interpretation no less, just as I love what they say when it is true; not because it is theirs, but because it is true. If, however, they do indeed love it because it is true, then it is both theirs and mine, for it is the common property of all truth-lovers."[23] Again we encounter this lovely vision of the church, and of individual churches, as shouldering together the happy burden of interpretation, and sharing together in the plurality of readings that arise from such an undertaking. Let the differences abound, and let us love one another in the midst of those conversations, and even sometimes heated debates, about those differences. On the other hand, Augustine warns, "whoever claims as his own that which you have set out for the enjoyment of all, and wants for his own

---

21. Augustine, *Confessions*, 309.
22. In R. S. Pine-Coffin's translation of the *Confessions* (Penguin, 1961), 296.
23. Augustine, *Confessions* (trans. Burton), 309–10.

what belongs to everyone, is driven away from what belongs to all and back to what belongs to himself; that is, from truth to falsehood."[24]

Finally, Hippo's sainted bishop offers up his prayer to Truth that will bring us full circle to Matthew's rendition of Jesus's citation of Moses's commandments:

> "Give ear, O God, Judge supreme and very Truth, and hear what I say to this opponent" (Jer. 18:19). Give ear and listen; it is before you that I speak and before my brothers, those who "use the law lawfully" to achieve the "goal of love" (1 Tim. 1:5–8). The answer I give him is fraternal and irenic:
>
> "If we both see that what you say is true, and if we both see that what I say is true, tell me where we see it. I do not see it in you, nor you in me; we both see it in the unchangeable Truth itself that is above our understanding. Seeing, then, as we are not arguing over the light that comes from our Lord and God, why should we argue over our neighbour's thoughts, which we cannot see in the way that we can see the unchangeable Truth?"[25]

Setting aside, if we are able and willing, the Platonic underpinnings of Augustine's notions of "light" and "the unchangeable Truth," we find nonetheless a deep wisdom in his prayer. Just as he prays to God who is Truth far beyond his capacity to comprehend or imagine, so in his prayer he imagines conversing with his interpretive opponent. They both believe that truth exists, precisely because they both believe in God, specifically God as revealed in the incarnate Word who said, "I am the Truth" (John 14:6). While they may "see" this Truth in some way—perhaps as "in a glass, darkly" (1 Cor 13:12)—they do not particularly see this truth in each other's interpretations. When the interpretive community functions healthfully, we all acknowledge that we are creatures of dust, feeble and frail, limited and biased in our readings of things, including Scripture. This is not a bad thing; it is a function of existing as these creatures that we are, interpreting our way through every moment of our individual and collective experiences. As Buber has already reminded us, "We are created along with one another and directed to a life with one another."[26] Hence, we really do need each other—including in the mutual bearing of the happy burden of interpretation. We acknowledge, as Augustine prayed, that "the unchangeable Truth

---

24. Augustine, *Confessions*, 310.
25. Augustine, *Confessions*, 310.
26. See fn. 10 of this chapter.

itself... is above our understanding," and so we are left, we are entrusted, with the ongoing task of interpreting together. This is why Augustine, in his prologue to *Teaching Christianity*, warns against sanctified self-sufficiency, "[L]et us not be too proud to learn what has to be learned with the help of other people." Imagine that God did not teach us through the agency of others; then "love itself, which binds people together with the knot of unity, would have no scope for pouring minds and hearts in together, as it were, and blending them with one another, if human beings were never to learn anything from each other."[27]

Back in *Confessions*, Augustine continues to address both God and his imagined human opponent: "Even if Moses himself were to appear and say 'This is what I meant', we would still not see the Truth in the same way, and yet we would believe."[28] What a wonderful line! Even an audience with Moses the author, face-to-face, would not rid us of the necessity of interpretation. Augustine encourages us to acknowledge, perhaps even to celebrate, the ambiguities and pluralities of meaning inherent in any relationship between the interpreter and the interpreted. Unless we believe in Vulcan mind-melds, the "other" is always accessible to me only through acts of interpretation—and very likely the same would hold also in a Vulcan mind-meld![29] We are readers, we are interpreters, of necessity, for we can always only "know in part" (1 Cor 13:12).

> Let no one, then, be "filled with pride against his brother over what is written" (1 Cor. 4:6). Let us "love the Lord our God with all our heart, with all our soul and with all our mind, and our neighbor as ourselves." Unless we believe that whatever Moses meant in the Scriptures, he meant it for the sake of these two commandments, that we should love God and neighbor, we "make the Lord a liar" (Jn. 5:10), if our attitude towards our fellow-servant's views is not what Moses taught us it should be. There are so many true meanings to be extracted from these words; see how foolish it is, then, to be in a hurry to assert which of them Moses really meant, and with destructive controversies to offend against the spirit of love—when it was for the sake of love that Moses said all the things we are trying to elucidate![30]

---

27. Augustine, *De Doctrina Christiana* (trans. Hill), 102, 103.
28. Augustine, *Confessions*, 310.
29. I grant that this allusion is effective only for people familiar with *Star Trek* lore.
30. Augustine, *Confessions*, 310–11.

Since "all the Torah and prophets hang on these two commandments," and since Genesis is the opening book of the Torah, and the creation stories are the opening of Genesis—then all we read there, from *In the beginning* onward, has been written for the sake of love for God and all neighbors. Augustine took a bold but praiseworthy interpretive step in proposing that if this is the rule for reading the Torah and the prophets, it can and should also be the rule for reading all of Holy Writ. So in *Teaching Christianity* he claims that "Scripture . . . commands nothing but charity, or love, and censures nothing but cupidity, or greed, and that is the way it gives shape and form to human morals." Growth in the Christian life, then, is "making progress in the love of God and neighbor, and in the knowledge of [God and neighbor],"[31] and this is Holy Scripture's purpose. In dealing with difficult passages of Scripture that seem not to point us in this direction, Augustine wrote that "you should take pains to turn over and over in your mind what you read, until your interpretation of it is led right through to the kingdom of love."[32] Indeed, admitted Augustine, there are texts whose "secret meanings have to be winkled out for the nourishment of love"[33] for God and all neighbors.

Augustine's rule of interpretation is formulated in direct reliance upon Jesus's citation of the laws of Moses regarding love for God and neighbor—but, even more specifically, upon Matthew's unique testimony that Jesus added that all of the Torah, and the prophets too, hang on these two commands. In Hillel's memorable phrase, "The rest is commentary." This, I think, is a worthy hermeneutic for the church of tomorrow. What if our interpretations of Scripture were governed by the assumption that the dual command of love represents God's *telos* for the church, for all people, indeed for all creation? This of course would not lead us all to agree on the meaning(s) of any given text—perish the thought!—but it would, as Augustine has written, also provide us proper guidance for navigating those inevitable differences with love, that is, with kindness, patience, empathy,

---

31. Augustine, *De Doctrina Christiana*, 176.

32. Augustine, *De Doctrina Christiana*, 179. In this and the following quotation, Hill's translation actually employs the word "charity" rather than "love."

33. Augustine, *De Doctrina Christiana*, 177. As I write this in Manchester, UK, I find myself consulting an online dictionary to learn that "winkle" is a distinctively British verb meaning "to extract or obtain something with difficulty."

and a commitment to trying to understand the other. What a rule for interpretation—and what a rule for life.[34]

---

34. Meier warns against the tendency "to treat Matthew 22:34–40 as the summit and summary of Jesus' moral teaching. It is rather the summit and summary of Old Testament morality, in keeping with the question that was asked. . . . [W]e should remember that the gospel as a whole shows us that Jesus himself, not any OT command, however lofty, is the center of Christian morality" (*The Vision of Matthew*, 158). I believe this is an unnecessary bifurcation. For one thing, all three Synoptic Gospels feature some version of this dual command citation, and it seems unlikely that early Christian readers and hearers would have thought this citation to be beside the point of Christian discipleship. Further, it seems safe to say that Christians believe that Jesus did not simply quote these commands of Moses, but that his very life was a compellingly faithful embodiment of these commands. If Christ is the center of Christian morality, as it surely is correct to say, it is not a Christ devoid of the Jewish tradition or of a life deeply motivated by the commands of love for God and neighbor.

4

Wisdom's Love for All

For if you love those who love you, what reward do you have?

GIVEN THE IMPORTANCE ACCORDED the commands to love God and neighbor in Matthew's gospel—"on these two commandments hang all the law and the prophets" (22:40)—it is no surprise that Matthew's Sermon on the Mount should put some serious flesh and bones on what neighborly love entails. It is also no surprise that Matthew should root deeply in the nature of God this calling upon Jesus's disciples to love as God loves.

The Sermon on the Mount (Mt. 5–7) unpacks Jesus's expectation that his disciples will practice a righteousness exceeding that of the scribes and Pharisees (5:20). An expectation so phrased is, of course, unique to Matthew, who never shies from framing discipleship to Jesus in distinctly Jewish terms. If Jesus's vow that "not one letter, not one stroke of a letter, will pass from the law until all is accomplished" (5:18) has caused fits for many Christian interpreters over the centuries, let there be no doubt: Matthew's interpretation and proclamation of Jesus the Messiah does not negate, nullify, or erase the Torah or any of its commandments. To suggest that "all [was] accomplished" in Jesus's death and resurrection, such that the Torah's requirements have indeed passed away, just might make some sense in John's gospel (Jn. 19:30) but makes very little sense here; indeed, in Matthew the Torah and all its details remain in effect "until heaven and earth pass away" (5:18). Thus, decades after the end of Jesus's earthly ministry this gospel can still warn that "whoever breaks one of the least of these commandments, and teaches others to do the same, will be called least in the kingdom of heaven" (5:19). Granted, such teachers as relax the Torah's requirements are not consigned to damnation, but there is no question that the Jesus we encounter in this passage is deeply Jewish in his approach to the matter. The Torah stands. Attempts to avoid or soften these statements in Matthew require "hermeneutical gymnastics" that, in J. Andrew Overman's words, "seem excessive, if not tortured."[1] This is why Matthew (alone) has Jesus insist that "I have come not to abolish but to fulfill . . . the law [and] the prophets" (5:17). The widespread Christian notion that all was fulfilled in his death and resurrection, thereby freeing his followers from the divine commands of the Torah and the prophets, essentially flies in the face of this entire gospel.[2]

Nonetheless, our previous chapter should alert us to the fact that Matthew understands Jesus as having taught, and more crucially embodied, a new way of reading Torah even while doggedly insisting on its enduring authority. "The law is to be respected, not abolished," Donald Senior writes, "but its interpretation is to be ruled by the love command."[3] All of the Torah, and all of the prophets' pronouncements as well, hang like garments on the two pegs of love for God and all neighbors. Everything else is merely commentary on this dual command. At the heart of divine revelation, at all times and in all places, is love: God's lavishly indiscriminate love for all people, and God's calling upon Jesus's followers to participate in such wondrous love by extending it, reflecting it, to all others. This comes to most pointed expression in Matthew 5:43–48, which passage Overman accordingly describes as the unveiling of "what [Matthew] believes to be the hermeneutical key to all the laws and the prophets."[4] Again, it actually turns out that when interpreted through the lens of love, the Torah's commands become even more exacting, thereby, in Matthew's view, "exceeding . . . the righteousness of the scribes and Pharisees" (5:20)—presumably because

---

1. J. Andrew Overman, *Church and Community in Crisis: The Gospel According to Matthew* (Valley Forge, PA: Trinity Press International, 1996), 77.

2. The Book of Mormon reflects a typically Protestant evangelical reading of the Matthean text: "It is expedient that there should be a great and last sacrifice; and then shall . . . the law of Moses be fulfilled; yea, it shall be all fulfilled, every jot and tittle, and none shall have passed away" (Alma 34:13).

3. Donald Senior, *The Gospel of Matthew* (Nashville: Abingdon Press, 1997), 106.

4. Overman, 82.

such a reading probes the heart's deepest intentions, motivations, and desires. This is not some easy-believism in which the demands of God are ignored or effaced; it is a 'narrow way' that indeed may be so difficult as to be, or at least seem, virtually impossible.[5]

A Teaching for Disciples

It is critical to keep in mind that Jesus is teaching his disciples, his students, here. His primary audience is not the world in general, but his own community of learners. Like Moses on Sinai towering over the people of Israel, Jesus has ascended this mountain (5:1) to deliver his Torah wisdom. His is the community of the new covenant—a covenant that soon enough be ratified and sealed by his own blood (26:28), comparable to the ratification of the Sinai covenant with the blood of bulls (Ex. 24:6-8). In both cases, the covenant is God's gift to a people who are being instructed in how to live in the world as God's people. If in contemporary North American culture there is a distinct tendency to read the Sermon on the Mount as offering an individualistic ethic, or on the other extreme to read it as applying, say, to the behaviors of an entire nation (such as the United States),[6] then how important it becomes to insist, against both of those readings, that the Sermon is indeed Wisdom's calling placed upon her people, a social reality, a community—but not this country or that nation-state. It is a calling upon Jesus's own community, the renewed Israel, his *ekklesia*. Thus, for example, it is to his disciples, gathered at his feet as his community, to whom Jesus says, "You [plural] are the light of the world. A city build on a hill cannot be hid.... [So] let your [plural / collective] light shine before others, so that

---

5. See David Wenham, "The Rock on Which to Build: Some Mainly Pauline Observations about the Sermon on the Mount," in *Built Upon the Rock: Studies in the Gospel of Matthew*, eds. Daniel M. Gurtner and John Nolland (Grand Rapids/Cambridge: Wm. B. Eerdmans Publishing Co., 2008), 187-206. Wenham observes, "A teacher making such demands must surely be on a different planet from most of us; the teaching can seem very depressing" (197).

6. I think of the popular bumper sticker that says, "When Jesus said 'Love your enemies,' I think he probably meant 'Don't kill them.'" There is no doubt that Jesus meant as much; the question is, To whom is this command to love our enemies given? Why should, say, the masterminds and fledglings of the United States industrial-military complex take these words as having been addressed to them? No country's military could remain military if it took up the task of actually loving the enemy. Jesus is speaking specifically to those who, having recognized his Lordship, are committed to doing the will of his Father in heaven (Mt. 7:21).

they may see your good works and give glory to your Father in heaven" (Mt. 5:14).

While there is much in the Sermon on the Mount that is unique to Matthew, our focus in this chapter will be on that "hermeneutical key to all the laws and the prophets"[7] offered to us in the concluding passage of Matthew 5. As he has done already in teachings on anger (5:21), adultery (5:27), divorce (5:31), oaths (5:33), and retaliation (5:38), Jesus begins with what was taught of old before offering his antithesis. "You have heard that it was said, 'You shall love your neighbor'"—this much coming from the Torah, the Laws of Moses (Lev. 19:18). But then Jesus adds that his audience has additionally heard it said to "hate your enemy" (Mt. 5:43). While the people of Israel are never commanded by God to hate their enemies, there certainly are commands in the Torah about exterminating them (Deut. 7:1–6, 20:1–18); further, it would not have been difficult for faithful Jews to appeal to the famous prayer of David,

> *O that you would kill the wicked, O God,*
>   *and that the bloodthirsty would depart from me ...*
> *Do I not hate those who hate you, O LORD?*
> *And do I not loathe those who rise up against you?*
> *I hate them with a perfect hatred;*
>   *I count them my enemies.* (Ps. 139:19, 21–22)

Quite apart from such texts, once 'neighbor' is understood (as it is in Leviticus 19:18) to be the fellow-Israelite, or more broadly as the one with whom I exist in proximity and with whom, at least in large measure, I agree, then it becomes an easy step to hate all those beyond this near sphere. Perhaps it won't be an active hatred; perhaps it will be simply fear or suspicion, possibly dehumanization. In any case, the walls go up and we do what we must to bolster them. Particularly if such fears are encouraged by religious difference, it may become exceedingly difficult not to assume that a seething hatred of this ungodly other is precisely what God requires. The Torah would not need to legislate it; it comes naturally enough. But we know that Jesus taught, and lived, a very different reading of Torah, of the natural world, and of God:

> But I say to you, Love your enemies and pray for those who persecute you, so that you may be children of your Father in heaven;

---

[7]. See footnote 4 of this chapter. Ulrich Luz further adds that "the Antitheses as a whole serve as examples of love" in *The Theology of the Gospel of Matthew* ("New Testament Theology" series, Cambridge University Press, 1993), 54.

> for he makes his sun rise on the evil and on the good, and sends [the blessing of] rain on the righteous and on the unrighteous. For if you love those who love you, what reward do you have? Do not even the tax collectors do the same? And if you greet only your brothers and sisters, what more are you doing than others? Do not even the Gentiles do the same? Be perfect [Gr., *teleios*], therefore, as your heavenly Father is perfect [*teleios*]. (Mt. 5:44–48)

The daunting conclusion of the above passage—"Be perfect as your heavenly Father is perfect"—is an obvious and intentional echo of Leviticus 19:2, God's calling upon Israel to "be holy, for I the LORD your God am holy." Just as the people of Israel were to share in divine holiness by a collective life of obedience to God's laws, so now this renewed Israel, symbolized by "The Twelve," are to share in the *teleios* of God—specifically identified as indiscriminate love. The Sermon on the Mount, then, replaces the adjective 'holy' (Heb., *qadosh*) with the term that in the Septuagint "is used to translate a Hebrew concept that refers to what is whole, intact, undivided."[8] If we may apply this term to God as Matthew does (5:48),[9] then the immediate context makes it clear that God is whole, intact, and undivided in *love for all people*. This is who and what God is. Thus there is no one who exists outside of, or apart from, this love of God that in fact *is* God. It is deeply significant that Jesus teaches that the most faithful way of becoming God's children, i.e., imitating God's character, is by *indiscriminately loving all people, as God does*. Jesus contrasts such living with that of tax collectors and Gentiles, who do what comes naturally by loving and welcoming those who are like them, those with whom they are comfortable, those with whom they feel safe and secure. But of course this is the natural course for any human; thus, the importance of the term 'Gentiles' here as a stark contrast to Israel's calling to be a light to all the nations (i.e., Gentile peoples) through faithful obedience to God's Torah. (This is a critical theme to which we will return later in this chapter.) The surprising move that Jesus makes, of course, is to teach us that this obedience now is to include loving our so-called 'enemies',

---

8. Eduard Schweizer, *The Good News According to Matthew*, trans. David E. Green (London: SPCK, 1976), 135.

9. Interestingly, in the Book of Mormon's version of the sermon, ostensibly preached by the risen Christ to Israelite descendants in the New World, Jesus's role is elevated: "Therefore I would that ye should be perfect even as I, or your Father who is in heaven is perfect" (3 Nephi 12:48). It is unclear by syntax whether the meaning is that Jesus is perfect as the Father is, or that Jesus is here identified with the Father. There are texts in the Book of Mormon that make the latter claim (e.g., Mosiah 15:1–4).

welcoming those who are strange or alien to us, praying for those who persecute us. This is a far cry from much that passes for Christianity today, where far too often xenophobia is the prevailing atmosphere and we yet revel in what Bonhoeffer called 'cheap grace'. The church of tomorrow shall, indeed must—if it is truly to be Jesus's community—make God's expansive and inclusive love its sole priority. Everything else is commentary.

The Perfection of Love

To read "be perfect, therefore, as your Father in heaven in perfect" as a counsel for despair—as though Jesus is setting up an impossible standard of perfection to frustrate his listeners into utter reliance upon divine mercy—is to misunderstand this text. This is not absolute divine perfection being held over our heads like a guillotine. *Teleios*, then, is not "the flawlessness of a rounded personality brought to the utmost pitch of perfection";[10] it is the practice of loving as, and loving whom, God loves. This may indeed be a far more demanding perfection!—but if it is not easy, it is at least relatively simple. Thus John Wesley could sum up his "plain account of Christian perfection" as nothing more, less, or other than *love*.

> It would be well for you to be thoroughly sensible of this: the heaven of heavens is love. There is nothing higher in religion; there is, in effect, nothing else. If you look for anything but *more love* you are looking wide of the mark; you are moving out of the royal way. And when you are asking others, Have you received this or that blessing?, if you mean anything but *more love*, you mean wrong; you are leading them out of the way . . . [11]

Such love as this may indeed be "the heaven of heavens," but it is also intensely practical. It is striking that Jesus here mentions an act so mundane as greeting people. Do we offer greetings only to those who are our brothers and sisters, those with whom we share religious commitments and community? If so, says Jesus, we do no more than anyone else. (In other words, we are not practicing excessive righteousness.) Or, in Wesley's fine insight, it is possible for "bigotry and party-zeal" to restrict our love to only "a small number whose sentiments and practices are so much our own, that

---

10. Schweizer, 135.

11. John Wesley, *A Plain Account of Christian Perfection*, edited and annotated by Randy L. Maddox and Paul W. Chilcote (Beacon Hill Press of Kansas City, 2015), 135–136.

our love to them is [nothing] but self-love reflected."[12] If the greetings that Jesus has in mind include the bestowal of a blessing,[13] then this teaching becomes all the more radical. What might it mean for the church of tomorrow to follow Jesus in this matter? Can Jesus's followers offer greetings, bestow blessings, upon people and communities who are not Christian? What will such greetings entail? Essentially, will we become a people of hospitality toward those who think, believe, pray, or practice differently than we? This is what I hope for the church of tomorrow.

Or will we rest content with bestowing greetings and blessings upon those of our own circle? This cannot be the church of tomorrow.

A Community of Communities

United Methodist theologian Marjorie Hewitt Suchocki has wondered if we might come to understand Jesus's *ekklesia* as one community within a "community of communities," i.e., of religious communities, upon the earth.[14] While this suggestion need not and ought not to remove our (or any other religious tradition's) evangelistic verve, it would likely reorient our understanding and practice of evangelism especially in relation to serious practitioners of other paths. We would begin by acknowledging the real possibility that the plurality of religious traditions and communities in the world is in some way a function of God's will and work. If we were to accept Suchocki's challenge to imagine such a possibility, we might find it intriguing that the Qur'an offers support for this theological position. For example: "O humanity! Truly we created you from a male and a female, and We made you peoples and tributes that you may come to know one

---

12. John Wesley, *Explanatory Notes upon the New Testament* (London: Epworth Press, 1976), 241–242.

13. In Schweizer's words, "Greeting others plays an important role among the rabbis, and being the first in speaking to another is a mark of special honor." *The Good News According to Matthew*, 134.

14. Marjorie Hewitt Suchocki, *Divinity and Diversity: A Christian Affirmation of Religious Pluralism* (Nashville: Abingdon Press, 2003). The Church itself is, clearly, a "community of communities" with considerable plurality, which is inevitably true as well of all other religious traditions. This seems theologically significant, insofar as such plurality arises out of many factors but always includes differences of interpretation. Since differences of interpretation arise directly from our situation as historical creatures with limited perspectives, it seems inevitable that, if we believe in God as Creator of all things, we must assume that the differences of interpretation are a necessary feature of creaturely existence and thus a situation willed by, or at least not undesirable to, the Creator.

another" (49:13).[15] This text first affirms the solidarity of all human beings, an equality of biological origin—but then also insists that God has made human beings into a variety of ethnicities and cultures, precisely with the intent that those differences would impel us to try to overcome our fears of 'the other' and come to know one another. The differences, of course, do not vanish and should not; but if we invest in the demanding labor of listening to the other, living alongside and loving the other as one who is like unto our very own selves, we probably also will come to the recollection that we are all human beings together, born of mothers and fathers. Human nature is not a monolith, to be sure; yet there are human experiences of family, of love, of food, of shelter, of vulnerability, hopes and dreams that we in some sense do profoundly share as a human family. Recall again the words of the Torah: "Love the stranger as yourself, for you yourselves once were strangers in the land of Egypt" (Lev. 19:34).

In another passage of the Qur'an God instructs Muhammad to recite, "We believe in that which was sent down unto us and was sent down unto you; our God and your God are one, and unto Him we are submitters" (29:46). We who follow Jesus as God's Messiah and Lord, however, believe that submission to God, i.e., doing the will of Jesus' Father in heaven, is fulfilled by hearing Jesus's words and acting upon them, like a wise person who builds her house on a rock instead of sand (7:21–28). We have come to believe that this teaching of his is the narrow gate, a demanding road of obedience that is hard but "leads to life," and that "there are few who find it" (7:13–14). There are real and manifest differences between the paths of teaching laid down by Jesus and Muhammad, even if there is some shared ground too. There are many religious paths that are "narrow" and "hard," that demand a great deal of those who walk upon them. These paths are not identical; sometimes they may crisscross or even move parallel for a while, but they are unique roads with their own distinct ends, their own visions of divinely-intended life and of what practices most effectively get us there.[16] They are not all leading in the same direction or trying to head to the "same place" (although "to God is our return," a typical qur'anic phrase). Yet for the Qur'an, it is God who has bestowed upon the human community these many different paths that entail, in history, quite differing communities.

---

15. All qur'anic quotations in this chapter, and in this book, are from *The Study Quran: A New Translation and Commentary*, eds. Seyyed Hossein Nasr, Caner K. Dagli, Maria Massi Dakake and Joseph E.B. Lumbard (New York: HarperOne, 2015).

16. On this see Mark Heim, *Salvations: Truth and Difference in Religion* (Maryknoll, NY: Orbis Books, 1995).

Perhaps the most dramatic example of this qur'anic teaching is in 5:48: "For each [people] among you We have appointed a law and a way. And had God willed, He would have made you one community, but [He willed otherwise], that He might try you in that which He has given you. So vie with one another in good deeds. Unto God shall be your return all together, and He will inform you of that wherein you differ" (Q 5:48). For the Qur'an, then, human beings' religious differences are unavoidable and in fact attributable to God, who could have willed the world to be otherwise. Given the strong doctrine of sovereignty in the Qur'an, it is not surprising to find on its pages precisely this fascinating theological position: the plurality of religious traditions (convictions, practices, liturgies), in some mysterious way, exists by the will and work of God "to try [human beings] in that which He has given" to each community.

But what part might plurality play in this testing? Could not God test all humans as one community, with one path as the criterion of testing? Presumably—*unless* a critical aspect of the testing, the sifting, the shaping, is how we humans will deal with those who differ from us, sometimes radically. How will we respond to those who are strangers to us? Further, when the differences include questions of ultimate meaning, value, and devotion, the testing and trying of our character becomes exceedingly difficult. Such testing, I submit, is not so much about determining who is worthy to enter the life to come as it is about God's educational process, God's nudging, of us toward peaceable relations in this world, now. True, the Qur'an insists that we all shall ultimately return to God—who alone is able to "inform [us] of that wherein [we] differ." In the meantime the Qur'an calls Muslims, Jews, Christians, Zoroastrians, and even the fairly mysterious "Sabeans"[17] to "vie with one another in good deeds." Surely there is a profound wisdom in this admonition. We need not assume the Qur'an to be divine dictation to appreciate this wisdom. If only we strove to outdo one another in works of goodness and compassion, rather than to prove that "we" are correct and "they" are wrong! I am reminded, again, of Jesus's instructions to his

17. There is no scholarly consensus on the identity of the "Sabeans" who are mentioned several times in the Qur'an, where they are generally associated with the "People[s] of the Book." It is certainly possible that they are the predecessors of today's Mandeans, a population of 60–70,000 who lived primarily in southern Iraq and the Iranian province of Huzistan until the Iraq War of 2003. Since then the Mandean community has dispersed in many directions, with the largest contingent finding refuge in Sweden. If this identification holds, then we can say of the Qur'an's "Sabeans" that they had distinctively strong Gnostic ideas and practices, including astrology, and venerated John the Baptist as God's final and authoritative teacher.

disciples to "let your light shine before others, so that they may see your good works and give glory to your Father in heaven" (5:16). Perhaps we can embark on some friendly, even holy, competition? For that matter, perhaps we, too, who follow Jesus might see the "good works" of those in other religious communities and give glory to God for them?[18]

Wisdom Theology & Wisdom Incarnate

We should note that Jesus, in arguing that the love of God is freely lavished upon all people irrespective of their character or deeds, appeals to the natural phenomena of sunshine and rain. Granted, the Jesus of the synoptic gospels is known to make the birds of the air and the flowers of the fields features of his teaching; he could build parables out of a mustard seed as well as from observations of farmers and their crops of wheat (and weeds!). But here a most significant theological proposition—God's indiscriminate love for all—is buttressed by the simple observation of the agricultural blessings of sunshine and rain. This teaching is unique to Matthew, and of course the appeal to natural phenomena is a typical feature of wisdom literature. We encounter in this passage "the wisdom motif of the goodness of the God who creates, . . . but only by way of support of a love that goes beyond all bounds and includes enemies as its object."[19] On this basis, Jesus asks, "[I]f you love [only] those who love you, what reward do you have?" (5:46). In this bit of wisdom theology, Matthew anticipates another major theme in the Qur'an. In a fashion and to a degree that far outstrips the Bible, the Qur'an repeatedly insists that the natural world is filled with "signs" or evidences of the Creator. Here is one example, among a great host of others. "He it is Who spread out the earth and placed therein firm mountains and streams, and of every kind of fruit He placed therein two kinds. He causes the night to cover the day. Truly in that are signs for people who reflect" (Q13:3). Intriguingly, the term "signs" is a translation of the Arabic term *ayat*, which is also used to refer to the verses of the Qur'an. For Muslims, just as the Qur'an is filled with *ayat* that point to God precisely because they present God's speech, so also is the natural world brimming with *ayat* that

---

18. In this connection, see John Wesley's radically inclusive sermon "A Caution Against Bigotry," *The Works of John Wesley* Vol. V (London: Wesleyan Conference Office), Sermon XXXVIII, 479–492.

19. Rudolf Schnackenburg, *The Gospel of Matthew* (Grand Rapids: William B. Eerdmans Pub. Co., 2002), 62, 63.

point to God because they are created by God to do so. The Qur'an, like creation itself, is a book filled with signs of God, signs to be read by people willing to do the reading and reflect upon it. Similarly, at the very heart of Jesus' Sermon on the Mount is this appeal to the signs of sunshine and rain as evidence for God's indiscriminate love—a love we are called upon to imitate in our relations with all people. In Russell Pregeant's words, "The appeal is not to Jesus' presence or even to the Torah or the history of Israel, but to an order of creation perceptible in nature itself and therefore, by implication, available to all persons in all times and places."[20]

While Pregeant's insight is important and helps to forge a connection in Christian-Muslim conversation (and well beyond), it should not obscure the fact that Christian faith points to Jesus as the everlasting and most true Sign of this matchless love of God. We are to follow *him*. If Matthew presents Jesus as doing a little wisdom theology here, we already have seen that Matthew presents Jesus as God's very Wisdom among us as this human being. If indeed the Church is to be a community among communities on God's good earth, our purpose is to be that people who learn from, and in turn proclaim, this one whom we confess to be Divine Wisdom incarnate.

To be such a community as this will require some hard work. Earlier in the sermon Jesus underscores the radical nature of his wisdom community with a hyperbolic teaching unique to Matthew. He cites the commandment forbidding murder but then, employing the lens of love, Jesus radicalizes this command to include anger, or insults, against a fellow disciple ("brother," vv. 22, 23). Killing another human being is generally not a random act from out of the blue; in nearly every instance, such an extreme act begins in the heart ravaged by anger, envy, or great pain. Jesus takes his disciples (then and now) to the seeds and roots of murder in order to nip it in the bud. "So when you are offering your gift at the altar, if you remember that your brother or sister has something against you, leave your gift there before the altar and go; first be reconciled to your brother or sister, and then come and offer your gift" (5:23-24).

Imagine the setting. Jesus is teaching his disciples somewhere in Galilee, roughly 80 miles from Jerusalem. This means a walk of three days or so—tack on a couple more if one took a safer, less contested route around Samaria. In this distinctively Jewish teaching, Jesus's disciples would have to imagine that they have walked at least three days to reach Jerusalem

---

20. Russell Pregeant, *Christology Beyond Dogma: Matthew's Christ in Process Hermeneutic* (Philadelphia: Fortress Press, 1978), 78.

and the Temple there. Having made it through whatever further obstacles were entailed in reaching the Temple's altar where the priest stands, ready to perform the sacrifice, the listener's imagination now is startled: *if you remember that your brother or sister has something against you* . . . It is not simply "if you remember that you have something against your brother or sister," but if they have something against you. In this undeniably radical teaching, Jesus tells his disciples to stop in their tracks, make the three-day (or longer) trek back to Galilee, find this fellow disciple and seek to make things right. Only then should the disciple feel permitted to return those three days-plus, back to the Jerusalem and its Temple, to offer altar worship to God.

Notice that in this hypothetical (but readily imaginable) scenario, the issue is not necessarily about me and my attitudes toward this other. I might bear no ill-will whatsoever. But if this other person does toward me, Jesus says, God deems it more important to go make that relationship right than to offer up my holy gift of worship. I may think this other person got it all wrong, that there is no good reason for his or her bad feelings. I may think myself entirely in the right. But, as Eduard Schweizer puts it, "the crucial point is that attention is no longer focused on us, . . . but on the *other* person, and how his living is whittled away by our conduct."[21] Remember the teaching is about anger. Here Jesus instructs his followers to be sensitive to the danger being done to a fellow disciple if we simply allow him or her to stew in anger against us, even if we happen to think their anger is misplaced or unjustified.

But it seems terribly extreme to stop the act of ritual worship at the Temple in Jerusalem in order to make that long and arduous trek back to Galilee just because someone is unhappy with us. We might pause, too, to note that Jesus is not represented as saying that Temple worship is worthless or even unnecessary; everything in this teaching presupposes a traditionally Jewish perspective on the Temple and its altars. But Jesus radically prioritizes human relations over ritual worship; we remember that later in this gospel Jesus will on two occasions cite Hosea 6:6, "I desire mercy, and not sacrifice." Here the "mercy" in question is directed toward the fellow disciple whose anger, disappointment, or resentment at me—whether I think it legitimate or not—is eating away at his or her heart and mind. What shall I do? Drop everything—even my gift for God at the altar—and

---

21. Schweizer, 176.

go the distance to work through the hard feelings with the purpose of making things right again. "Then come [back!] and offer your gift." Schweizer comments,

> Now the Pharisees taught that a sacrifice could be interrupted, but only for ritual reasons—to interrupt it simply on account of a neighbor would be inconceivable, because its purpose, for them, was above all the offering of a pure and unsullied ritual. When a cultic act is stopped for the sake of one's brother, as Jesus requires, cultic ideology has been fundamentally overcome.[22]

And what is it, again, that overcomes "cultic ideology"? It is mercy, *hesed*, right relations among Jesus's followers. It is imperative that this community practice right relations because, otherwise, it cannot possibly be "the light of the world." If in fact Jesus was calling the Twelve to be the embodiment of Israel's renewal, then it is inevitable that the purpose of this renewal would be to become a people who, together in their social relations, reveal the goodness, mercy and love of God to the Gentile peoples of the world. "The reign of God," in Gerhard Lohfink's words, would not be "established worldwide in one fell swoop. It would not fall from the clouds; rather, it would be mediated historically. It would be established by shining forth from one concrete people," thereby "revealing its nature to the world."[23] It is not nearly enough to preach good news to the world's many peoples; there must be a representative community, a "city set on a hill," a mobile Jerusalem that portrays in real, actual living together the nature of God's gracious rule.

Divine Wisdom for the Gentiles

This leads immediately to another reason why Matthew matters. Following the Sabbath stories about the disciples plucking grain and Jesus healing someone's withered hand in the synagogue,[24] Matthew informs us that Jesus, aware of the Pharisees' growing conspiracy against him, departed from the area with many folks following. "He cured all of them" and "ordered them not to make him known" (12:15–16). Then, in a citation from the

---

22. Ibid., 177.
23. Gerhard Lohfink, *Jesus and Community* (Philadelphia: Fortress Press, 1984), 71–72.
24. Recall Chapter 2 of this book.

prophet Isaiah that is unique to Matthew's gospel, we read the rationale for this secretive Messiah:

> *Here is my servant, whom I have chosen,*
>   *my beloved, with whom my soul is well pleased.*
> *I will put my Spirit upon him,*
>   *and he will proclaim justice to the Gentiles.*
> *He will not wrangle or cry aloud,*
>   *nor will anyone hear his voice in the streets.*
> *He will not break a bruised reed*
>   *or quench a smoldering wick*
>   *until he brings justice to victory.*
> *And in his name the Gentiles will hope.* (Mt. 12:18–21)

For Matthew, Jesus is God's servant, anointed with God's Spirit, sent to become God's emissary to all the non-Jewish peoples of the world. In this regard Jesus is portrayed as having fulfilled Israel's calling to be "a light to the nations" (Is. 42:6). Matthew's source is Isaiah 42:1–4, the first of the so-called "servant songs" of Isaiah. The most immediate motivation for citing this passage is to indicate that Jesus's silencing of the crowds was already prophesied: "He will not cry or lift up his voice, or make it heard in the street" (Is. 42:2). This certainly also fits well with the self-description of Wisdom Incarnate in Matthew 11, "I am gentle and humble in heart, and you will find rest for your souls" (v. 29). The portrait is of a deliverer, a champion, a savior who does not trumpet his own arrival, but who in fact labors quietly, gently, unobtrusively in the world. This divine gentleness—to be understood, possibly, as a direct result of the Spirit's presence upon and within him—is portrayed beautifully in the servant's refusal to snap off a reed already barely hanging on, or to blow out a candle whose faint flame is all but extinguished. This one acts in quiet yet hopeful determination, nurturing and protecting whatever slim signs of life may remain in any situation. This is Wisdom "gentle and humble in heart," fanning a flickering flame and binding the barely walking wounded.

Of course the Isaian passage also mentions "the nations" (Is. 42:1) and "the coastlands" (42:4), rendered as "the Gentiles" in Matthew. That may seem entirely incidental to Matthew's use of the passage, and perhaps even counterproductive given Jesus's instructions to the twelve prior to their first missionary venture—"Go nowhere among the Gentiles, and enter no town of the Samaritans, but go rather to the lost sheep of the house of Israel"—instructions, not surprisingly, found only in Matthew (10:5–6). But if we understand this first sending as part of Jesus's attempt to renew Israel in its calling to be God's light to the nations, it fits nicely into Matthew's overall narrative. For, in the end, Jesus will indeed send forth his "eleven" to go "and make disciples of all nations" (Matt. 28:16–20).[25] If we understand Matthew's citation of Isaiah 42 in this fashion, then the work of the Spirit-anointed servant is a work carried on essentially by Jesus's renewed Israel, his community of disciples. If this servant is "gentle and humble in heart," it seems unavoidable that one of the most important things we are to learn of him is to become, like Wisdom Divine, also "gentle and humble in heart." Jesus's community, sent out into and among the world's peoples ("the nations"), ought not "wrangle or cry aloud" in loud voice or bullying behavior. Jesus's community also ought not to snap off the barely lingering leaf or quench the smoldering flame; the church of tomorrow must take seriously its calling to be a people who labor humbly, quietly, unobtrusively, yet determinedly to nurture hope in the face of despair and life in the face of violence and death.

The portrait of Jesus and his community here is poignant, compelling, and beautiful. But there is one more critical component in the Isaiah 42 passage: three times we read that God's servant will "bring forth" or "establish" *mishpat*, or justice, among the peoples. This *mishpat* invariably implies a knowledge of the God of Israel that immediately includes right and just relations among human beings. We learn in the verses that follow, not cited by Matthew, that the servant in mind is the people Israel: "I have called you in righteousness, I have taken you by the hand and kept you; I have given you as a covenant people, a light to the nations, to open the eyes that are blind, to bring out the prisoners from the dungeon, from the prison those who sit in darkness" (42:6–7). This *mishpat*, justice grounded in divine wisdom, is to become realized among all the world's peoples through God's covenant people Israel. For Matthew, then, Jesus is God's renewal of this calling upon Israel such that, through the *ekklesia* that he builds, he extends God's nurturing love and light to all people everywhere. Such at least is the hope.

Notice, however, that if this servant / community makes its presence felt not in loud cries or demonstrations of power, but in nurturing wounded existence and protecting the barely flickering flame, then its existence must be marked by patience, humility, persistence, and solidarity with

---

25. I will explore this critical idea in more detail in Chapter Nine of this book, "Wisdom's Commission."

the powerless and marginalized. This Spirit-anointed servant community, Jesus's own community through the earth's generations of the past two millennia, ought to have been characterized by precisely this gentle, humble love. Sometimes it has; too often is has not. Our record in this regard is deeply blemished. The church of tomorrow must acknowledge first our collective failures, and in repentance strive to take instead this path described in Matthew's citation of Isaiah. Indeed, if Matthew's citation is correct, then whatever the church has been doing, *Jesus the Anointed One* has been laboring gently, humbly, quietly within the world "until he brings justice to victory" (12:21). Or, in the words of Isaiah, "He will faithfully bring forth justice. He will not grow faint or be crushed until he has established justice in the earth" (42:3–4).

Further, if Matthew's citation of Isaiah is taken seriously, then it is precisely this humble, gentle Anointed One "in [whose] name the Gentiles will hope" (Mt. 12:21). Often that hope has taken a rather dramatic apocalyptic form replete with divine violence and retribution against evil-doers, and understandably so. Yet we should ask if such a hope is truly coherent with the portrait of the servant described jointly by Isaiah and Matthew. The eschatology implied in this passage is for the long haul, rather than for apocalyptic doom. The one who in, and as, Divine Wisdom is gentle and humble in heart is not likely to force, and enforce, *mishpat*. This is why, as we will explore more fully in Chapter Nine, the resurrected Jesus with all power and authority entrusted to him makes his first move that of sending out his Jewish renewal community to all the nations—not to strike them down or force them into compliance with God's rule, but to go "teaching them to obey everything that I have commanded you" (Mt. 28:20). And then this Spirit-anointed and Spirit-resurrected servant, intent on proclaiming God's *mishpat* and bringing it to victory in the world, offers this eschatological promise: "And remember, I am with you always, to the end of the age" (Mt. 28:20). May the church of tomorrow find the courage in the presence of the living Jesus to bind up the bruised reeds, to protect and nurture the faltering flame, until this mysterious servant "has established justice in the earth" (Isaiah 42:4).

5

Wisdom and Foolishness

> ... *the road is hard that leads to life, and few there are who find it.*

GIVEN MATTHEW'S DEPICTION OF Jesus as the embodying of divine Wisdom itself, it is no surprise that those who follow Jesus should be deemed wise, "like a wise man who built his house on rock" (Matt 7:24). But where there are those who are wise, there inevitably also are the foolish ones who build on sand. How shall we best, or most wisely, most lovingly, interpret these final words of the Sermon on the Mount?

Wisdom's House

This parable of building on rock or building on sand is not unique to Matthew; it also concludes the Sermon on the Plain in Luke. But true to the wisdom theme in Matthew, the descriptors "wise" and "foolish" are found only in this gospel's version of the parable—and naturally, "the wise person is a regular character in wisdom literature."[1] Jesus here identifies the wise person, the sage, as one "who hears these words of mine and acts on them" (7:24). Given the placement of this parable as the conclusion to the sermon, it is reasonable to assume "these words of mine" are most immediately

---

1. Carter, *Matthew and the Margins*, 193.

everything Jesus has just finished teaching. Certainly one might extend this to include everything Jesus teaches in this entire gospel; this would cohere well with his commission at the end of Matthew "make disciples of all nations, . . . teaching them to obey everything that I have commanded you" (28:20). In either case, of course, the criterion for wisdom is the teaching of Jesus—and the point is not whether or not we *believe* in his words, but whether or not we *obey* them.

Significantly, in Proverbs 9, Woman Wisdom "has built her house" and invites folks to enter: "You that are simple, turn in here!" (Prov 9:1, 4). Later, Sirach would elaborate on this house that Wisdom built: "Happy is the person who meditates on wisdom and . . . reflects in his heart on her ways, . . . who listens at her doors [and] camps near her house, . . . and so occupies an excellent lodging place" (Sir 14:20–21, 23–25). Warren Carter adds, "Here [in Matthew 7] the wisdom tradition receives Christological modification to represent the teaching which disciples hear, and on which they build their lives."[2] Correspondingly, the foolish one "hears these words of mine and does not act on them" (Matt 7:26). The difference is not between those who hear and those who do not. Indeed, those who do not hear Jesus's teachings seem not to be under consideration in this passage. We will return to them later.

Lord, Lord

This concluding parable, then, coheres with the passage that immediately precedes it. "Not everyone who says to me, 'Lord, Lord,' will enter the kingdom of heaven, but only the one who does the will of my Father in heaven" (7:21). While Luke features a comparable saying—"Why do you call me 'Lord, Lord,' and do not do what I tell you?" (6:46)—Matthew has provided a more explicitly eschatological setting: entering the kingdom of heaven "on that day" (7:22) is conditioned on doing "the will of my Father in heaven." There really can be no question, in this context, regarding the will of God: it is all that Jesus has just taught his disciples (and the outlying crowd, 7:28) in this demanding sermon. In John Meier's words, "The ultimate criterion of what *is* the will of the Father is the authoritative word of Jesus."[3]

What are we to make of this phrase, "Lord! Lord!" found in both Matthew and Luke? It sounds like an evocative cry of worship, perhaps not

2. Carter, *Matthew and the Margins*, 193.
3. Meier, *The Vision of Matthew*, 65.

unrelated to Paul's teaching that "if you confess with your lips that Jesus is Lord and believe in your heart that God raised him from the dead, you will be saved" (Rom 10:9). *Not so fast*, Matthew may be warning. Of course, Paul also had plenty more to say about Christian obedience, but Matthew's warning seems appropriate, and necessary, in every age—including and perhaps particularly our own. Christian faith too readily slides toward cheap grace; the church of tomorrow must be willing to hear the hard words of Jesus here, and to live accordingly. This is what it means to learn from him, to shoulder his yoke (Matt 11:29).

But this passage is more than simply a rebuttal of easy-believism. "On that day many will say to me, 'Lord, Lord, did we not prophesy in your name, and cast out demons in your name, and do many deeds of power in your name?'" Deeds of power and wonder can attract the crowds; this saying subtly acknowledges the "wow factor" of sensational religious phenomena. Carter suggests that the thrice-repeated "in your name" implies "using his name as a formula of power or invoking his authority,"[4] perhaps in an almost-magical way. It evokes a sense of easy familiarity with the invocation of Jesus's name as possessing inherent power. Certainly such abuse of Jesus's name thrives in some contemporary preaching, especially on the TV-evangelism circuit. But Matthew's Jesus is unfazed by such remarkable demonstrations. As Schnackenburg observes, "Matthew refuses to be impressed by signs and wonders that seducers, too, can perform (24:24); . . . for him, moral observance is the only thing that counts."[5]

We must acknowledge that this emphasis upon obedience to the divine will may appear to rub against the grain of evangelical Protestantism's doctrine of salvation by grace through faith. Does Matthew's Gospel offer us instead some notion of salvation by "works"? Add to this question those of Ulrich Luz: "Faced with the Sermon on the Mount, are we not forced to admit that our house is built on sand? . . . And are those condemned whose 'fruits'—meaning their deeds—are deemed insignificant or slothful by the Son of Man at the end of time? Is the Sermon on the Mount devoid of grace and mercy?"[6] Is Jesus simply laying down a new set of even more demanding rules, demanding the impossible?

Surely part of our reply to such questions will demand a renewed appreciation for the role of Torah in the life of Israel and in subsequent

---

4. Carter, *Matthew and the Margins*, 191.
5. Schnackenburg, *The Gospel of Matthew*, 79.
6. Luz, *The Theology of the Gospel of Matthew*, 46, 47.

developments of Judaism. The Jewish tradition celebrates the Torah not as God's intolerable burden but as God's gracious gift of the way of life, the way in which Israel has been called by walk in covenantal relation with its Redeemer. The laws of Sinai are predicated upon, and grounded in, God's gracious liberation of the people Israel out of Egypt's bondage (Exod 19:4–6). Correspondingly, Matthew proclaims Jesus as Emmanuel, "God with us" (Matt 1:23), who has come to "save his people from their sins" (1:21). Jesus's calling of the twelve disciples is a powerful testament to the hope of a renewed calling upon Israel to walk faithfully with its gracious, loving God. Small wonder that Jesus ascended a mountain, echoing Sinai, to teach his disciples how to become a collective "light of the world" and "a city built on a hill" (5:14). The reason why those who do the will of Jesus's Father will enter the kingdom of heaven is that it is precisely such living together as Jesus describes that embodies God's gracious reign in this world. Entering the eschatological kingdom is not so much a *reward* for a life well lived in obedience to the Father's will as it is the natural (if such an adjective can be used) *result* of having lived a kingdom life in the present. The Sermon on the Mount portrays that sort of life—a life that Jesus's disciples are called upon to share in together for the sake of all the world's peoples (28:19).[7]

Of all of our Gospel writers, Matthew is the most concerned to portray this wise living as continuous with the history of God's interaction with the people Israel. In Matthew alone, Jesus warns his hearers, "Do not think that I have come to abolish the law or the prophets" (5:17); in Matthew alone the Torah commands to love God and neighbor are the hinges upon which "all the law and the prophets hang" (22:40). Further, as we now engage the material that closes the Sermon on the Mount, we once more encounter this phrase "the law and the prophets." Whereas Luke's version gives us "Do to others as you would have them do to you" (Luke 6:31), Matthew's Jesus adds "for this is the law and the prophets" (7:12). If the so-called (and too often underappreciated and trivialized) Golden Rule *is* "the law and the prophets," this may shed interesting light upon Jesus's stated intention *not* to abolish the law or the prophets. For that matter, if the commands to love God and all neighbors are the hinges upon which the law and the prophets hang, then we are being invited to understand love for all others, and acting toward "others as [we] would have them do to [us]," to be deeply intertwined, if not essentially identical.

---

7. See Chapter 9 of this book, "Wisdom's Commission."

The Golden Rule

Many are the commentators who rightly indicate that this Golden Rule is far from unique to Jesus. It appears in both positive ("do to others") and negative ("do not do to others") formulations in Hellenistic and Jewish writings predating Jesus.[8] "It must therefore appear quite odd," observed Krister Stendahl, "when the Golden Rule is used as an epitome of what was new with Jesus."[9] In an important sense, of course, Jesus in fact denies that it is anything new, since it is "the law and the prophets." While acknowledging all of this, Carter argues for the importance of context:

> Some claim that it is a universal ethic which expresses the wish of all people to be treated with decency and justice. While that may be so, [that reading] does not adequately express [the rule's] meaning in this context near the end of the sermon and in relation to Jesus' vision of an alternative way of life.[10]

Carter undoubtedly has a point, but perhaps we should not so quickly shy away from the universalist slant on this teaching. The fact that many other wise teachers in human history have appealed to an ethic of reciprocity need not, in itself, undercut Jesus's (possibly) unique twist. The question may become one of applicability: how difficult have we human beings found it to practice doing to others as we would have them do to us in the situations where those others are truly, frighteningly *other*? Is this perhaps where we typically draw the line? Carter finally argues that the context for this saying is "a way of life that embodies God's gracious, transforming, indiscriminately loving, generous, and good empire (5:43–48)."[11] But we noted in the previous chapter of this book that Jesus's appeal to God's indiscriminate love—precisely in 5:43–48—is itself rooted in the universal, everyday blessings of sunshine and rain given to all and observable by all.[12] In other words, it is a wisdom ethic that in principle is universally pertinent. If God loves the evil and the good, the righteous and the

---

8. In Hellenism, Herodotus, *Hist.* 3:142; Isocates, *Demonicus* 14; Diogenes Laertius, *Lives* 5.21; in Judaism, Tobit 4:15; Sirach 31:15. Comparable formulations of this Golden Rule, or an ethic of reciprocity and mutuality, are found in Buddhism, Confucianism, Islam, Zoroastrianism, Hinduism, and many other traditions.

9. Cited by Hill, *The Gospel of Matthew*, 149.

10. Carter, *Matthew and the Margins*, 184.

11. Carter, *Matthew and the Margins*, 185.

12. See Pregeant, *Christology beyond Dogma*, 76–80.

unrighteous—evidenced in, of all things, the weather—then to be a child of God, to perform the will of Jesus's Father, is to love even one's enemy as God loves. There is in Matthew a wisdom theology that moves from the observation of the goods of the natural world to a radical calling upon us to love all people—including (and perhaps especially) those we find least lovable.

Indeed, in the Golden Rule's context in Matthew, here are the words that immediately follow: "Enter through the narrow gate; for the gate is wide and the road is easy that leads to destruction, and there are many who take it. For the gate is narrow and the road is hard that leads to life, and there are few who find it" (Matt 7:13–14). While it may be typical to consider the Golden Rule a broad and inclusive ethic, universally acknowledged and taught—as I am willing to consider in this chapter—what if we were to consider it to be, nonetheless, "the narrow gate"? What if it is widely acknowledged but very rarely practiced? The wide gate and easy road leading to destruction—the path most people take, Matthew's Jesus observes—is one that rejects the very idea of engaging the other, the stranger, the enemy, as one who is like unto myself and who is thus in radical need of basic requirements like food, water, and shelter, to say nothing of love, kindness, and respect. To reject my commonalities with this other, this stranger, this enemy, is the easy path that does indeed lead to destruction, for it amplifies mutual hostilities and feeds reciprocal anger and pain. It reinforces my desire for safety and plenty at the cost of those I am willing to discount. It may appear to reap immediate advantages. Yet it cannot but lead finally to destruction.

The narrow gate, the hard road to tread, is the one on which the followers of Jesus must "in everything do to others as you would have them do to you"—and on this narrow road, there is no "other" who is disqualified. It is loving enemies, doing good to those who hate us, blessing those who curse us, praying for those who abuse us (Luke 6:27–28). *Perhaps this is well nigh impossible.* But it is the road that leads to life precisely because it is the road *of* life, of true life—for life truly thrives only where it is radically and lavishly shared with all. This is the road that Jesus trod, this road of life, and of course it got him killed as a young man. So it is in a world plagued by sin that leads us on toward death. But none of this changes the fact that true human life and flourishing ultimately depend upon living with all others in mutuality and reciprocity. Indeed, God's raising of the executed Jesus validates the path Jesus taught and embodied, radically demanding as that path surely is. Can the church of tomorrow walk upon such a difficult yet life-giving path? Much repentance would be required. J. Andrew Overman observes that in the late first century "apparently few followed the way Matthew articulated, which was hard but would lead to life."[13] Few then, and presumably few today—and few tomorrow as well. What kind of church might we become if we acknowledged that this is indeed an exceedingly narrow path with few travelers? Can we walk in this way?

I am proposing that this so-called Golden Rule is indeed widely known, frequently taught, perhaps nearly universally affirmed. Perhaps it is even practiced often, to some extent, by many. But perhaps, again, that is just the issue—the *extent* to which human beings are apt, and able, to reach and touch *all others* in this spirit of reciprocity. Considered this way, we seem not at all distant from Jesus's earlier command to love our enemies "so that you may be children of your Father in heaven; . . . For if you love those who love you what reward do you have? . . . Be perfect, therefore, as your heavenly Father is perfect" (Matt 5:43–48). So the question reasserts itself: Is Jesus asking of his disciples the impossible? Is this simply the imposition of a divine ideal intended only to frustrate us into a sense of inability, of our imperfections, so that we will be driven to acknowledge our need of grace?

Even if this has been a typically Protestant, and particularly Lutheran, way to read Matthew 5:43–48, let us recall that at the sermon's conclusion Jesus insists that "only the one who does the will of my Father in heaven . . . will enter the kingdom of heaven" (7:21). Remember that the wise person is the one who hears all of these teachings of Jesus and acts on them (7:24). It seems likely that Matthew's Jesus fully expects his followers to do these things, to do unto *all others*—whether friend, family, neighbor, stranger, or even enemy—in the light of the recognition that they are all "like unto myself." Jesus expects his followers to live fully and entirely out of this experience of seeing myself in all others and all others in myself. This is the narrow path. Is this within human possibility?

Wesley and Prevenient Grace

As a theologian within the Wesleyan tradition, I appeal once more to John Wesley for help in addressing these issues. Initially, we should note that Wesley would not be surprised at the virtually universal moral ideal of reciprocity and mutuality. Indeed, he would expect it.[14] Expanding upon

13. Overman, *Church and Community in Crisis*, 100.

14. We should acknowledge that other grounds can be, and have been, suggested as

the notion of prevenient grace he inherited from the Dutch theologian James Arminius (1560–1609), Wesley stipulated that this "grace that comes before" is nothing other than the very presence of God, the Holy Spirit, lovingly laboring in every human life. For Wesley, it is God, in whom "we live and move and have our being" (Acts 17:28), who awakens each and every human being to the reality of the neighbor, the other.

In his sermon "On Conscience," for instance, Wesley drew upon the work of British moral theorist Francis Hutcheson (1694–1746), who had taught that beyond the typical five senses we experience a "public sense, whereby we are naturally pained at the misery of a fellow creature and pleased at his deliverance from it."[15] Hutcheson assumed that this was a natural and universal capacity in human beings. Wesley, however, differed from Hutcheson by proposing that this "public sense," or what he otherwise sometimes calls "fellow-feeling"—and what we would likely call empathy—is not simply an inherited human capacity. It is, instead, an expression "of that supernatural gift of God which we usually style, preventing grace."[16] The light or presence of God enlightens and awakens human beings to a lively sense of the other as "one like unto myself." For Wesley, there is no human being who has ever existed who was not deeply loved and immediately graced by God; indeed, he was often quick to cite Matthew 5:43–48 to support his conviction. Thus, no human being lives without the Spirit's wooing to live compassionately and justly with (all) others. "No man living," he insisted, "is entirely destitute of what is vulgarly called 'natural conscience.' But this is not natural; it is more properly termed 'preventing grace.' . . . Everyone has some measure of that light, some faint glimmering ray, which sooner or later, more or less, enlightens every man that cometh into the

---

the rationale for the existence of this ethical ideal. It is not difficult to suppose, for instance, that evolutionary processes led human beings in a variety of cultures to recognize the survival value of caring for others, even others outside one's own clan or tribe. Karl Jaspers's influential notion of an axial age in human religious and moral development during, roughly, the eighth to the third century BCE, suggests a flowering of such values that may readily be interpreted as having occurred due to evolutionary constraints. See Armstrong, *The Great Transformation*. To be sure, for theistic evolutionists an approach like Wesley's, which we are about to examine, is not at all to be construed as excluding evolutionary or other naturalistic factors.

15. This is Wesley's characterization of Hutcheson in "On Conscience," *Works* Vol. VII, 189.

16. Wesley, "On Conscience," *Works* Vol. VII, 189. The terms "prevenient" and "preventing" were synonyms in Wesley's time, meaning "coming before."

world."[17] Most critical to our purposes here is the idea that human conscience is never simply human, because God is efficaciously present always to all people in every culture, society, and relational matrix.

Wesley, like Hutcheson before him, believed that in addition to this "public sense," or empathy, conscience included a "moral sense," or a universally shared yearning for justice. Wesley reiterated that "both the one and the other" are manifestations of prevenient grace in human lives, cultures, societies, and religious traditions. Indeed, even to exercise the most intimate of capacities associated with conscience—that of self-knowledge, or "discerning . . . [one's] own tempers, thoughts, words and actions"—"is not possible for [one] to do," insisted Wesley, "without the assistance . . . and the continued influence of the Spirit of God."[18] The crucial point to grasp here, though, is that this "continued influence"—we might construe the phrase as *continuous inflowing*—of God's Spirit does not undo the identity, negate the agency, or squelch the energies of the human creatures. Indeed, this influence of the Spirit instigates and heightens human responsibility.

For Wesley, then, the human conscience is a *con-fluence*: there is the influence, the inflowing, of all of our experiences, education, and relationships, but there is also the inflowing of the Spirit to quicken, to address, to call, to convict. In practice, indeed in reality, these influences are inseparably intertwined. In "On Conscience" Wesley states this explicitly. First, he indicates that the etymology of the word "conscience" is "to know together with" another. Then he proposes that this "other" is God—but *not* "none other than" God! God always works with the human condition in its finitude and particularity. Thus, as we have seen, on the one hand Wesley rejects the phrase "natural conscience" because, "properly speaking, it is not natural, but a supernatural gift of God, above all [the human's] natural endowments. No, it is not nature, but the Son of God, that is 'the true light, which enlighteneth every man that cometh into the world.'"[19] On the other hand, conscience "is that faculty whereby we are at once conscious of our own thoughts, words, and actions, and of their merit or demerit. . . . But this varies exceedingly, according to education and a thousand other circumstances."[20]

---

17. Wesley, "On Working Out Our Own Salvation," *Works* Vol. III, 207. Here, of course, Wesley's more immediate biblical text is John 1:9.

18. Wesley, "On Conscience," *Works* Vol. VII, 189–90.

19. Wesley, "On Conscience," *Works* Vol. VII, 187–88.

20. Wesley, "On Conscience," *Works* Vol. VII, 187.

Education and a thousand other circumstances! There are undoubtedly more than just a thousand such circumstances: events significant and not so; memories (often at least half forgotten); countless conversations; habits of thought and behavior; political, religious, and moral authorities; all kinds of relations with others, and so on (and on!). These all contribute their presence, their effects, their energies into our psyches and bodies. But Wesley of course intended the number of "a thousand" not as a limit, but as an exorbitant and wild gesture toward the infinitely incalculable particulars of each of our lives. If *con-science* is, on the one hand, a "knowing with" the Spirit of God who searches all hearts and all things, it is, on the other, a "knowing with" those numberless particulars of each and every human being in history. And because God does not negate or cancel the contributions of those "thousand other circumstances," conscience is not a stable, unvarying universal standard. Indeed, it "varies exceedingly"!

And yet!—on that other hand, it is God who speaks, who moves, who draws and woos us from within "the boundaries of our habitation" (Acts 17:26). God the Creator respects the inflowing of those "thousand other circumstances" in their felt presence in our lives. Wesley garnered further support for this idea by alluding to the famed words of Micah 6:8, "So that we may say to every human creature, 'He,' not nature, 'hath showed thee, O man, what is good.'" For Wesley it is significant that the one addressed in the text is "O man" (or, much more faithful to the point, "O human"; Hebrew, *adam*)—and *not* "O Christian" or "O Jew." In Wesley's reading of the Micah text, the Holy One quietly labors in the world to show all human beings the good path on which to walk: "to do justice, and to love kindness, and to walk humbly" with one's deity.

Indeed, Wesley takes the Micah text a step further. He notices that "Balak king of Moab" and "Balaam the son of Beor" are mentioned a few verses earlier (6:5); thus, not without some justification he assumes that this "beautiful passage" is given "a peculiar force" when we "consider by whom and on what occasion the words were uttered." Wesley suggests that Balaam the pagan prophet was "then under divine impressions," and that "probably Balak too, at that time, experienced something of the same influence. This [i.e., prevenient grace] occasioned his consulting with, or asking counsel of, Balaam,—his proposing the question to which Balaam gives so full an answer . . . ."[21] Wesley, then, assumed that this classic prophetic text calling its hearers to "do justice, and to love kindness, and to walk humbly

---

21. Wesley, "On Conscience," *Works* Vol. VII, 188.

with your God" was originally and long ago the answer given by the pagan prophet Balaam to King Balak's tortured query, "With what shall I come before Yahweh?" (Mic 6:6–8). This is a fascinating reading, for it implies that this well-known and well-loved text is essentially a textual fragment of prevenient grace.

My point is not to argue that Wesley was correct in all the particulars. It is to suggest that his reflections offer an intriguing possibility for Christians of the Wesleyan tradition, and beyond, to consider: might not the so-called Golden Rule, in all of its various expressions in a great variety of cultures, be interpreted as a crucial instantiation of the work of the Spirit in human existence through many millennia? We can be certain that Jesus was familiar at least with Hillel's formulation of the rule,[22] and his radical equivocation of the rule with "the law and the prophets" seems to settle the issue as to whether or not he considered the idea unique to himself. He did not. But my argument is that this is nonetheless "the narrow gate" and the hard road "that leads to life," for few there are who actually live in this way to its fullest extent: in *everything* doing to *all* others as we would want done to ourselves.

Would this amount to salvation by works? Does it really all depend upon how well or how thoroughly a person has lived the Golden Rule? It must be remembered that, for Wesley, even the simplest deed of mercy or justice toward the neighbor is already and always itself a response to the prevenient grace of God benevolently laboring in one's existence. It is not a deed that I initiate; nonetheless, it is a deed for which I am responsible. We move very close to an idea not unlike the meditations of Levinas and of Buber before him: God as prevenient grace confronts us in the neighbor, the stranger, the other, even the enemy. God as prevenient grace calls us to respond to the light of this divine prompting to see and to feel this other as one truly "like unto myself," whose creaturely vulnerabilities I feel as my own—and to respond accordingly. "Since [God] is invisible to our eyes," Wesley wrote, "we are to serve God in our neighbor, which God receives as if done to himself in person, standing visibly before us."[23] The more widely and radically we extend the category of "neighbor," the more difficult and narrow the path becomes—and yet it is the path to life in its fullest, life as it was meant by our Maker to be lived. We believe this because it is the sort of life that Jesus "the Messiah, the Son of the living God" lived; this in turn fits

---

22. See Chapter 3 of this book, under the heading "Matthew Matters?"
23. Wesley, *A Plain Account of Christian Perfection*, 111.

him well to be the one who, we read in Matthew later, "will repay everyone for what he has done" (16:16, 27). If "everyone" really means *everyone*, and if it really means for what everyone has *done* (as opposed to what each has thought, or believed, or hoped, or prayed), then presumably there is some kind of measure or standard of judgment. Again, Wesley's suggestion is that the standard will depend upon the quality and quantity of "light" that a person has received from God from within the particularities of her history, culture, society, education—"and a thousand other circumstances."

Further, a doctrine of prevenient grace such as Wesley's might shed light on Paul's intriguing declaration that "gentiles, who do not possess the law," may at least in principle "do instinctively what the law requires" for, "though not having the law, are a law to themselves" because "what the law requires is written on their hearts, in which their own conscience bears witness" (Rom 2:14–15). We need not have recourse to some notion of natural law, nor to an overly static idea of eternal principles etched in every human conscience. It may be enough to suggest that the living Spirit of God dwells in the midst of human lives and communities, ever awakening us to the neighbor, the stranger, the other, ever enlivening us to the call of justice, ever present in the face(s) before us.

The Wise, the Foolish, and All Those Others

We return to a point made early in this chapter: Jesus's Parable of the Wise and Foolish Builders encompasses two sorts of people: "everyone ... who hears these words of mine and acts on them" and "everyone who hears these words of mine and does not act on them" (7:24, 26). This leaves out a great many people, both in Jesus's own time and in the centuries since— to say nothing of all those virtually countless lives before Christ. What of all those folks? I grant that this question was not on Matthew's radar; the point of such a teaching for Matthew is to drive home its critical, existential import for those who do hear, rather than to speculate on the fate of those who do not. We might even guess that Matthew assumed that eventually— perhaps sooner than later—the great commission that concludes his gospel would be fulfilled. The fact remains that the vast majority of human beings who have ever lived have not heard these radical teachings of Jesus; for that matter, many of those who have heard of Jesus and his words, who may indeed even possess a rudimentary understanding of the gospel, might in fact have received a terribly garbled and distorted message. They have so misheard that they have heard without hearing. The fact that this issue is not forefront in Matthew's Gospel does not mean we cannot or should not engage it ourselves.

Wesley's ideas about the efficacy of prevenient grace do seem promising. Those who have never been confronted by the words of Jesus (Matt 7:24) have nonetheless been confronted by the Spirit or light of God in countless ways, perhaps most often and specifically in the bodily presence of fellow human beings—whether as neighbor, other, stranger, friend, or enemy. This "light" may shine brightly, or dimly, upon every human being at any or every given moment, depending upon (again, in Wesley's fine phrase) "education and a thousand other circumstances." Wesley appealed to Luke 12:48—"from everyone to whom much has been given, much will be required"—to argue that lesser light implies a reduced measure of answerability. For both "modern Heathens" of his own age, and for "ancient Heathens" of millennia prior, "no more therefore will be expected of them, than the living up to the light they had."[24] Thus God's judgments are just, holding people accountable only for what they knew, not for what they did not know. Nonetheless, this remains a demanding standard! Neither Wesley nor we have any good reason to suppose that people generally live up to the light they have received. Our own experience tends not to be terribly encouraging. Thus, the divine light of prevenient grace, even as it draws people toward the mercies of God, may typically leave people with a greater sense of their moral failure and unworthiness. To this human failure the Gospel's reply is Jesus's invitation to drink from the cup of his "blood of the covenant, which is poured out for many for the forgiveness of sins" (Matt 26:28). Even here, to be sure, Matthew's Gospel is adamant in its demand regarding what is expected of those who have received divine forgiveness. Matthew uniquely insists on God's forgiveness being conditioned on our forgiving others; "but if you do not forgive others, neither will your Father forgive your trespasses" (6:15). Divine grace and human response are deemed inseparable.

Again, we should acknowledge that the vast majority of human beings have not during their lifetimes heard of such forgiveness through Jesus, nor of the life of forgiveness that such grace demands and expects. Refusing to assume that all such people are inevitably damned—which would, after all, simply be a new form of predestination—but also rejecting the possibility of postmortem conversion, Wesley assumed that God would judge

---

24. Wesley, "On Faith," *Works* Vol. VII, 197.

fairly, and compassionately, all of the unevangelized on the basis of their responsiveness to the degree of gracious light that shone upon their lives. This would help Wesley (and perhaps us) to make sense of Jesus's words that soon follow the Sermon on the Mount: "I tell you, many will come from east and west and will eat with Abraham and Isaac and Jacob in the kingdom of heaven, while the heirs of the kingdom will be thrown into the outer darkness" (8:11–12).

It is significant that Wesley never understood this idea of prevenient grace to imply that unevangelized people would be better off not hearing the gospel. More light is always better!—even as it heightens one's responsibility before God and other people. Better then, in an important sense, to be a fool who hears Jesus's words and refuses to act on them than never to hear his words at all. For only in hearing these words do we undergo the possibility of entering the narrow gate and walking the difficult way that leads to life. Such a life—let us call it salvation—is not simply or even primarily about some eternal destiny. If it were, perhaps it would be better for some never to hear Jesus's words at all, and take their chances, as it were, with the possibilities afforded by prevenient grace. But that is to assign salvation only a postmortem significance. The life of wisdom is a life lived well and faithfully in the here and now. Even if such a life may be vaguely apprehended and attended to by virtue of prevenient grace (cf. Acts 10:34–35; 17:26–27), Matthew's Gospel testifies to the irreplaceable efficacy of Jesus's words and deeds to reveal the great light and life of salvation now, in this world. The wise ones who put his words into practice, that is, his community of disciples, then in turn have become "the light of the world" as they allow their light to shine before others (Matt 5:14, 16). This is about a life, particularly a corporate life, lived well together in this world as a social testimony to the God of Israel, the God of Jesus, as the true Creator (and re-Creator) of all things.

What we are describing here truly is salvation by grace. But grace must be understood as the very presence of God, the Spirit of Christ, encountering, speaking, calling, convicting all people everywhere—awaiting, demanding, and enabling their response. This is grace that in its very nature calls for human response in terms of concrete deeds in relation to the neighbor. We could call it typically Wesleyan, but it is surely also (and much earlier!) typically Jewish. We hope it is typically Christian! Even so, one of the leading Jewish theologians of the twentieth century, Eugene Borowitz (1924–2016), wrote that "Wesley's emphasis on the deeds that sanctifying grace should produce has something of the emphasis on 'deed' that Judaism makes primary. In any discussion of Christian and Jewish ethics John's Wesley's thought might be a useful, near-middle ground with which to begin."[25] It is pertinent to Borowitz's observation that what he identifies as "sanctifying grace" is nothing other than justifying grace or prevenient grace or any other sort of grace. "Grace" for Wesley is always *God*—God lovingly, actively, wooingly present in every human being in all times and places. The shifting adjectives for grace describe the mode of response that is possible for any particular human being in the exigencies of her existence. Thus, there surely also are deeds that prevenient grace should produce, as indicated earlier: "God has showed you, O human, what is good."

Wesley's confidence in God's prevenient grace never inhibited his determination to proclaim the gospel anywhere he could to all the people he could. The church of tomorrow likewise will go forth to proclaim, in deed and in word, that Jesus *is* the narrow path we follow, "teaching [all the world's peoples] to obey everything that I have commanded you" (Matt 28:20). The more light, the better!—because this light evokes and enlivens the possibility of greater and deeper love for God and all neighbors. Greater light calls for deeper responsibility—but such response-ability is precisely what is needed for such love to occur, let alone to flourish. This narrow path that leads to life, this life lived together by the community of the wise, is for the sake of the world and its healing.

---

25. Borowitz, *Contemporary Christologies*, 118. I intend the present chapter of this book to be an elaboration and extension of Borowitz's claim.

6

Upon This Rock (Wisdom's Risk)

But who do you say that I am?

JESUS'S FAMOUS CONVERSATION WITH his disciples regarding his identity and mission, including Peter's confession that Jesus is God's Messiah, is common to all three Synoptic Gospels.[1] Our intent here, of course, will be to isolate and engage the material in this story that is unique to Matthew in order to appreciate further why Matthew matters. Let us begin, however, with the one line that is identical (right down to the last iota!) in all three versions of this story: Jesus's question pressed upon his disciples, "But who do you say that I am?"

Given the typical variation among the Gospels' account of this conversation, the fact that Jesus's question is worded identically in all three Synoptics underscores the critical and enduring importance of the question. One might argue that it is the question that Jesus continues to ask his followers

---

1. Matt 16:13–20; Mark 8:27–30; Luke 9:18–21. It is arguable that John offers at least a roughly parallel conversation in ch. 6, after Jesus feeds the multitudes (which actually tracks with the Synoptics' placement of the conversation) and becomes embroiled in controversy over his shocking demand that people are to "eat my flesh and drink my blood" (John 6:56). At hearing such things, "many of his disciples turned back and no longer went about with him" (6:66). Jesus then asks the twelve, "Do you also wish to go away?"—hardly the same question as "Who do you say that I am?" admittedly. But at this point Peter offers his confession, "Lord, to whom can we go? You have the words of eternal life. We have come to believe and know that you are the Holy One of God" (6:67–68).

down through the centuries. This question, in Elizabeth Johnson's words, "resounds through the centuries inviting a response from every generation of believers and from every disciple. Who do you say that I am?"[2] We may think we now have the answer down pat, given Peter's confession. Yet even among the slight variations of each gospel's description of Peter's confession of faith, we encounter slippage, difference, interpretive distinctions. Further, Peter himself soon betrays a sizable gap between his preconceptions about what a Messiah does and how Messiah is envisioned by God. The risk of divine Wisdom, I shall argue in this chapter, is that of having entrusted to human beings this critical and necessary task of interpretation: of Jesus, of texts, of God, of the church. Further, this story shall remind us of the always-looming possibility that we might not have it quite right in any one of these matters.

Jesus first asks his disciples about the general public's perceptions of him. They avoid the less savory interpretations—that Jesus is insane, or even possessed by the devil—and stick with the more salutary. All three Synoptics include the populace's speculations that Jesus might be John the Baptist or some other ancient prophet returned from the dead, or perhaps the return of Elijah from his heavenly journeys in a fiery chariot, coming now as prelude to the end of the world. Only Matthew includes the name of Jeremiah as a candidate. Daniel Harrington observes that "the addition of Jeremiah to the list is consistent with Matthew's general interest in Jeremiah as a figure of Jesus."[3] Jeremiah is named here but also in Matthew 2:17 and 27:9, with several other allusions to the book of Jeremiah (7:15–23; 11:28–30; 23:37–39). Given Jesus's warning against those who cry out "Lord! Lord!" but fail to do God's will (Matt 7:21), Jeremiah's prophetic judgment against the temple in Jerusalem is particularly apt:

> Thus says . . . the God of Israel: Amend your ways and your doings, and let me dwell with you in this place. Do not trust in these deceptive words: "This is the temple of the LORD, the temple of the LORD, the temple of the LORD." For if you truly amend your ways and your doings, if you truly act justly with one another, if you do not oppress the alien, the orphan, and the widow, or shed innocent blood in this place, and if you do not go after other gods to your own hurt, then I will dwell with you in this place . . . . (Jer 7:3–7)

---

2. Johnson, *Consider Jesus*, 3.
3. Harrington, *The Gospel of Matthew*, 247.

For Matthew, then, the weeping Jeremiah is the perfect precursor to the prophet, and more than a prophet, that is Jesus. So it is no surprise that very soon in this gospel, Jesus will begin to disclose to his disciples the intense suffering awaiting him in Jerusalem. But that is to get ahead of our story.

Who Do You All Say That I Am?

Jesus then asks his follow-up, *the* Christological question: "But who do *you* say that I am?" It hardly need be added that the *you* is plural in the Greek, the "y'all" of the American South. Jesus is asking his community of disciples, together, this question. It is undoubtedly the question he still is asking, but it is critical that we come to understand that the question cannot finally be answered with mere words; what is required is a kind of life lived together by the community he will soon call his *ekklesia*. Just as Jesus answered the question "Are you the Coming One, or shall we look for another?" with his deeds, so Jesus's query "Who do you say that I am?" can only be answered truly by our deeds.

But words have their place too. Peter confesses:

"You are the Messiah." (Mark 8:29)
"The Messiah of God." (Luke 9:20)
"You are the Messiah, the Son of the living God." (Matt 16:16)

It is obvious that Matthew's version features the most theologically developed confession by Peter, but let us begin with what is common in all three Synoptics: Jesus is Messiah (*Christos*). The term means "one who is anointed," still evident in its Greek root in christenings of both babies and boats. To be anointed with oil poured upon one's head, in the history and traditions of Israel, was to be chosen, acknowledged, and set apart by God for God's purposes. It is noteworthy that by very definition, one who is anointed does not stand alone, for one does not anoint oneself. The term implies one who is anointed, another who anoints, and the (an)ointment that the anointer outpours. To call Jesus the Christ or Messiah, then, is to acknowledge that he cannot be properly understood simply on his own, or as some isolated, heroic individual. Luke's version of Peter's confession gets at this idea most directly with the terse reply, "The Messiah of God." Jesus is God's Anointed One. In fact, in the sequel volume of Acts this same Peter preaches that "God anointed Jesus of Nazareth with the Holy Spirit and with power" such that Jesus "went about doing good and healing all who were oppressed by the devil, for God was with him" (10:38). It is arguable, then, that the church's confession that God is Triune is rooted primordially in its confession that Jesus is the *Messiah*, anointed by *God* with God's own *Spirit*.

Matthew's account of Peter's confession adds, "the Son of the living God," which of course would contribute to later Trinitarian reflections and, more immediately, in Harrington's estimation "'corrects' any false impressions related to 'Messiah'"[4]—though he elaborates no further. Presumably, Harrington means that the term "messiah" by itself is liable to be interpreted as a "low" Christology—Jesus as nothing other, nothing more, than a human being anointed by God for a task. Harrington's is certainly a possible reading, given language we have already encountered in Matthew 11: "All things have been handed over to me by my Father; and no one knows the Son except the Father, and no one knows the Father except the Son and anyone to whom the Son chooses to reveal him" (11:27). For that matter, after Jesus calmed the storm on the Sea of Galilee, delivering his disciples from their fear of the elements, "those in the boat worshiped him, saying, 'Truly you are the Son of God'"(14:32–33). This is one who is master over the chaotic elements of wind and sea, who calls out in the divine voice over the crashing waves "I am" (*ego eimi*, 14:27), who is the very embodiment of Psalm 77—"When the waters saw you, O God, when the waters saw you, they were afraid; the very deep trembled. . . . Your way was through the sea, your path, through the mighty waters; yet your footprints were unseen" (Ps 77:16, 19). This is very God, "the Son of the living God," in our midst.

Unavoidably, the theological seeps seamlessly into the political. Warren Carter notes that the place in which this confession occurs is Caesarea Philippi, the locale where King Herod had erected a marble temple to commemorate Augustus; it should be little surprise, then, that the phrase "the son of the living God . . . was commonly used to honor and elevate emperors, especially Augustus. It was part of a cluster of terms that recognized the emperors' identity as agents of the gods' will and power expressed through Rome's rule."[5] To confess Jesus to be "the Son of the living God," and to do so precisely in this region architecturally dedicated to Roman supremacy, "is to contest and challenge those claims of sovereignty and agency. . . . To recognize Jesus as God's [son] confirms that he, not the emperor, manifests

---

4. Harrington, *The Gospel of Matthew*, 247.
5. Carter, *Matthew and the Margins*, 333.

God's purposes."[6] (Need it even be said that the temptation to worship political empire has perhaps never been greater in the history of the United States, including far too many U.S. churches, than it is in these early decades of the third millennium?)

Jesus the *Christos* and Peter the *Petros*

One of the most glaring and dramatic differences between Matthew and the other Synoptic Gospels occurs in the next moment of interchange. In Mark and Luke, Jesus responds to Peter's confession with an immediate prohibition against his disciples' spreading this notion to anyone else. The fact that Matthew has the same prohibition makes it all the more telling that, between Peter's confession and Jesus's adamant hushing of the twelve, we encounter these striking words that *clearly matter to Matthew*:

> Blessed are you, Simon bar-Jonah! For flesh and blood has not revealed this to you, but my Father who is in heaven. And I tell you, you are Peter (*Petros*), and on this rock (*petra*) I will build my church, and the powers of death shall not prevail against it. I will give you [singular] the keys of the kingdom of heaven, and whatever you bind on earth shall be bound in heaven, and whatever you loose on earth shall be loosed in heaven. (Matt 16:17–19)[7]

Few biblical passages have packed a more controversial punch than this one found in Matthew alone. Some observations, though, seem incontrovertible. One is that Jesus clearly is enthusiastic in his reply. Another is that Jesus attributes the insight in Peter's confession to divine revelation. (Neither Mark nor Luke even hint at anything of the sort.) Another is that

---

6. Carter, *Matthew and the Margins*, 333.

7. John Meier, drawing upon W. Grundmann, *Das Evangelium nach Matthaus*, suggests that Jesus's response is a trio of triplets:
   v. 17: a. Happy are you, Simon, Son of Jonah,
      b. for flesh and blood did not reveal [this] to you,
      c. but my Father who is in heaven.
   v. 18: a. And I say to you that you are [the] Rock,
      b. and upon this rock I will build my church,
      c. and the gates of Hades shall not prevail against it.
   v. 19: a. I shall give you the keys of the kingdom of heaven,
      b. and whatever you bind on earth shall be found in heaven,
      c. and whatever you loose on earth shall be loosed in heaven.
(Meier, *The Vision of Matthew*, 110).

Jesus is entrusting to Peter a role and responsibility unlike anything else in the New Testament.

But what does all of this mean for us today?

Perhaps more than any other single passage in Holy Writ, "the confessional standpoint of the interpreter has quite often coloured his exegesis."[8] What is the "rock" upon which Jesus intends to build his church? Protestant attempts to dodge what seems to be the "plain meaning of the text"—historically a typically Protestant concern—are less like rock and more like shifting sand, weak and ill-founded. Jesus tells Peter that he is *petros*, "Rock."[9] It takes intellectual gymnastics comparable to the abilities of a circus contortionist to argue that this *Petros* is not the *petra* (the difference lies simply in Greek case endings) upon whom Jesus will do his building project. To try to suggest that the *petra* is somehow simply Peter's confession of faith in Jesus, or that Peter is symbolic here of any and all of Jesus's disciples, is willingly to ignore both the Greek syntax and the rest of the story. David Hill concurs: "Attempts to interpret the 'rock' as something other than Peter in person (e.g., his faith, his confession, the truth revealed to him) are due to Protestant bias, and introduce to the statement a degree of subtlety which is highly unlikely."[10] For Jesus immediately adds, "I will give *you*"—second-person singular noun, inescapably meaning Peter himself—"the keys of the kingdom of heaven" (16:19). Uniquely in the Gospel of Matthew, Jesus is handing over to Peter an immense responsibility, whatever we might take that responsibility to entail.

It is difficult to ignore echoes of the concluding parable in the Sermon on the Mount,[11] where Jesus identifies the sage as one "who hears these words of mine and acts on them" and compares her to someone who has built her house on rock (*petran*, 7:24, 25). Indeed, these are the only two passages in the entire New Testament, let alone Matthew, in which "build" (*oikodomeo*) and rock (*petra*) are used in direct combination. If we are bold to connect the two passages, then it seems likely that, at least for the Matthean community and tradition, Peter was recognized as the

---

8. Hill, *The Gospel of Matthew*, 258. Hill is describing the judgment of Oscar Cullmann after the latter's having surveyed the field of New Testament interpreters in his *Peter: Disciple, Apostle, Martyr*.

9. The Johannine version: Simon's brother Andrew "brought [Simon] to Jesus, who looked at him and said, 'You are Simon son of John. You are to be called Cephas' (which is translated Peter)" (John 1:42).

10. Hill, *The Gospel of Matthew*, 261.

11. Recall the previous chapter of this volume.

authoritative interpreter of Jesus's teachings. He would be the one to help guide the community of discipleship in how to act on Jesus's words in new and changing circumstances—the rain, floods, and winds of historical and social contingency. But the fact that Matthew's Gospel was likely written about fifty years after Jesus's ministry—and if so, about fifteen years after Peter's martyrdom—raises the critical question of Peter's perduring pertinence. Why would Matthew find it necessary, or even important, to include this blessing of responsibility upon Peter, well after Peter's death? What point would it serve? Roman Catholic tradition, of course, finds the necessity of Petrine authority in the notion that this authority has been passed down through history via the chain of bishops of Rome. Thus even when, or perhaps especially when, Protestant interpreters grant Peter's primacy in this passage, we are left with conundrums. Is there a contemporary relevance in Matthew's story of Jesus and Peter? In the moderate, well-measured words of Harrington, who was himself a Roman Catholic, "The quarrel among Christians through the centuries revolves around two further questions: Has Peter's primacy been handed on to successors? Has this primacy been carried on by the bishops of Rome? Catholics answer these questions in the affirmative, whereas other Christians do not."[12]

Peter and Paul

I will not be the first by far to suggest that while Matthew's church(es) undoubtedly honored Peter as "the keeper of the keys of the kingdom" in ways that the Markan and Lukan traditions do not even begin to imagine, this need not lead further into affirming some continuing significance for a long chain of Petrine heirs. It must be granted that Peter's primacy must have still mattered to Matthew well after Peter's death—which raises the question regarding an heir to Petrine authority during the time of Matthew's writing—yet this gospel offers nary a hint about such any particular person inheriting Peter's "keys." It seems more plausible to interpret this passage as indicative of a continuing argument among early Christian traditions regarding the relative importance and authority of Peter, particularly in relation to Paul. But Harrington offers the intriguing possibility, "Perhaps the leaders [of the Matthean community] traced their spiritual pedigree back through Peter much as the rabbis did through their teachers."[13]

---

12. Harrington, *The Gospel of Matthew*, 252.
13. Harrington, *The Gospel of Matthew*, 251.

If Harrington is right, then we can suggest with a high degree of certainty that Paul was not impressed. Perhaps it is a coincidence that Paul informs the Corinthians that "no one can lay any foundation other than the one that has been laid" and that this "foundation is Jesus Christ" (1 Cor 3:11), but if so, it is an intriguing coincidence. Indeed, Paul boldly writes that "like a skilled master builder I laid a foundation"—the foundation of Jesus Christ—"and someone else is building on it" (3:10). While immediate context would suggest that it is primarily Apollos on Paul's mind (3:4; 4:6), he has already mentioned Peter as a competitor for the Corinthians' affections (1:12) and will soon enough do so again (3:21). By identifying the foundation with Jesus and relativizing the importance of Peter, it is arguable that Paul has some awareness of the claims of the Matthean community. In any case, Paul warns that "each builder must choose with care how to build" on the foundation (3:10); indeed, a builder ("God's servants" like Paul, Peter, and Apollos) who builds a church poorly or unfaithfully may even barely escape divine judgment "as through fire" (3:15). When Paul informs the Corinthians that they together "are God's temple" and warns that anyone who destroys God's temple will be destroyed by God (3:16–17), we may wonder how far Peter was from Paul's mind, if he was far at all.

We properly consider Matthew our most "Jewish" gospel and, given that Peter obviously enjoyed a place of significance in this early Jewish Christian tradition, it is not difficult to postulate Paul's problem with all of this. Indeed, it comes to a head in Paul's letter to the Galatians when he writes of the time he was constrained to stand up to Peter publicly regarding the latter's overly tender Jewish sensitivities about fellowshipping with gentiles (Gal 2:11–14). Essentially, Paul publicly shames Peter who was, for Paul, among "those who were supposed to be acknowledged leaders—what they actually were makes no difference to me," he adds, "for God shows no partiality—those leaders contributed nothing to me" (2:6). If Jesus had given Peter the "keys of the kingdom," Paul had not received the memo! His pushback against Petrine primacy could readily perpetuate a feud for decades between these early streams of Christian community. This possibility could, I believe, sufficiently explain the importance for Matthew, among the Synoptics, of insisting upon this bestowal of authority upon Peter with no further textual concern for identifying a successor. If all of this is even approximately the case, then the point is made: churches could share the confession that Jesus is God's Anointed One without full agreement—indeed, with significant disagreement—regarding the implications

Upon This Rock (Wisdom's Risk)

of that confession. What began as a tension between Matthean-Petrine communities and Pauline communities—a tension inscribed in the very pages of the New Testament—has continued through the centuries as the conflict of interpretations within Christian tradition most broadly construed. Obviously, such conflicts continue into our contemporary setting. Is this situation a result of a risk undertaken by divine Wisdom—the risk of entrusting to human minds, hearts, and hands the burden of interpretation? Does God dwell peacefully among our differences and arguments? Is God content not to settle arguments such as these found even in the earliest generations of the Christian faith?

Binding and Loosing

The specific function of "the keys of the kingdom of heaven" entrusted to Peter is elaborated in the words that immediately follow: "whatever you bind on earth shall be bound in heaven, and whatever you loose on earth shall be loosed in heaven" (16:19). This authority to bind (or "tie up") and loose (or "untie") was in fact claimed by various schools of Pharisees contemporary with Jesus and in the centuries after. In rabbinic usage, "binding and loosing" entails the authority either to forbid or permit a certain action in the light of the Torah. By extension, then, it is the power to "bind" a person in guilt before God and the community, as well as the power to "untie" the transgressor through the processes of forgiveness and reconciliation. Not surprisingly, given Matthew's deep ties to communal Jewish identity and practice, this gospel mirrors the synagogue's concern for proper boundaries for, and healthy interactions within, the community of God's people. But of course in the stead of the term *synagogue*, Matthew uses the term *ekklesia*—Jesus's community of disciples that is to be built upon Peter—and is the only canonical gospel to employ this term. Its usage is likely intended as a deliberate contrast to "synagogue," even as the concern being expressed for community identity and boundaries is essentially the same. Nearly all commentators on Matthew, then, concur that "binding and loosing" has to do with judgments about the community's rules and exemptions, or with imposing or lifting excommunication, or both—and they are closely related anyway. "Peter has authority to make pronouncements (whether legislative, . . . or disciplinary) and these will be ratified by God in the Last Judgment."[14] Once again, we may surmise that it is the risk of

---

14. Hill, *The Gospel of Matthew*, 262.

divine Wisdom to entrust such deliberations and responsibilities to Peter, at least among these early Jewish Christians who were to become, more or less, the Matthean community.

Occasionally one finds Christian commentators who invert the logic of this authority given to Peter such that what Jesus actually is saying is that the binding and loosing occurs first in heaven, and then somehow is communicated to Peter to enact what God has decided on any given matter. This interpretive move seems motivated by a legitimate religious concern to uphold divine priority and authority. But it also misses by a mile the Jewish genius for grappling with the implications of a covenantal God. The rabbinic tradition developed a penchant for citing Deuteronomy 30:12, "It is not in heaven," to indicate that the God of Israel has entrusted to Israel (its scholars in particular, naturally) the collective responsibility to govern itself according to the dictates of Torah—as interpreted by the rabbis. The late Episcopalian theologian Paul van Buren (1924–98) wrote of Deuteronomy 30:12,

> This absolutely crucial word of Torah about the Torah meant for the rabbis that Torah was not only given into Israel's hands, but that the interpretation too was up to Israel. God has given to his covenant partner the freedom and responsibility to say what his holy word shall be, and as it is decided on earth, so shall it be in heaven. God's word shall now be settled in human words. God's holy covenant is to be worked out entirely by creatures in the creaturely realm.[15]

We should add that such a reading coheres nicely with the rest of the Deuteronomic passage: "It is not in the heaven, that you should say, 'Who will go up to heaven for us, and get it for us so that we may hear it and observe it?' . . . No, the word is very near to you; it is in your mouth and in your heart for you to observe" (Deut 30:12, 14).[16] There is a classic rabbinic story that gets to the heart of this idea.

---

15. Van Buren, *A Theology of the Jewish-Christian Reality, Part III*, 225. In this light van Buren suggests that, "if the Church could muster such rabbinic daring" (172), it might come to see, for examples, its ideas about Jesus's death having saving significance and even its ideas about Jesus's identity and nature (e.g., at the Councils of Nicea and Chalcedon), historically contingent as such formulations are, as having been honored, ratified, and even "assumed" by God—taken up by God as the means by which "to draw innumerable Gentiles to their knees before him" (172).

16. In Romans 10:5–10 Paul gives the Deuteronomy passage a distinctively Christological spin. For a comparison between the Pauline and rabbinic readings of Deuteronomy

Upon This Rock (Wisdom's Risk)

Eleizer and His Critics

The Talmud tells the story of a teacher named Eliezer who became embroiled in a debate with other rabbis about—of all things—the ritual cleanliness, or not, of a particular oven. That's the controversy. Eliezer insists the oven is kosher, while all the others disagree with him. In an effort to gain votes for his side, Eliezer performs several wonders bound to turn a few heads. He successfully commands a tree to become uprooted and fly through the air for several hundred feet; he convinces a stream to begin flowing in the opposite direction; he causes the walls of their house of study to lean inward upon themselves, as though collapse is imminent. Surely someone who could curry such favor and power from God cannot be wrong about an oven! Yet his fellow rabbis are unfazed and unconvinced.

So Eliezer attempts a *coup de gras*. He calls upon God to settle the argument in his favor. "Suddenly a heavenly voice went forth and said to the sages, 'Why are you arguing with Rabbi Eliezer? The Halakha [legal ruling] is in accordance with him in all circumstances.'" This might seem to close the deal; Eliezer wins the argument. Instead, Rabbi Yehoshua stands and simply cites the text from Deuteronomy, "It is not in the heavens" (30:12). Eliezer has illegitimately appealed to heaven for a deciding vote, because God has already entrusted the hearing, interpreting, and doing of the Torah to the people Israel. Perhaps having done so is a risk, but it is a risk that God apparently has willingly undertaken. Eliezer's appeal is out of order, for no further appeals to heaven may be made, precisely because God's word "is not in the heavens." Eliezer is voted down by the others, and God's vote cannot change the outcome because God's vote does not count.

But how did God feel about this? We find out in the rest of the story. Later, a certain Rabbi Nathan encounters the prophet Elijah, still employing that fiery chariot under God's direction to accomplish occasional tasks on earth for God. Nathan recalls that famous controversy between Eliezer and his halakhic opponents, asking Elijah for the inside scoop on how the result had gone down up there in heaven: "What did the Holy One, blessed be He, do at that time?" Elijah's reply suggests that the rabbis who told this story believed that God has a healthy sense of humor and a humble willingness to abide by the rabbinic rules of textual interpretation and debate: God, Elijah recalls, "laughed, saying: '*My sons have defeated me, My sons have defeated*

30, see my *Claiming Abraham*, 40–42.

me.'"[17] American-Israeli philosopher David Hartman (1931–2013), who did much to introduce this story into contemporary religious reflection, wrote that the story "signifies God's self-limiting love for the sake of making His human covenantal partners responsible for intellectually developing the Torah," such that "students of the Torah are called upon to exercise human initiative and creativity."[18] Surely this bespeaks the character of a good parent ("my sons have defeated me!"), who nudges her children to grow and mature toward responsible adulthood. We should be suspicious of any portrayal of God that threatens to keep human beings in servitude and self-loathing. It is my hope that the church of tomorrow will be open to learning from the rabbinic spirit of innovation, creativity, and boldness before God as children to whom God beckons to grow into maturity and godlikeness.

Matthew's Gospel, deeply rabbinic as it is, can be interpreted to be gesturing in just such a direction. There is no apparent hesitation on Jesus's part in entrusting this power of binding and loosing into Peter's hands. God is not interested in keeping Jesus's disciples in self-abnegating servitude, waiting upon God's direction for every move we make. Because in fact it turns out that this authority of binding and loosing is not given only to Peter.

Whatever You All Bind on Earth

It is both intriguing and crucial that in Matthew 18 we encounter the language of binding and loosing again. Not surprisingly, this same passage has Matthew's only other use of *ekklesia*—the only two places where this term translated "church" is to be found in the four Gospels. Because binding and loosing has so much to do with protecting the religious identity, the moral integrity, and the proper boundaries of the community, it is natural to find this phraseology connected with the church. "This is how things must be done in a community that wishes to make manifest its own sacredness," Ulrich Luz has written. "The Qumran community was such a community. So was Matthew's."[19] Of course it is glaringly significant that in Matthew 18 the authority of binding and loosing is given to the church (Matt 18:17–18)! In the context of dealing with an unrepentant offender within the community, Jesus tells his disciples that "whatever you [plural] bind on earth will be

---

17. The Talmud, *Baba Mesia 59b*.
18. Hartman, *A Living Covenant*, 33–34.
19. Luz, *The Theology of the Gospel of Matthew*, 105.

bound in heaven, and whatever you [plural] loose on earth will be loosed in heaven" (18:18). Indeed, Jesus promises his living presence with his gathered disciples as they navigate the challenges of living as a holy community amidst the hard realities of human failure and transgression: "For where two or three are gathered in my name, I am there among them" (18:20).[20]

This dual usage of "binding and loosing" poses fascinating questions: What happened to Peter's apparently unique role as described in Matthew 16? Is this an authority granted to one person, or in fact to the entire church? If to one person, how then to read Matthew 23's injunctions that "you are not to be called teacher, for you have one teacher, and you are all students, ... nor are you to be called instructors, for you have one instructor, the Messiah" (23:8, 10)? If to the entire church, how would differences of interpretation or application be avoided, or at least navigated? Who, if anyone, would have "the last word"? Is that perhaps the import of Jesus's promise to be present with the church in its deliberations, that somehow he will guide them to the correct judgments? But how well would that fit with the binding and loosing authority already granted, or with the declaration that "if two of you agree on earth about anything you ask, it is done for you by my Father in heaven" (18:19)? Might it be, then, that this second "binding and loosing" passage represents the process the Matthean community practiced post-Peter? That is, did the authority granted particularly to Peter become somewhat, somehow democratized after his martyrdom? Luz has suggested that this binding/loosing authority was "probably worded in the plural (see John 20:23) and reformulated in the singular by Matthew in 16:19, where Peter, Jesus' 'typical disciple', is given the authority to bind and loose."[21] But is Luz playing loose with "bind and loose"? Is not Peter portrayed as much more than the "typical disciple," particularly in Matthew 16, where he is the *Petros* upon whom Jesus shall build his church?

There is a morass of questions here. Suffice it to say that the idea of Peter's individual authority in Matthew 16 aligns better with traditional Roman Catholic commitments, while the collective authority described in Matthew 18 bodes better for Protestant predilections, given especially Martin Luther's teaching about the priesthood of all believers. Perhaps

20. This promise provides the basis for Chapter 7 of this book, "Wisdom's Presence."

21. Luz, *The Theology of the Gospel of Matthew*, 106, fn. 7. Luz, a luminary in contemporary Matthean studies, died October 13, 2019—as it turns out, just a week before my Didsbury Lectures at Nazarene Theological College upon which this book is based. I mention this only to stress my gratitude for the significant help Luz's writings have been to me in this project.

more fundamentally for both passages, we encounter here an entrusting of interpretive and disciplinary authority to finite and frail human beings (whether Peter alone, or Peter and his spiritual successors, or the *ekklesia* itself, in some way). "It is not in the heavens."

Divine Revelation and Human Interpretation

There is, though, one final consideration. Matthew matters because only in this gospel does Jesus attribute Peter's confession to divine revelation (16:17). It is no coincidence that Matthew signifies that it was "from that time on" that "Jesus began to show his disciples that he must go to Jerusalem and undergo great suffering . . . , and be killed, and on the third day be raised" (16:21). Nor is it surprising that the talkative Peter is first to object: "God forbid it, Lord! This must never happen to you" (16:22). Just as Jesus was enthusiastic in his approving reply to Peter's earlier confession, so now is he in his harsh rebuttal: "Get behind me, Satan!" If it was not human opinion but divine revelation that prompted Peter's confession of faith, Jesus now turns the tables and informs Peter that "you are setting your mind not on divine things but on human things" (16:23). There is no question that we are to view these two conversations in juxtaposition. What has happened between the first and the second?

What I want to underscore is that, according to Matthew, Jesus truly did affirm Peter as a special recipient of divine revelation. Did Peter forget what had been revealed? No. The critical point to appreciate is that revelation did not give Peter full and perfect knowledge about what his own confession entailed. It seems unavoidable that Peter's protesting Jesus's prediction is attributable precisely to his assumptions about what *Christos* should entail. God's revelation apparently did not rid Peter of those presuppositions. There is no need to assume any uniformity in Jewish ideas about the Messiah in Second Temple Judaism in order to appreciate the likelihood that suffering was not included in most people's expectations, and certainly not in Peter's. The point is that whatever was entailed in the revelation granted to Peter, there was much he had yet to learn. Divine revelation did not render him an automaton.

This too, we might say, is an aspect of the risk of divine Wisdom: revelation does not dehumanize its human receptor but in covenantal relation works patiently and painstakingly with the creaturely contours of human existence. The human element is always present, never preempted or bypassed by God. It appears that God has no interest in undoing or de-creating human capacities and gifts. As Gregory of Nazianzus put it in his *Theological Orations*, God does not relate to us from a place of insecurity or envy of our intellectual gifts—which were given to us, after all, by God. God therefore relates to us and labors with us "not out of envy, for envy is far from the divine Nature . . . especially envy of that which is the most honorable of all God's creatures. For what does the Word prefer to the rational and speaking creatures? Why, even their very existence is a proof of God's supreme goodness." Divine Wisdom, accordingly, does not hoard power but actively seeks ways to share it, to encourage dignity and responsibility in all human creatures, for all are created for the purpose of reflecting God's goodness and love. Thus, Gregory adds, "It . . . is utterly sophistical and foreign to the character, I will not even say of God, but of any moderately good human being, who has any right ideas about himself, to seek his own supremacy by throwing a hindrance in the way of another."[22] Far from throwing a hindrance in our path, God enjoins us toward the path of becoming creatures who can speak and act in God's stead. Our doctrine of the incarnation of the Logos as truly human among us places this conviction front and center.

We may surmise that this is God's chosen way of communing, and communicating, with us—with all of its attendant risks. If God entrusts such tasks as "binding and loosing" to the church, then it seems that our differences of interpretation over the centuries were inevitable. We certainly have not come to any agreement regarding the contemporary meaning and implications of Jesus's words to Peter in Matthew 16. The church of tomorrow will need to come to terms with this passage and others like it, and thus with the real diversity within early Christianity, along with the inevitability of that diversity continuing, and even spreading, into the present. We must theologize accordingly.

There was no way for Peter, and no way for us today, to come to appreciate the implications of our confession that Jesus is the Christ apart from actually following in the steps of this messiah. Perhaps "Get behind me!" should be interpreted in that light. Only as Peter gets behind Jesus and follows—rather than trying to get in his face and counsel him about being the indomitable messiah Peter takes him to be—will Peter understand the implications of his confession. So it is for us. The upshot is that divine revelation ultimately is Jesus himself—divine Wisdom incarnate—and only in

---

22. Gregory of Nazianzus, *On God and Christ*, second oration, sec. 11.

taking up our cross and following him will we ever truly learn from this One who is gentle and humble in heart. And we will still have our differences.

7

Wisdom's Presence

For where two or three are gathered in my name, I am there among them.

THE ONE WHO PROMISES to be present among a gathering of only two or three disciples is the same one who is "gentle and humble in heart." In this intriguing promise, unique to Matthew, we are encountered by divine Wisdom incarnate who, as Emmanuel, "God with us," dwells in the very midst of his disciples.[1] It is clear that Matthew is burdened to stress this point about the divine presence in Christ, and as Christ. In a later chapter we will focus attention on Jesus's promise at the very end of this gospel—also, not surprisingly, unique to Matthew: "Remember, I am with you always, to the very end of the age" (Matt 28:20). *Emmanuel:* God is with us (1:24). "I am with you all, always," Jesus promises as he sends out his Jewish disciples to the nations. From beginning to end, and in the middle, Matthew's matter is *promised presence*, the very presence of God. Divine Wisdom seeks a dwelling-place among human beings (Sir 24:7–8).

The promise to be among "two or three gathered in my name" occurs in the very midst of Matthew (Matt 18). As usual, though, context is critical. Here we encounter Jesus instructing his disciples about how to deal

---

1. This chapter is adapted from my presidential address for the 2013 annual meeting of the Wesleyan Theological Society, held that year at Seattle Pacific University, entitled "Spirit/Shekhinah/Sakina: Perhaps There Really *Is* No Holiness but Social Holiness."

with the inevitability of offenses or transgressions within the community of disciples. Yet another reason why Matthew matters is that only this gospel includes such a detailed strategy for dealing with offense: first the offended, the sinned against, should seek out the offending brother or sister quietly, alone, and try to work for reconciliation in that sequestered setting. Of course, in such a scenario there is less potential for public shaming. "But if you are not listened to, take one or two others along with you"—much like Deuteronomy instructed the Israelites—"so that every word may be confirmed by the evidence of two or three witnesses" (18:16). We remember that if that doesn't work, now we can "tell it to the church; and if the offender refuses to listen even to the church, let such a one be to you as a Gentile and a tax collector" (18:17). The deeply Jewish nature of Matthew's Jesus shines here once again; even if Jesus created a community that was porous toward tax-collectors and eventually would go out into the worlds of the gentiles, in this passage these are still identified as people who are outside the bounds of the wisdom community. This passage teaches the church to take seriously the matters of harm done within and among its members (especially to the vulnerable "little ones," 18:4–6), to face these difficult matters head-on, to seek full reconciliation and restitution—and, failing that, to discipline unrepentant offenders with exclusion.

So we are in the middle of instruction regarding how this community of discipleship is intended to do the hard and necessary work of reconciliation, of healing and restoring relations. How will this *ekklesia* function when the going gets rough, and especially when the "rough" is not coming from the outside but gets going from the community's very midst? How do we live together as brothers and sisters, yoked together with Jesus, learning from divine Wisdom who is gentle and humble in heart? The next words attributed to our Teacher are these: "Truly I tell you, whatever you [you all, that is] bind on earth will be bound in heaven, and whatever you [all] loose on earth will be loosed in heaven" (18:18). Of course we have encountered such remarkable instruction before! What was initially predicated of Peter alone is now extended to the wisdom community as a whole: a "power [that] would seem to concern either the imposing (and lifting) of decrees of excommunication or the forgiving (and not forgiving) of sins."[2]

Matthew's Jesus continues: "Again, truly I tell you, if two of you agree on earth about anything you ask, it will be done for you by my Father in heaven" (18:19). Surely here is a sentence that sorely needs to be taken

---

2. Harrington, *The Gospel of Matthew*, 269.

always in its context! The reference to "two of you" seems to match perfectly with the earlier reference to the offended disciple taking "one or two others along" in the second phase of attempted reconciliation. So also, then, that well-beloved promise of Christ's presence, "For where two or three are gathered in my name, I am there among them" (18:20). Harrington comments, "The ideas of agreement, common prayer, and Christ's presence are here in the service of exercising the power to bind and loose in the case of the brother [or sister] who sins," and so "the context continues to be judicial, not directly liturgical."[3]

This remarkable promise of the presence of Jesus among a gathered few, then, occurs in the context of some gritty directives about dealing with difficulties, and perhaps difficult people, within a community characterized and shaped by mutual forgiveness. This forgiveness is neither easy nor cheap. "Since such processes were used by the Essene and early rabbinic communities," Harrington observes, "it was only natural that the Matthean Christians should have their own procedures and that their rules might help to define their community identity for both insiders and outsiders."[4] In this case, then, the risen Christ as Wisdom incarnate promises presence—"I am there among them"—in the difficult conversations involving confrontation, third-party observers, sorting out the issues, trying to determine and then assign guilt or innocence, forgiveness, reconciliation—or, sadly, excommunication of an unrepentant offender.

This is probably not the Matthew 18:20 that most of us grew up with. More than likely, we are more familiar with the promise of Jesus being with us even in Wednesday night prayer meetings where in fact one might lean heavily on the assurance that only two or three folks are required to guarantee his presence. Even this was an important idea, though, given our hard Western leanings toward individualism. We know Jesus called a dozen disciples to become a renewed Israel, a revived people of God together, a city set on a hill, a community of disciples living together under the yoke of Jesus's teaching, receiving divine forgiveness and, ideally at least, extending that forgiveness to one another. We remember that he taught them to pray, "Our Father, . . . forgive us our trespasses as we forgive those who trespass against us." As I learned such things through college and seminary, it certainly became attractive to read Matthew 18:20 as the promise of divine presence in Jesus Christ, by the lovely power of the Spirit, amongst

---

3. Harrington, *The Gospel of Matthew*, 269.
4. Harrington, *The Gospel of Matthew*, 269.

the company of disciples—even if only two or three. It went together so well with John Wesley's dictum, which by then I had learned as something of a mantra: "No holiness but social holiness." I am certainly not opposed to a kind of liturgical adaptation of this promise—Christ's presence in our communal worship—but have come to appreciate the fact that the promise more directly addresses this process of doing the hard work, having the difficult conversations, making the tough calls, that enable a community of disciples to perdure through the inevitable issues of hurt, anger, pride, shame, forgiveness, reconciliation, and justice. Further, the primary concern at stake here is the protection and nurturing of those most easily victimized, the "little ones" in our midst.

A Similar Promise of Presence

This promise of Jesus, unique to Matthew, offers one of the more fascinating connections between this gospel and rabbinic Judaism. In the Talmud—that great encoding of generations of rabbinic discussion and debate regarding the identity and vocation of the people Israel, especially in the glaring absence of the temple—we peer through a textual window into the Jewish community as it strove over generations to wrestle with the questions of everyday life before God, as the people of God. In the earlier layer, historically speaking, of the Talmud, called the Mishnah (which was edited, compiled, and set to writing around the year 200 CE), we read: "If two sit together and words of Torah pass between them, then the Shekhinah is in their midst."[5] What is this Shekhinah? It is another promise of presence.

It is notoriously difficult to establish a point of origin for *shekhinah*, a term derived from the Hebrew verb meaning "to dwell." Second Maccabees may provide the best clue; it includes a prayer of Jerusalem priests for the "Temple of your indwelling" (*naon tes ses skenoseos*). As Joseph Sievers has observed, "*Skenosis*, an abstract feminine noun, finds its closest Hebrew parallel in meaning as well as in form in *Shekhinah*."[6] If this is the case, then we may conclude that this term, which may have developed in part as a circumlocution for God's dwelling in Israel's midst, had been closely associated, if not virtually identified, with the temple in Jerusalem. If the term originated in the Jewish conviction that the temple was the divine *skenoseos*,

---

5. *Pirkei Avot* 3.3.

6. Sievers, "'Where Two or Three . . .'; The Rabbinic Concept of *Shekhinah* and Matthew 18:20," 172.

God's place of dwelling, then the destruction of the temple pressed hard the painful question, "Where is God now?" Does God dwell among us without a temple? The earliest generations of rabbis, whose deliberations were codified in the Mishnah, agonized over this question, as did early Jewish followers of Jesus. Certainly the community of disciples for whom, and likely by whom, the Gospel of Matthew was written also wrestled with this question.

As the house of holiness of Israel's God lay in ashen ruins, the rabbis, these sages of Torah, developed their fascinating conviction that the Shekhinah, God's presence, dwelt in Israel's midst—but particularly in the sages' midst as they engaged together in the study of Torah, doing so for the sake of God's people in new and alien places, facing unanticipated threats to their well-being, asking the burning questions of a people in exile. Indeed the Shekhinah, they were bold to believe, had wandered into exile with them. It is notoriously difficult to date historically the sayings that were gathered, edited, and collated as the Talmud, but we do know this much: It was Rabbi Hananiah ben Teradyon, a contemporary of the great Rabbi Akiva, in the early second century, who was reported to have taught that if two sages engage the Torah together, then the Shekhinah is dwelling in their midst. Similarly, Hananiah's contemporary rabbinic colleague Halafta ben Dosa is reported to have taught, "If ten men sit together and occupy themselves with the Torah, the Divine Presence rests among them as it is written (in Psalm 82:1), 'God has taken his place in the divine council.'"[7] Halafta proceeds to argue, Abraham-style, that the Shekhinah is present also for a gathering of only five, then for just three, then "even to two," and finally "even of one." It is striking, however, just how often some variation of this teaching on the Shekhinah appears, and almost without exception the divine presence is associated with a social context, a gathering of, say, two or three. Several decades ago, as I was writing my doctoral dissertation at Emory University on related matters, I offered this commentary on Rabbis Halafta and Hananiah: "In either case it is [within] a communal interpretive process—a religious community confronting, and being confronted by, its sacred text—[that] . . . God's presence is experienced."[8]

Of course, the Mishnah's affirmations regarding the Shekhinah as divine presence are intriguingly similar to Jesus's promise in Matthew 18:20. The texts cry out for an answer: Is there a relationship between the sayings

---

7. Hananiah's version of the teaching on the Shekhinah is found in *Mishnah Tractate Avot* ("ethics of the fathers") 3.3; Halafta's closely follows in *M. Avot* 3.6.

8. Lodahl, *Shekhinah/Spirit*, 56.

of these Mishnaic rabbis, who (perhaps not coincidentally) lived and taught in the region of Galilee in the early second century, and Jesus's promise to be "there" in the midst of the judiciary/reconciliatory process of the community of disciples? If there is a relationship, how might we construe it? What happened here?

The problem is intractable, "a question remaining essentially unsolved."[9] Part of the problem is that when the Talmud attributes a saying to a particular rabbi, there is no way to know whether the saying necessarily originated with that rabbi—and often there is at least circumstantial evidence to suggest earlier precedents. In this case, Sievers asserts that "the idea of the Shekhinah with two people . . . is a concept that can be traced to the first century,"[10] i.e., earlier than either Hananiah or Halafta and perhaps very near to the time of Jesus and virtually contemporaneous with the composition of Matthew. How do we think these two sayings side-by-side? How are we to relate them to one another? What are at least some of the leading possibilities?

- Perhaps there was already a notion of the Shekhinah dwelling among two or three sages talking Torah even in Jesus's own time, and Jesus himself adapted this idea to himself. Perhaps, but not likely—especially in light of the likelihood that this idea of a mobile Shekhinah would really be necessary only after the destruction of the temple.

- It would be more likely that the author of Matthew, as conversant as he obviously was with the earliest developing rabbinic schools in the middle to second half of the first century CE, drew upon a saying of growing popularity—that the Shekhinah dwells outside the temple ruins and among the people Israel, particularly as they are engaging Torah—and adapted it to Jesus as "Emmanuel," the embodying of the divine Wisdom (and, of course, the Torah itself) in the world. In this scenario we have, in W. D. Davies's catchy verbal sketch, "a Christified bit of rabbinism."[11]

- David D. Kupp offers this alternative minority position: "It is worth asking, 'Why could Jesus himself not have postulated this future

---

9. Kupp, *Matthew's Emmanuel*, 194.

10. Sievers, "'Where Two or Three . . .'; The Rabbinic Concept of *Shekhinah* and Matthew 18:20," 174.

11. Davies and Allison, *The Gospel according to Saint Matthew*, Vol. II, 790.

gathering of his followers 'for his name's sake'?"[12] In this scenario, presumably, the origin of the statement rests upon Jesus's lips, and the "two or three gathered together" is not necessarily a riff on a growing Jewish sentiment regarding the Shekhinah, but would presumably be a function of his earlier mention of the offended disciple taking along a witness or two "so that every word may be confirmed" (18:16; cf. Deut 19:15). On the other hand, of course, we must acknowledge that this is one of a great many passages that is unique to Matthew's Gospel, and so, we might say, is idiosyncratic to Matthew's particular vision of Jesus the Messiah. That in itself does not mean that Jesus did not or could not have said these words—but I suspect that we also must proceed to acknowledge that the quest to ascertain "what Jesus actually said" is deeply problematic, for we are aware that historical occurrence, disciple testimony, and authorial theology are strands so thoroughly intertwined that they cannot readily (if at all) be teased apart. We may suspect, perhaps quite rightly, that this passage owes much to the writer's apparent concern to write a gospel that will underwrite a Matthean school of Jesus-yoked Torah sages who "bring forth out of [their textual treasures] what is new and what is old" (13:52).

- If it were in fact the case that the Gospel of Matthew provided the origin of this idea of divine presence dwelling in the midst of gathered sages, then "it is possible," in Davies's words, "that the saying of R. Hananiah b. Teradion was called forth by the gospel saying as a kind of counterblast." The rabbis would have been adapting a claim they have heard that Jesus made, transforming it into Shekhinah lingo. It is not impossible. Davies, however, hastens to add, "—but more probably [Hananiah's saying] expresses what was a rabbinic commonplace."[13]

- Finally, it is possible that this sort of formulation was simply "in the air" of mid- to late-first-century Jewish thought and speech. Interestingly, its earliest usage seems to arise from teachers of the region of Galilee, so perhaps it even had its beginnings there. In this scenario, we do not seek an easily identifiable line of influence from one teacher or tradition to another, but something more like a common cultural wellspring for gesturing toward the holy presence of God—again,

---

12. Kupp, *Matthew's Emmanuel*, 193.
13. Davies and Allison, *The Gospel according to Saint Matthew*, Vol. II, 790.

particularly in the trying times after the temple's demolition. It is intriguing that, in the consideration of this possibility, we may appreciate a potentially profound significance in the association of divine presence with, and within, the interpersonal engagement of those who love God: in one setting, it is those who love God as the gracious bestower of Torah and, in another setting, it is those who love God as the gracious bestower of Jesus. *This is the same God*, is it not? Is it *not*?

We should remember, incidentally, that "Torah" here was not understood to be only the Pentateuch; it included also the oral interpretations of Torah passed down through generations of rabbis and their disciples. This "oral Torah" itself, the rabbis eventually came to believe and to teach, was also given to Moses on Sinai—a distinctly creative way of stipulating that divine revelation continued, indeed continues, through the rabbis' wrestlings with Scripture and with each other's interpretations thereof. So much of this wrestling was concerned with the everyday matters of maintaining Jewish identity amidst almost countless threats to this seasoned community of interpretation! Interestingly, Sievers points out that "a text dealing with the question of the Shekhinah among judges states that 'court proceedings also are Torah,'"[14] i.e., that the rabbinic rulings regarding "binding and loosing" were believed to have been blessed and guided by the presence of the near-dwelling God of Israel. This would provide a comparable context for each of the sayings in Matthew and the Mishnah. It is tempting to follow Davies in this judgment that "Jesus . . . has simply been substituted for the *shekinah*, and gathering together 'in my name' for the study of the Torah. As in the Mishnah, so in Matthew: the zone of the sacred is not dictated by geography but is mobile."[15]

Tempting, but this is not a closed case. Kupp is correct: "Evidence for the source of Matthew 18:20 is too scanty, the origin of the Shekinah concept is too clouded, and the contexts of the two sayings too distinct to point to any specific historical-literary relationship."[16] Nonetheless, we can concur with Davies on his judgment that in both the rabbinic and Matthean formulations, "the zone of the sacred is not dictated by geography but is mobile." Freed, as it were, from the temple, God can be(come) on the move. Both the rabbis and the Matthean sages seek—and perhaps testify to—the

---

14. Sievers, "'Where Two or Three . . .'; The Rabbinic Concept of *Shekhinah* and Matthew 18:20," 176.

15. Davies and Allison, *The Gospel according to Saint Matthew*, Vol. II, 790.

16. Kupp, *Matthew's Emmanuel*, 195.

divine presence *precisely in their midst as communities of ongoing interpretation*. And this, of course, is not "interpretation" merely as a pastime or a "head game," but interpretation as a life lived together. We understand these promises of presence to be a reassuring reply to the quest for divine Wisdom in the midst of fragile and frail human beings who are striving to maintain communal identity and continuity over the ravages of time and in the face of the persistent acids of tragedy and ambiguity.

Matthew and the Mishnah

But as we encounter these textual claims to a divine presence, we are constrained to ask: Is there a Presence beyond the text? And if so, can we say in good conscience that only our community, our tradition, provides the place of dwelling for divine Wisdom? When set side by side, these passages from Matthew and the Mishnah, do they become words of harsh, exclusivist confrontation? Questions continually spin out of these texts like a vortex in reverse, such as: For either of these communities, is the promise merely a *claim*, a *stipulation*—or is it something more like a *testimony*? Is it an attempt to describe what we might boldly call an "experience of God"? Was there a mysterious, elusive Presence that Jewish sages sensed, even if ever so slightly and fleetingly, as they studied and argued face to face? Did they experience (what they took to be) the very presence of God? Or is the rabbinic claim upon the Shekhinah's presence really nothing more than a textually generated argument? And if so, does textual study in the presence of others generate some kind of "experience" that might be interpreted, or misinterpreted, to be an awareness of divine presence? What is going on in these texts? What is going on beyond them? Is there a Presence *before* these texts?

Warren Carter has written that the rabbinic sayings about the Shekhinah related to the question regarding "where and how God's forgiving presence and will were [to be] encountered now that the Temple was destroyed. Matthew's answer is Jesus."[17] So the question perhaps now becomes, was Matthew's answer intended to *supplement* the rabbis' answer, or to *supersede* it? We probably should guess that the latter was intended, which only leaves us to wonder whether we can, in good faith, follow in this supersessionist claim. If Jesus as Emmanuel essentially embodies exhaustively the presence of Wisdom divine, then these rabbinic claims regarding the

17. Carter, *Matthew and the Margins*, 369.

Shekhinah may readily be considered empty errors. We might even have to call them lies. But can we do such a thing? Ought we? Especially if it were to turn out that the Gospel of Matthew has adapted "a rabbinic commonplace" (Davies) and transferred it wholesale to Jesus, it would seem disingenuous, now, to trumpet such triumphalism.

But what are our options? We cannot, must not, collapse these two claims into some sort of generalized divine presence that does not do justice to the distinctiveness of the respective communities—their histories, texts, practices, traditions. The Shekhinah is not simply the presence of Jesus Christ, nor *vice versa*—even if it is the presence of God that is named in both the Shekhinah and Jesus Christ. But how can these things be? Kupp is correct, I think, to suggest that "the striking correspondence" between Matthew 18:20 and early second-century rabbinic claims "points at minimum to two distinct religious circles . . . dealing with similar questions about divine presence in terms of their own community identity and experience."[18] But we could also legitimately ask at this juncture about what "experience" Kupp has in mind and how much legitimacy we can properly grant to such a slippery category. As a Christian community of interpretation, we are of course liable, and legitimately so, to assume the possibility of a veridical experience of the resurrected Christ in the midst of his gathered disciples as they wrestle with issues of "community identity"; indeed, Christians of the Wesleyan tradition may be even more inclined to trust in the possibility of such experiences. We do, after all, believe in "hearts strangely warmed"! But that knife cuts both ways. If we follow Wesley in trusting in the veracity of an experience of divine presence—let us call it, with Wesley, following Paul, "the witness of the Spirit"—then are we not obligated at some point to consider the possibility of a valid and compelling "testimony of the Shekhinah" in the Jewish community? Or is that an abandonment of Christian convictions regarding the singularity, irreplaceability, and utter uniqueness of Jesus Christ? Kupp seems correct to detect a "rhetorical antithesis" between Matthew and Mishnah, perhaps even "possible reference to the very real historical antithesis between the two religious worlds of Matthew's communities and their counterparts in Judaism."[19] They were, and continue to be, two religious worlds. But they are not airtight. Communication is possible. We can even open our community's texts to practitioners of that other "religious world," and they to us. Not all Jews and Christians are interested

18. Kupp, *Matthew's Emmanuel*, 195.
19. Kupp, *Matthew's Emmanuel*, 196.

in doing this, and perhaps not all need to be. But as one striking example among others, the movement known as Scriptural Reasoning represents a faithful and courageous attempt to do precisely this.[20] Perhaps we can wonder whether there is presence divine in the midst of such a gathering.

Matthew and the Mishnah—and Muhammad

But the quandary does not quit here. I still remember the moment, probably about twenty years ago, while reading Frederick Denny's *Islam and the Muslim Community*, that I encountered this striking claim: "When the Qur'an is recited properly, God's presence, in the form of his *sakina*, is believed to descend upon the reciter and hearers. This *sakina* is a 'tranquility,' literally, which includes the sense of a protecting and guiding spiritual presence." Denny then adds this parenthetical aside: "Compare this with the Jewish notion of *shekhinah*, 'the Presence of God in the world.'"[21] As though any encouragement were needed!

Indeed, the comparison cries out to be made. *Al-Sakina* is derived from an Arabic root that denotes "stillness," "quiet," "calm"—with a secondary meaning: "to settle down, to dwell in a habitation." It seems unavoidable that the terms *sakina* and *shekhinah* bear some kind of very close historical/semantic relationship to one another, but to speculate upon this is well beyond my ken. It is more important to observe that Muslim tradition has tended, virtually unanimously, to understand *sakina* as a divine gift of peacefulness and calm. It is a kind of divine reassurance in the face of unbelief and opposition, but is decidedly not interpreted as signifying God's very presence. But that is the Islamic tradition of interpretation of the term *sakina* as it appears in the Qur'an—and while this tradition surely should be respected, one has to wonder to what extent theological considerations have placed constraints upon possible alternative significations of *sakina*. Jewish scholar Reuven Firestone, self-admittedly not working from within the Islamic tradition, is not convinced that "quiet" or "tranquility" always works as an adequate translation of the term in its qur'anic usage; he suggests a *shekhinah*-friendly shade of meaning, "a divine indwelling."[22] He appeals to passages such as these:

20. See especially Ochs, *Another Reformation* and Ochs and Levene, eds., *Textual Reasonings*. See also Ford and Pecknold, eds., *The Promise of Scriptural Reasoning*.
21. Denny, *Islam and the Muslim Community*, 62–63.
22. Firestone, "Sakina," 590.

It is [God] Who sent down *al-sakina* into the hearts of the believers, that they may increase in faith . . . . (48:4)

. . . Muhammad said to a fellow believer, "Do not grieve, for God is with us." Then God made His *sakina* to descend upon him and supported him with forces you did not see. (9:40)

God sent down *al-sakina* upon His Messenger and upon the believers, and charged them with the word of piety, of which they were . . . its true keepers. (48:26)

Beyond these passages, the one that provides the most fascinating possibilities for intertextual engagement is found in the Qur'an's second *surah* or chapter, widely known by its nickname "The Cow." By far the longest *surah* in the Qur'an, "The Cow" is filled with biblical allusions and stories, including a version of the appointment of Saul as king of Israel. "The prophet said to [the people of Israel], 'The sign of [Saul's] kingship is that the Ark will come to you in which there is *al-sakina* from your Lord and a relic from the family of Moses and the family of Aaron, borne by angels. In this is a sign for you if you are true believers" (2:248). Firestone's instincts seem sound; does it make much sense to translate *sakina* here as "tranquility"—"the Ark will come to you in which there is tranquility from your Lord"? Especially if we assume that Muhammad was drawing upon (undoubtedly oral) biblical narrative as it was interpreted and shaped by the rabbinic tradition, it is difficult to avoid the real possibility that *sakina* here shades very closely to *shekhinah*—the divine presence among the people Israel—particularly since the passage has to do with "the Ark of the Presence." While Muslim tradition has consistently avoided this interpretation of the term—just as, similarly, the phrase "holy spirit" (al *ruh al quds*) has been traditionally interpreted to signify the angel Gabriel—the question I am pursuing is whether or not it is possible that the qur'anic text is bearing witness to a more immediate presence of God than what Muslim interpreters have generally allowed. To put it bluntly: is *al-sakina* a gift of tranquility from God, quite distinct from God?—or is *al-sakina* better understood to be a signification of God's very presence, *a la* Shekhinah? In a fashion comparable to the difficulties encountered in the similar sayings of Matthew and the Mishnah, in this case once again the weight of the evidence is inconclusive. As Firestone observes, "Western scholarship considers the term [*sakina*]to have derived from the rabbinic concept of *shekinah*, based on Q 2:248, but has had difficulty fitting such a concept into all the other verses."[23]

So the ontological status of *sakina* remains an open question; in any case, there may be only one qur'anic text that seems immediately amenable to Denny's claim that, for Muslims, "When the Qur'an is recited properly, God's presence, in the form of his sakina, is believed to descend upon the reciter and hearers."[24] In 48:26 we read that "God sent down *al-sakina* upon His Messenger and upon the believers, and charged them with the word of piety [or self-restraint], of which they were . . . its true keepers." If "the word of piety" can be equated with revelation, and it likely can, then we have here at least one qur'anic text that does indeed associate the descent of the *sakina* with qur'anic recitation. This is an intriguing possibility. Further, the idea is found much more explicitly in a *hadith* or traditional story about Muhammad.[25] In the hadith collection of al-Bukhari (d. 870 CE; 256 in Muslim calendar), we read of a man during the time of Muhammad who was reciting Surah 18 while his tethered horse stood nearby. During his recitation, a descending cloud encircled and engulfed him; his horse was visibly startled and unsettled by the sight. So the next morning the man sought out Muhammad and told him what had happened, to which the prophet replied, "It was the Sakinah that descended for the Qur'an." I suppose we could say that in this case, while there were two who were gathered, only one of them was human.

Where, finally, do all these meanderings among Matthew, the Mishnah, and Muhammad lead us? These intertextual paths, for all of their possible intersections, interweavings, and cross-cuttings across several centuries, seem to lead to a testimony like this: The presence of divine Wisdom is experienced in the gathering of disciples around the locus of divine revelation. For Matthew, it is a gathering "in my name" that is assured of the very presence of the living Jesus Christ; for the Mishnah, it is a gathering "for the sake of Torah" that is assured of the Shekhinah, the very presence of God; for Muhammad, it is a gathering to hear the faithful and proper recitation of the Qur'an that is assured of the *Sakina*, the gift of divine calm, divine peace—and perhaps even of divine presence. Is it possible that divine Wisdom has made multiple dwelling-places in our creaturely midst?

---

23. Firestone, "Sakina," 590.
24. See Denny, *Islam and the Muslim Community*.
25. Firestone, "Sakina," 591.

What shall we make of these things, we who are Christian believers rooted in the Wesleyan tradition? Happily, or at least hopefully, we are under no constraint to agree entirely about how to answer this question. But I would like to conclude this chapter with these three relatively brief suggestions:

- However narrowly or broadly we might construe the idea of a community of divine Wisdom, if something definitive occurs "when two or three are gathered" then perhaps Wesley has put us, his inheritors and successors, on a good path by insisting that "there is no holiness but social holiness." Admittedly, Wesley had in mind only the social phenomenon we call "the church"—a relatively narrow construal of the possibilities we have considered in this chapter. Our present ruminations are intended not at all to deny this Christian conviction, but to ask whether we can legitimately restrict "social holiness" to the church alone. We are asking here about the synagogue and the mosque, even as we acknowledge the morass of difficulties such a question may well create. It seems to me that the church of tomorrow cannot avoid this question, both with its difficulties as well as its intriguing possibilities.

- Though Wesley did in fact have only the church in mind when he stipulated "no holiness but social," his liberating vision of divine grace opens up other possibilities. Think for just a moment about his sermon "Free Grace," in which Wesley proclaims that divine grace "is free in all to whom it is given" (and it is given to all!) and "does not depend on any power or merit in man," for all such human goodness or virtue

    > flow[s] from the free grace of God;...Whatsoever good is in man, or is done by man, God is the author and doer of it. Thus is his grace free in all; that is, no way depending on any power or merit in man, but on God alone, who freely gave us his own Son, and "with him freely gives us all things." But is it free for all, as well as in all? To this some have answered "No...."[26]

    But of course Wesley answered with a rousing "Yes!" If such grace truly is free *for all* and free *in all*, then it seems inevitable that this grace (which is the Spirit of God) should be freely active and experienced within the social realities and constraints of all human beings. Wesley could even speak of a "social grace" whereby "[God] draws some

26. Wesley, Sermon CXXVIII, "Free Grace," in *Works*, Vol. 7, 373–74.

souls through their intercourse with others."[27] Is it possible that the Shekhinah is indeed that "social grace" present and active within the Jewish community's wrestling with its texts over these many centuries, and thus profoundly a Torah-shaped Presence? Perhaps the greater challenge for us to consider: Is it possible that the Sakina is indeed that "social grace" present and active within the Muslim *umma*'s recitation, hearing, and obeying of the Qur'an over these many centuries, and thus a Qur'an-shaped Presence?

- Finally, if these possibilities seem insufficiently faithful to the Matthean proclamation of Jesus Christ as "Emmanuel, God with us," hopefully we can follow Wesley as our guide at least as far as his sermon "On Faith" would lead us. In it, he suggests a perhaps healthy agnosticism, insofar as "it is not so easy to pass any judgment concerning the faith of our modern Jews." Indeed, admits Wesley, "it is not our part to pass sentence upon them, but to leave them to their own Master."[28] Now that is a fascinating phrase, "their own Master"![29] It speaks to a uniquely formed relationship between God and the Jewish people, does it not? As to Islam, Wesley in this same sermon dropped some intriguing hints about the possibilities of grace; he acknowledged that some Muslims "were . . . being taught of God, by His inward voice, all the essentials of true religion." Here Wesley mentions a Muslim author "who, a century or two ago, wrote the *Life of Hai Ebn Yokdan*" which, Wesley judged, "contains all the principles of pure religion and undefiled."[30]

27. Wesley, *A Plain Account of Christian Perfection*, 106.
28. Wesley, Sermon CVI, "On Faith," in *Works*, Vol. 7, 197, 198.

29. I have written in another context regarding this phrase, "Of course 'their own Master' is, for Wesley, none other than the God and Father of our Lord Jesus Christ; nevertheless, as *the Jewish people's own Master* God is addressed and obeyed—the experience of God is shaped, the perception of God framed—by an education other than Christian teaching, . . . God is 'their own Master' as the God of the Torah, the God who liberated a slave people out of Egypt and called them to become God's own covenant people. This is *their own Master*, one who has become their own Master through a particular historical (rabbinically formed) 'education and a thousand other circumstances' uniquely a part of Jewish memory and identity." Lodahl, "To Whom Belong the Covenants?" 204.

30. Wesley, Sermon CVI, "On Faith," in *Works*, Vol. 7, 197. The author of the story was a twelfth-century Muslim philosopher, Ibn Tufail. See Yates, "The Wesleyan Trilateral: Prevenient Grace, Catholic Spirit, and Religious Tolerance"; see also Murphree, "'Pure Religion and Undefiled': A Wesleyan Analysis of Ibn Tufail's *The Improvement of Human Reason*."

Divine Wisdom makes its presence felt. If these hauntingly similar testimonies across traditions have anything to teach us, it might be that this Presence is most distinctly felt in the difficult labors that communities of interpretation undertake, that indeed "there is no holiness but social holiness." We might be inclined to argue long and hard against the notion that Wisdom makes its appearance in communal traditions other than the church. Or we might feel ourselves more generously inclined toward the synagogue but much less certain about the mosque. I am not trying to settle the issue; I am only trying to raise it. But this is not simply a theoretical matter. If the promised presence of Christ is for the "two or three who are gathered in [his] name" as they strive hard to maintain a faithful community of forgiveness and reconciliation, then our Christian claims on the divine presence turn out to be damnably empty if we do not practice the things our Lord Jesus Christ has taught us. Denying the divine presence to synagogue and mosque does not automatically guarantee divine presence to us. If indeed "there is no holiness but social holiness," then finally the onus is on us.

8

Hardened Hearts (Wisdom's Concession)

It was because you were so hard-hearted that Moses allowed you to divorce your wives,
but from the beginning it was not so.

JESUS'S CONVERSATION ABOUT DIVORCE with some Pharisees is not unique to Matthew, for before him the Gospel of Mark had told the story. But as is often the case in close comparisons of the Synoptic Gospels, the variations—sometimes minor, sometimes more noticeable—can accumulate to the point where the same story isn't the same story any more. So it is with this story. Let us begin by laying the two accounts side-by-side:

Mark 10:2–12	Matthew 19:3–9
Some Pharisees came, and to test him they asked, "Is it lawful for a man to divorce his wife?"	Some Pharisees came to him, and to test him they asked, "Is it lawful for a man to divorce his wife **for any cause?**"

Mark 10:2–12	Matthew 19:3–9
	He answered, "Have you not read that the One who made them at the beginning 'made them male and female,' and said, 'For this reason a man shall leave his father and mother and be joined to his wife, and the two shall become one flesh'? So they are no longer two, but one flesh. Therefore, what God has joined together, let no one separate."
He answered them, "What did **Moses command** you?	
They said, "**Moses allowed** a man to write a certificate of dismissal and to divorce her."	They said to him, "Why then did **Moses command** us to give a certificate of dismissal and to divorce her?"
But Jesus said to them, "Because of your hardness of heart he wrote this commandment for you. But from the beginning of creation, 'God made them male and female.' For this reason a man shall leave his father and mother and be joined to his wife, and the two shall become one flesh.' So they are no longer two, but one flesh. Therefore, what God has joined together, let no man separate."	He said to them, "It was because you were so hard-hearted that **Moses allowed** you to divorce your wives, but from the beginning it was not so.
Then in the house the disciples asked him again about this matter. He said to them, "Whoever divorces his wife and marries another commits adultery against her; and if she divorces her husband and marries another, she commits adultery."	And I say to you, whoever divorces his wife, except for unchastity, and marries another commits adultery."

We note first the difference between Mark and Matthew regarding the question the Pharisees asked. For Mark, "Is it lawful for a man to divorce his wife?" For Matthew, "Is it lawful for a man to divorce his wife *for any*

Hardened Hearts (Wisdom's Concession)

cause?" To be sure, in both cases the question is posed from the perspective of the husband, who alone is presumed to possess the potential prerogative of divorce. Warren Carter observes, "The Pharisees ask a question that assumes divorce is normative.... Their question is male-centered, concerned with what a man can do," and so presumes a "'natural right' to exercise unrestricted male power over his ... wife in a patriarchal household."[1] In Mark's case, though, the question is balder, bolder: Is divorce permitted by the Torah at all? Matthew's version poses the question in a different way, indeed in two different possible ways of interpreting the question: 1) Is there any cause or reason that a man can justifiably offer for wanting a divorce? Or 2) Will any old reason do?

We have mentioned the two leading (or at least best-known) schools of Pharisaic instruction during the early first century CE, those of Shammai and Hillel.[2] If in our earlier reference Hillel seemed the more attractive option ("Do not do to others what is distasteful to you"), in this controversy Shammai seems the better. The school of Shammai put strict limitations on permissible rationales for divorce, teaching essentially the same as what Matthew presents Jesus as teaching, both here and in 5:32. That single rationale is *porneia*, often translated "unchastity." While its precise meaning may finally elude us, it seems likely that adultery is intended. In any case, it does not matter for our present purposes. What is important is that this restrictive interpretation of "something objectionable" in Deuteronomy 24 contrasts dramatically with the school of Hillel, which granted husbands a wide berth for justifying their wandering preferences.

But did Jesus actually match the school of Shammai in his teaching about divorce? In the Gospel of Matthew, yes. If, however, we follow the convincing scholarly consensus on such matters, we recognize that Mark's Gospel was the earliest written and that Matthew drew upon Mark as one of his sources. If this be the case, then it appears that Matthew has done some slight editing of his Markan source on divorce. Mark offers no exceptions or escape clauses: divorce is prohibited, period. Matthew, writing a decade or two later, already apparently reflects some reservations that likely were felt in the earliest generations of Jesus-followers. If Mark's Jesus seems extreme on the issue, Matthew's is a mildly moderating voice. Even so, in Matthew the disciples' response to Jesus's teaching is, "If such is the case of a man with his wife, it is better not to marry" (19:10). This is a remarkable

---

1. Carter, *Matthew and the Margins*, 378.
2. See Chapter 3 of this volume, "Wisdom's Commands."

mentality: if there are such heavy restrictions on legitimizing divorce, then let's not bother! If the disciples' view here mirrors attitudes within the earliest churches, how much more difficult would have Jesus's "no excuse" approach in Mark have sounded!

The Human Element

We seem to be dealing with the difficulty that at least some early Christian communities felt with such extreme language. This is the first indication of several instances that will build toward a common theme for this chapter: let us call it *the human element*. In this first case, it is simply a matter of Matthew's differing with Mark, having added "for any cause" to the question of divorce and then having provided that the sole cause is "unchastity."

Then follows a second indication of the human element. In Mark, Jesus's initial reply to the Pharisees' question is, "What did Moses command [*enetailato*] you?" (Mark 10:3). The Pharisees reply that "Moses allowed [*epetrepsen*] a man to write a certificate of dismissal and to divorce her" (10:4). Jesus uses the language of command and the Pharisees respond with the language of permission. Note, too, that both the Pharisees and Jesus seem content to discuss the matter in terms of Moses's actions, whether of commanding or simply permitting. This is not to deny that both parties would have assumed that behind Moses's authority stood the authority of God—it is only to recognize that both sides could speak unreservedly of Moses's role as the prophet and teacher of Israel, which certainly gestures toward another human element in the text. But again, beyond their mutual acknowledgement of Moses, even more intriguing is the fact that Matthew, presumably acting as an editor of Mark's earlier telling of the story, switches the verbs *command* and *permit*! In Matthew the language of command is placed on the Pharisees' lips—"Why then did Moses command [*enetailato*] us to give a certificate of dismissal and divorce her?" (Matt 19:7)—while Jesus corrects the Pharisees' assumption by indicating that "Moses allowed [*epetrepsen*] you to divorce your wives" (19:8). It is the same pair of verbs in both Mark and Matthew—but the verbs have been swapped in this game of "he said, they said." Which verb was really on whose lips? While it may seem relatively insignificant, there is sufficient theological difference here to set a fundamentalist's head to spinning. By switching the verbs as they appear in Mark, Matthew was able to make it clear that Jesus is the one who

Hardened Hearts (Wisdom's Concession)

rightly understands what is going on in the Deuteronomy text in question. This is not Moses commanding anything; it is Moses making a concession.

But of course, this notion of Moses "allowing" or "permitting" unveils yet another layer of the human element in the text. The human spiritual leader of Israel, Moses, is making an allowance for "your hardness of heart" (Mark 10:5), i.e., the stone-hard hearts of the men of Israel both in Moses's time and in Jesus's. It is critical to note that it is the *hard hearts of men* at issue here; nothing is said of women, and nothing need be said, when it was clearly men who benefitted from the Torah's patriarchy-weighted laws regarding divorce. This seems the proper juncture at which to recall the Deuteronomic passage that sparked the discussion to begin with:

> Suppose a man enters into marriage with a woman, but she does not please him because he finds something objectionable about her, and so he writes her a certificate of divorce, puts it in her hand, and sends her out of his house; she then leaves his house and goes off to become another man's wife. Then suppose the second man dislikes her, writes her a bill of divorce, puts it in her hand, and sends her out of his house (or the second man who married her dies); her first husband, who sent her away, is not permitted to take her again to be his wife after she has been defiled; for that would be abhorrent to the LORD, and you shall not bring guilt on the land that the LORD your God is giving you as a possession. (Deut 24:1–4)

Clearly, the text is not primarily about divorce. Divorce here seems to be a given. Indeed, the passage appears to be more about men's proclivity toward ending marriage relationships! The prohibition to remarry a woman whom one has divorced, and then who remarried only to become available again, just might have to do with the divorcee's or widow's economic compensation, as Tivka Frymer-Kensy has suggested: "Having once declared her an unfit wife, the husband cannot remarry her and profit from her once more."[3] Need it be said, though, that Deuteronomy offers no such rationale? Rather, the text presents the woman as an object who is radically vulnerable to the whims of her husband as well as to the charge of uncleanness; she is a thing that "has been defiled" by relations with the second man (who was after all her husband!), something that Deuteronomy stipulates "would be abhorrent to the LORD" (24:4). In all of this, the woman appears to be little more than a piece of property tossed from one owner-protector

---

3. Frymer-Kensy, "Deuteronomy," 60.

to another, possibly at the slightest whim (depending upon how one interprets "something objectionable in her"), and the one who ends up "defiled" in the process. It is not an uplifting picture, and Matthew wants his audience to understand that none of this qualifies as a command from Moses, let alone from God. "It was because you were so hard-hearted that Moses allowed you to divorce your wives, but from the beginning it was not so" (Matt 19:8).

Beginning at the Beginning

Indeed, Matthew inverts the entire conversation to begin it at the beginning, literally, with Genesis. Where Mark ends the interchange between Jesus and the Pharisees with Jesus's appeal to Genesis, Matthew puts Genesis's beginning right at the beginning; to the Pharisees' initial question about divorce, Jesus replies, "Have you not read that the one who made them in the beginning 'made them male and female' . . . so they are no longer two, but one flesh" (19:4, 6). He begins with a theology of creation and proceeds accordingly. Indeed, what Jesus proposes as having been "from the beginning" (19:8) stands in stark contrast with the situation Moses faced. God's creative intention, Jesus argues, is that the male and the female "become one flesh" (19:5). Drawing upon Phillis Trible and Walter Brueggemann, Carter writes,

> This one-flesh relationship is marked by "unity, solidarity, mutuality, equality," a strange, against-the-grain identity in a culture that stressed gender differentiation, male superiority and domination, and female subordination as norms in the patriarchal household. The one-flesh marriage forms a relationship of solidarity, trust and well-being.[4]

Perhaps a brief "theology of the flesh" is in order. In the Jewish Scriptures that the Pharisees and Jesus shared, "flesh" covers all creaturely existence (Gen 9:9–17) in its fragility, vulnerability, transience, and mortality. "All flesh is grass" (Isa 40:6) precisely because grass is here today, scorched or eaten tomorrow. So with "flesh": it is not evil by any means, but it is finite and frail. "Flesh" names our proneness to suffering, wounds, sorrow, and death—as well as our radical neediness for sustenance and protection. This is why the Israelites were counseled often not to put their trust in "the arm

---

4. Carter, *Matthew and the Margins*, 379.

Hardened Hearts (Wisdom's Concession)

of flesh" (Jer 17:5; 2 Chr 32:8). Flesh is soft, malleable, needy, vulnerable, limited. To become "one flesh" with another person, then, would include living all of this neediness and frailty together, sharing fully in the wounds as well as the joys and fulfillments of this other. It is to feel the vulnerability of this other one as my own vulnerability. It is living "softly," like flesh, with this other. We recall Ezekiel's prophecy to the Israelites in exile that God would "remove from your body the heart of stone and give you a heart of flesh" (Ezek 36:26). Christian tradition generally has interpreted this promise as having found its fulfillment in Jesus Christ. Such a belief cannot help but imply strongly that Jesus himself lived, and lives, among us as one whose heart is flesh: soft, open, vulnerable. This is a heart that feels the pain of others, and welcomes the others in, fully embracing them in all of their woundedness and vulnerability. "Is this not the fast that I choose: . . . to share your bread with the hungry, and bring the homeless poor into your house; when you see the naked, to clothe them, and not to hide yourself from your own *flesh* [*basar*]?" (Isa 58:6, 7). For Christian faith, it is as the incarnation of divine Wisdom that Jesus embodies this virtue of drawing near to and embracing, not of denying or eluding, the vulnerability of flesh.

A heart of flesh, however, does not preclude hard, biting words. Jesus accuses both Moses's contemporaries and his own interlocutors of possessing hardened hearts—hearts like stone. A hard heart, like an impenetrable boulder, keeps the other out. It is not a heart of flesh. The hard heart allows no one in. It is hardened against the suffering, sorrowful, vulnerable flesh of the other. This is the sort of heart that could look at the woman it once loved, to whom it once made tender promises, but now exclude and expel her. The hardened heart refuses to feel or to share in the pain that it inflicts. Jesus appears to be making such a judgment against the male hard-heartedness (the patriarchy) of Moses's Israel—but also against his Pharisaic contemporaries for being able to raise the question of divorce so cavalierly. "Moses allowed *you* to divorce your wives . . . because you were so hard-hearted" (Matt 19:8). And so the human element again looms: Moses made concessions for masculine hard-heartedness—a tragic insensitivity to the radical vulnerability of women's lives, an insensitivity bred of patriarchal weaponry.

All of these human elements begin to add up. *Moses* is freely acknowledged to be the spiritual leader the people of Israel. Among those people, the *men's hard-heartedness* toward women was taken into account by Moses. Mark's Gospel suggests that Jesus initially framed the conversation in terms of Moses's *command*, but Matthew switches the verbs to ensure that we understand Jesus interpreting this merely as Moses's *permission*. So even in this we detect the human element of *Matthew's editorial hand* re-shaping Mark and subtly offering his readers a radical hermeneutic for the Torah. Recall that it is only in this same Gospel of Matthew that we read of Jesus insisting that "until heaven and earth pass away, not one letter, not one stroke of a letter, will pass from the law until all is accomplished" (5:18).[5] If those words often feed a fundamentalist impulse toward the authority of Scripture, what we encounter in this debate about divorce, particularly as Mark's and Matthew's versions are compared, signifies otherwise. Jesus here is most definitely not encouraging the notion that every Torah command can simply be read right off the page as God's speech.

Reading Torah over Jesus's Shoulder

But how could Jesus make that statement about the Torah's eternal authority, down to the last jot and tittle, and yet later in the same gospel dismiss the teaching of Deuteronomy 24 as a Mosaic concession to the hard-heartedness of the patriarchal system? Surely the beginning of a reply to this question comes in what we have already encountered as Jesus's summary of the entire Torah and the prophets too: loving God with one's whole being and loving every neighbor as though that person were one's very own self (Matt 22:34–40). Surely there is no nearer neighbor than the spouse to whom we have pledged our troth. One simply cannot love this other as one's very self and yet also keep this other at an unfeeling distance by deadly virtue of a stone-cold heart. But one need not turn even that many pages of Matthew. We recall that the dictum about the inviolability of even the smallest letters and marks of the Torah is given near the beginning of the Sermon on the Mount (5:17–18), and near the end of that same sermon, we read that "the law and the prophets" are, essentially, that "in everything do to others as you would have them do to you" (7:12).[6] If this is the Torah and the prophets, the reasoning might go, then *Moses cannot have commanded Israelite men to divorce their wives.*

As we have observed already, even in Deuteronomy 24 Moses does not *command* divorce; rather, divorce is taken for granted and apparently assumed to be relatively common. However, there is *nothing in the*

---

5. See Chapter 4 of this volume, "Wisdom's Love for All."
6. See Chapter 5 of this book, "Wisdom and Foolishness."

Hardened Hearts (Wisdom's Concession)

Deuteronomy text whatsoever to suggest that this teaching is offered as a concession to the sinfulness of Israelite men. The text seems to reflect, without further comment or criticism, the patriarchal system's assumption of male power over women, the latter marked as "inferior, submissive, obedient, children-producing, home-focused."[7] Nothing in the text itself even vaguely hints that Moses, perhaps with a sigh and a shrug of his shoulders, conceded that "men will be men" and the best one can hope for is to curb their worst behaviors. To read Deuteronomy 24 simply off the page is get the impression that these are God's words of instruction to the people of Israel. Indeed, this would be the typical fundamentalist or even conservative reading of the text. But Jesus teaches otherwise. His rationale is grounded in a theology of creation derived from the early chapters of Genesis, to be sure, but also in the command to love one's neighbor as oneself—one of the pegs upon which everything from Genesis to Deuteronomy, and all the prophetic utterances as well, hang.

Jesus's reading of Deuteronomy should raise a critical question: If in this passage we do not actually encounter God's word/command to the people of Israel but rather a concession made by Israel's spiritual leader, Moses, to the hard facts of a sinful patriarchy, might a similar judgment be made of other Torah passages? Here I am adapting a typically rabbinic reading strategy to try to navigate otherwise very difficult biblical passages.[8] To put it simply and in the language of Matthew: surely this instance is not the only one in which Moses (or other biblical writers) "allowed" or "permitted" certain practices of the Israelites "because of the hardness of [their] hearts." The point here is not at all to suggest that ancient Israelite males were any worse (or any better) people than others. I am not interested in fomenting a new type of anti-Judaism. The point would be that Scripture always is written by—and written within the historical, social, political, and religious contexts of—fallen human beings. Christian tradition calls it sin, and no one is deemed exempt, except Jesus.

Allow an example. Only a few chapters earlier in Deuteronomy, we read rules of warfare that are presented as God's very word to Israel. If a nearby town accepts the Israelites' terms of peace and surrenders, "all of the people in it shall serve you at forced labor" (Deut 20:11). If not, then Israel's army was to besiege the city and "put all its males to the sword" (20:13),

---

7. Carter, *Matthew and the Margins*, 378.

8. For a remarkably thorough and insightful treatment of rabbinic interpretive strategies, see Samely, *Rabbinic Interpretation of Scripture in the Mishnah*.

after which the soldiers could "take as your booty the women, the children, livestock, and everything else in the town, all its spoil" (20:14). But in the towns within the land God was giving to Israel "as an inheritance" (20:16), nothing was to be left breathing. "You shall annihilate them—the Hittites and the Amorites, the Canaanites and the Perizzites, the Hivites and the Jebusites—just as the LORD your God has commanded" (20:17). How are we to read such passages?

I suggest that perhaps Jesus's words might apply here. "It was because you were so hard-hearted that Moses allowed you to destroy other people's cities, kill their men, and appropriate their families and goods as your own. It was because you were so hard-hearted that Moses permitted you to go in and slay the inhabitants of your promised land—men, women, and children—but from the beginning it was not so." A fundamentalist or even conservative response might be that this is playing fast and loose with the Scriptures, but a twofold reply suggests itself: 1) Jesus judges divorce as not what God intended "from the beginning," i.e., not in our Creator's original vision for what creation could and should become. It is hardly a stretch of the imagination to include warfare, wholesale slaughter, property appropriation, and enforced bondage, along with divorce, in this category. 2) Everything that Jesus said and did, as far as our four Gospels testify, was entirely against the grain of the violence of warfare described in texts like Deuteronomy 20. Indeed, Jesus's radical instruction to his disciples to love their enemies, arguing that such lavish, life-sustaining love characterizes God (Matt 5:43–48), would seem to make it clear that the behaviors of Israel in Deuteronomy 20 were not what God commanded, but what Israel's leaders (whether Moses or others) allowed its army to do because of the hardness of their hearts. (This would presumably include the leaders themselves.) Granted, such behaviors would be typical of virtually any Bronze or Iron Age peoples. Perhaps Israel's guidelines were even more moderate than many others. The point would remain that, generally speaking, cultures constructed out of hardened hearts were (and still are) the rule. But we can echo Jesus's judgement that "it was not so from the beginning"—not so much because Genesis teaches us this as that Jesus teaches, and incarnates, divine Wisdom as it truly was in the beginning.

The Gentleness of Wisdom Divine

If this is so, then divine Wisdom ultimately, and often, makes many concessions with human beings in the long and arduous road of earth's history.

Hardened Hearts (Wisdom's Concession)

"God works with the world as it is," Marjorie Hewitt Suchocki writes, "in order to lead it to where it can be."[9] Presumably, this is the way that God has always labored among us: starting with us where we are and gently, tacitly, quietly drawing us, guiding us toward God's vision for creation's goodness; or in the words of second-century Christian apologist Justin Martyr, God is "always urging the human race to reflection and remembrance, showing that he cares, and provides, for human beings."[10] This is a gentle, long-suffering labor for the long haul. If God works with the world where it is—whether cosmically or individually or collectively as peoples—then we should not expect to find the divine ideals for creaturely existence in every line or page of Scripture. The Bible reflects both the creaturely reality and the divine ideal. Divine Wisdom schools us gradually, respecting our cultural and individual limitations even as she beckons us toward better things. Our role in this divine labor is crucial, as the Gospel of Matthew repeatedly indicates. So in Jesus, divine Wisdom incarnate, we hear that we have been entrusted as his *ekklesia* with the tremendous responsibility of binding and loosing,[11] this happy burden of interpretation: creatively engaging and applying Holy Writ for the sake of sustaining faithful discipleship to Jesus as the model of the church of tomorrow. Perhaps such is at least a part of what Jesus meant when he said in Matthew (alone), "Therefore every scribe who has been trained for the kingdom of heaven is like the master of a household who brings out of this treasure what is new and what is old" (13:52). Though the task and process of "bring[ing] out . . . what is new" may seem formidable, risky, or perhaps even dangerous, it appears that this is precisely the risk that divine Wisdom is pleased to undertake so as to work in company, in covenant, with us frail and fragile creatures.

One of the more beautiful biblical demonstrations of this patient labor of Wisdom divine with human beings, in all of our frailty, is in what Luke's Gospel calls "the story about the bush" (Luke 20:37). In Matthew's version of the same conversation between Jesus and some Sadducees, Jesus asks them, "And as for the resurrection of the dead, have you not read what was said to you by God?" (Matt 22:31).[12] What is said to *us* by God, in this story

---

9. Suchocki, *In God's Presence*, 16, 18, 28, 31—these words are virtually a mantra in this beautiful little book on a process theological understanding of prayer.

10. Justin the Martyr, *The First Apology*, 270–71.

11. See chapter 6 of this volume, "Wisdom's Risk."

12. Jesus's fascinating question itself may be interpreted as acknowledging and welcoming the human element. He is debating the doctrine of the resurrection of the dead with members of a Jewish sect that denied this teaching. They restricted their canon

of the calling of Moses to become the spiritual leader of the people of Israel (Exod 3:1—4:17), is that God is the God of concessions. First, we should note the somewhat surprising desire of God that a human agent should be deemed necessary to Israel's liberation. "The cry of the Israelites has now come to me; I have also seen how the Egyptians oppress them. So come, I will send you to Pharaoh to bring my people, the Israelites, out of Egypt" (3:10). One would suppose that the Creator of all things could accomplish this liberation without human participation, yet instead we encounter the mystery of a Creator who proposes to act for Israel's liberation by way of a creaturely representative. This God in "the story of the bush" even respects Moses's distinct talent for raising objections, asking questions, throwing up roadblocks, and inventing excuses, patiently dealing with Moses's dodges one by one (3:11—4:13).

Finally, however, the story teaches us that humans ought not to beat around the bush forever. We read that God's holy anger burned against Moses, and we might expect Moses in the next instant to be reduced to ashes by a fiery flame from the burning bush. Instead, the Voice coming from the bush patiently proposes,

> What about your brother Aaron the Levite? I know that he can speak fluently; even now he is coming out to meet you, and when he sees you his heart will be glad. You shall speak to him and put the words in his mouth; and I will be with your mouth and with his mouth, and will teach you what you shall do. He indeed shall speak for you to the people; he shall serve as a mouth for you, and you shall serve as God for him. Take in your hand this staff, with which you shall perform the signs. (4:14–17)

Truly this story in Scripture testifies that the One we worship does not disregard, let alone fear, the human element. Perhaps this was Moses's first lesson in the divine art of concession, of compromise. "Moses *allowed* you to divorce your wives because of your hardened hearts." In ways that

---

to the books of Moses and did not believe that those books included teaching about the resurrection. There is something fascinating, then, in Jesus playing by their rules, restricting his argument to a passage in Exodus, part of their canonical text, and even happily acknowledging that God speaks to them within the strictures of their Scriptures. He does not appeal to the writings of the prophets, which he, like the Pharisees, accepts as divine revelation. He concedes the Sadducees' scriptural turf—and then offers a typically Pharisaic-rabbinic reading of the Exodus text to show the Sadducees that they are mistaken in denying resurrection hope in the God who is "God not of the dead, but of the living" (Matt 22:33).

thoroughly embarrassed the aforementioned Justin Martyr,[13] we are encountered by a Wisdom so "gentle and humble in heart" as to enter into give-and-receive, objection-and-reply conversation with Moses—and then finally, even as divine anger smolders, to offer a compromise with Moses. The Voice from the burning bush agrees to alter the plan for redeeming Israel, to include Moses's brother Aaron in this mighty work of redemption. Most critically for our purposes, we note that the Voice proclaims that as Aaron will serve as a mouth for Moses, Moses will serve as God for Aaron. This is striking language, and it means that Moses will *function* as God, will *represent* God, to Aaron. There is no likelihood that Moses will do this perfectly, for he is dust and ashes. But God in infinitely loving Wisdom is pleased to labor with the human, to invite and to include the human element into the very nature of divine labor in the world. The story of the bush, then, may even be read as a precursor to the responsibility of "binding and loosing" given by Jesus to his community (Matt 18:18–20). Divine Wisdom humbly and gently enters into conversation with the human element of finitude, frailty, ignorance, fear, and uncertainty.

The Conversation Continues

Indeed, for Matthew this conversation is not over. While Mark ends the story of Jesus's conversation about divorce with the Pharisees with blunt words about adultery, Matthew adds intriguing material utterly unique to this gospel and quite unlike anything else in Holy Writ. "Not everyone can accept this teaching, but only those to whom it is given. For there are eunuchs who have been so from birth, and there are eunuchs who have been made eunuchs by others, and there are eunuchs who have made themselves eunuchs for the sake of the kingdom of heaven" (19:11–12). Surprising

---

13. In his *Dialogue with Trypho*, a rabbi, Justin argues that "it will not be the Creator of all things that is the God that said to Moses that He was the God of Abraham, and the God of Isaac, and the God of Jacob," for such appearances and conversations are deemed by Justin, influenced deeply by Greek philosophical tradition, to be impossible for the true God. "He who has but the smallest intelligence," Justin continues, "will not venture to assert that the Maker and Father of all things, having left all supercelestial matters, was visible on a little portion of the earth." Justin's protests notwithstanding, here the rabbinic tradition is more helpful for our gaining an appreciation for the dialogical, covenantal character of Israel's God, who is the church's God. Perhaps Justin would have benefitted from a reminder about Matthew 23:1–3. (Chapter 60, "Opinions of the Jews with Regard to Him Who Appeared in the Bush." This fascinating record of second-century Jewish-Christian debate is accessible on several internet websites.)

imagery! Carter observes, "Eunuchs were permanent outsiders, dishonored marginal figures, often despised and socially alienated,"[14] and one wonders if Matthew's Jesus might be bringing out of the treasure of his Jewish tradition something new, and radically so. We turn back again to Deuteronomy, not far from the divorce/remarriage material of chapter 24, and find close by a listing of those who are excluded from God's holy people. This is how the list begins: "No one whose testicles are crushed or whose penis is cut off shall be admitted to the assembly of the LORD" (Deut 23:1). Whatever the reasoning behind these restrictions—possibly an indication of the esteem accorded male reproductive power, virility, "wholeness"?—Jesus seems to deconstruct the prohibition entirely. One wonders, again, whether Jesus could have added something like, "It was because your hearts were so hard that Moses allowed you to exercise your prejudicial exclusions, rooted as they are in the fear of your own inadequacies and impotence, as though they represented God's will."

Eunuchs were liminal figures, to be sure. In a patriarchal system that had cemented well-defined roles for males and females, husbands and wives, parents and children, eunuchs embodied strangeness. They were queerly other. "Eunuchs violated this order, threatened it (cf. Sir. 20:4) and the future of the household and survival of the race because they could not produce children."[15] It is noteworthy that Jesus, uniquely in this Matthew passage, suggests that eunuchs come in different ways and forms. "For there are eunuchs who have been so from birth"—just naturally so, without further elaboration. (Jesus doesn't theologize their existence.) There simply are such people. Then there are those "who have been made eunuchs by others," who, as Carter observes, "suffered personal violence and abuse"[16] through castration, violence inflicted upon their bodies in a most intimate way. Whether by the whims of nature or by the violent acts of others, eunuchs were sexually ambiguous, marginalized, outsiders. Hence their exclusion from the divine assembly and priestly service (Lev 21:20), though Isaiah prophesies of God's warm welcome to strangers and eunuchs: "Do not let the foreigner joined to the LORD say, 'The LORD will surely separate me from his people'; and do not let the eunuch say, 'I am just a dry tree.' For thus says the LORD: . . . 'I will give them an everlasting name that shall not

---

14. Carter, *Matthew and the Margins*, 383.
15. Carter, *Matthew and the Margins*, 383.
16. Carter, *Matthew and the Margins*, 383.

be cut off'" (Isa 56:3–5). Those who have been cut off will not be cut off by God.

Perhaps the Isaian prophecy energized and emboldened Jesus's own calling as well as his calling of us, his disciples, since he extends the imagery of the eunuch to those "who have made themselves eunuchs for the sake of the kingdom of heaven" (Matt 19:12). If the story often recounted is true, we may rightly assume that Origen took this counsel a bit too far, insofar as Jesus here presumably (and hopefully!) refers to those among his disciples who are unmarried or divorced and remain so in order to devote their energies entirely to the task of God's reign. But it is no less a jarring image, given that eunuchs embodied what was strange, ambiguous, outside easy categorizations of sexual identity and performance. They did not fit the norm. Further, those who make themselves eunuchs for the sake of God's reign and rule do not fit the norm precisely because the norm is inadequate to encompass God's expansive, loving reach. The church of tomorrow surely must find the resources within itself to stretch beyond both patriarchy and gender normativity for the sake of embodying God's surprisingly liberal and lavish love. Such stretching may make us uncomfortable at times. So be it. Indeed, we can almost hear Jesus adding, "Let anyone accept this who can" (19:12).

9

Wisdom's Commission

... teaching them to obey everything I have commanded you ...

THE RESURRECTED JESUS IS no less the personification, indeed no less the very incarnation, of divine Wisdom than was the earthly Jesus. Further, this Wisdom is and can be none other than "Love Divine, All Loves Excelling." Because this divine love is "gentle and humble in heart' (Matt 11:29), Jesus is no less gentle and humble in heart as the resurrected Christ than he was as the toiling, weeping, crucified Nazarene. Surely this is at least part of the significance of the wounds he yet bears in resurrection glory (John 20:19–29).[1] Indeed, Paul took great pains to stress that this Messiah hanging from a Roman crucifix is the very Wisdom of God (1 Cor 1:18–25). Divine Wisdom is "Christ and him crucified" (2:2; the New English Bible has it "Christ nailed to the cross"). It is this crucified one whom God has raised from death, and into whose nail-scarred hands God has entrusted all power and authority. In the light of such unexpected wisdom, in this chapter we will attempt an unusual triangulation: first, offering a theological reading of the words of the resurrected Jesus that conclude Matthew's Gospel; second, bringing those words into conversation with the great eighteenth-century

---

1. See Rambo, *Resurrecting Wounds*.

evangelist and Anglican priest, John Wesley; and third, considering how this conversation might be understood to engage the Islamic tradition.

Resurrected Wisdom

The description of the resurrected Jesus's appearance to his disciples on a mountain in Galilee is unique to Matthew. Mountains matter for Matthew! Geography becomes Christology: Jesus taught (5:1; 8:1; 24:3), prayed (14:23), healed and fed people (15:29), and was transfigured (17:1) upon mountains. But perhaps most importantly, this final appearance upon a mountain may provide a bookend for the first mention of Jesus on a mountain in Matthew: one of the wilderness temptations following Jesus's baptism, wherein Jesus is tempted with "all the kingdoms of the world and their splendor" (4:8). Now, at the conclusion of this gospel, all the kingdoms of the world are once again in view.

Matthew notes the presence of "the Eleven"—no longer "the Twelve" with the loss of Judas. Given that "the Twelve" represented Israel's twelve tribes and Jesus's intention to renew the calling upon the people of Israel to be the light of the world (Matt 5:14), the use of the term "Eleven" is noteworthy—Matthew's frank admission that Jesus's mission on Israel's, and now the world's, behalf has suffered fracture and loss. His wisdom community is incomplete, partial, eleven out of twelve. Yet in their situation of loss and fracture they have gone to the place where Jesus instructed them to go, presumably through the directions entrusted to the first witnesses of the risen Christ, a pair of women disciples (Matt 28:1–10). Presbyterian theologian Anna Case-Winters observes, "Apparently they believed these women. Though they have not seen the risen Lord, they see the effect of the risen Lord on these women. They do as the women have told them, and as a consequence they meet the risen Lord."[2] Case-Winters is right; the role of these women should not be glossed over. Warren Carter notes that Matthew's mention of "many" faithful women in 27:55–56, his description of them in terms of discipleship ("having followed him" and "served him"), and their prominence in 28:1–10 all "suggest that they have been present throughout, even if often invisible in the narrative" and that "it seems reasonable to guess that," along with the explicitly mentioned Eleven, "other

---

2. Case-Winters, *Matthew*, 337–38.

followers, women and men, also meet the risen Jesus" on this Galilean mount.[3]

So the resurrected-crucified one meets with his fractured, traumatized people up in the more familiar terrain of Galilee, far away from the site of his arrest, torture, and crucifixion. But distance has not distanced them from trauma and confusion; indeed, Matthew proceeds with an observation that is startling in its frankness. "When they saw him, they worshiped him; but some doubted" (28:17). In my judgment, this brief admission of doubt is yet another reason why Matthew matters. But why did this matter to Matthew? Why mention it? What is gained by this detail? If we understand this gospel to be the proclamation of good news, what purpose does it serve for Matthew to go there? After Matthew has gone to considerable lengths to describe the power and triumph of the resurrection (28:2–4)—especially in comparison to what we read in Mark's brief and mysterious account—why now divulge that "some doubted," or possibly (as the Greek does allow it) that they all worshipped, but that at the same time they all harbored doubts as well?

One might reply, "Well, because that is what happened!" But this would be to overlook the extent to which we believe Matthew (and every gospel writer) exercised human agency and creativity in what he wrote. For example, if we compare Mark's story of the cursed fig tree with Matthew's version, we find that Matthew left out Mark's aside that "it was not the season for figs," presumably because Matthew thought it embarrassing and unworthy of Jesus to suggest that his understanding of the agricultural cycles was subpar. Or consider Matthew's editing of Mark's language after Jesus's baptism; whereas Mark uses a notably forceful verb, "the Spirit *drove* Jesus into the wilderness," Matthew softens the description considerably with "the Spirit *led* Jesus into the wilderness." We detect his editorial hand. So, we ask again, what does Matthew's Gospel gain by acknowledging that, even in the very presence of the resurrected Jesus, some of his disciples doubted (or even that all of them had some doubts mixed in with their worship!)?

It may reflect an early tradition that would give rise later to John's story of a doubting Thomas, certainly. But here nothing further is said about it; indeed, that may be part of the point. Jesus does not seem put off, let alone dismayed, by the presence of doubt in his community of disciples. Jesus does not draw a dividing line to distinguish the doubtlessly good disciples

---

3. Carter, *Matthew and the Margins*, 550.

from those struggling with questions or uncertainty. Jesus does not send the wavering ones away to get their act together. Whatever Matthew's intent, this sounds like good news today. If there could be doubt in the presence of the risen Jesus on that Galilee mountain about two thousand years ago, it should not surprise us that there are elements of doubt in our churches, and even in ourselves, on any given Sunday as we gather in the presence of the Living Christ. We may bring our doubts to church with us. It is very good news that some doubted, but that Jesus did not single out the doubters nor ask them quietly to leave while he addressed the "true believers." Matthew simply registers the potentially embarrassing presence of doubt among Jesus's disciples, and allows this its place in the story he tells.

Let us dwell on this a little longer. The resurrection accounts in all of our gospels acknowledge the presence of doubt, uncertainty, or even simply of mistaken identity within their accounts of Jesus's resurrection appearances. Of course, the short ending for Mark—a cliff-hanger if there ever was one—offers even less assurance, concluding with frightened women fleeing the tomb in utter amazement. Luke tells the story of the two disciples on the Emmaus Road "whose eyes were kept from recognizing" (Luke 24:16) the stranger who joined them on their anguished hike homeward. Later, in the moment that "their eyes were opened" in the breaking of the bread, he suddenly vanished before their eyes (24:30–35). In John's Gospel, Mary Magdalene confused the risen Jesus with the gardener, realizing who he actually was only when she recognized his voice calling her by name (John 20:15–18). Later in John, in the story of the breakfast of toasted bread and fish on the Galilean shore, we read that "none of the disciples dared to ask him, 'Who are you?' because they knew it was the Lord" (21:12)—which is an odd thing to say at all if there really was no lingering doubt! Confusion, ambiguity, uncertainty—mystery. This really should not surprise us, given the nature of these experiences. Indeed, the resurrection theology in Luke-Acts seems pertinent here; Peter is portrayed as proclaiming to Cornelius and his household that "God raised [Jesus] on the third day and allowed [or 'permitted', or 'caused'] him to appear [lit., 'to be seen'], not to all the people but to us who were chosen by God as witnesses" (Acts 10:40–41). This sheds light upon the Emmaus road story, where their eyes "were kept from recognizing" Jesus and, correspondingly, "their eyes were opened." No doubt the passive verbs bespeak divine activity. There is a mystery, truly a divine mystery, involved in these encounters with the crucified-yet-living one. Further, if we take seriously this idea that God chose those witnesses whose eyes were opened (by God) to encounter the risen Jesus, then the prominent role of women in the Gospel stories is further heightened; this is not simply a matter of their having been in the right place at the right time, but of divine sovereignty. God elected these women to be the first witnesses, the first apostles of the living Christ.

The resurrection of Jesus from death is the definitive act of God—but it is also an act thoroughly shrouded in mystery, incomprehensibility, and ambiguity. The differences among our Gospels—including which women actually were these earliest witnesses—certainly attest to this. In his classic essay "Gospels' Ends," the late Presbyterian theologian William Placher wrote of these resurrection accounts,

> You need not deconstruct these texts. They fall apart in your hands.... [T]he Gospels' ends [employ] varied narrative strategies [that] we can recognize ... only if we respect the narrative logic of the individual gospels.... The Jesus we encounter in these stories rejects coercive power, and both the stories and the dominant Christian tradition also reject coercion. The different stories stand in their odd juxtaposition.... Only if we refuse to allow any single narrative to overpower the diversity of these texts can we authentically encounter the vulnerable one who turned away from the misuse of power, the one whose identity they narrate, and find ourselves living in a world in which just this victim of crucifixion is the one who has been resurrected.[4]

And so in the Gospel of Matthew the resurrected Jesus stands in the midst of all this ambiguity, even doubt, as the triumphant one. (Or is he more like "a Lamb standing as if it had been slaughtered"?) We may at least note that Matthew never makes the triumphal (and perhaps anticipated) claim that all their doubt was dispelled or overcome. Their doubts are not magically whisked away. The phrase "but some doubted" is allowed simply to remain there in the text, just as the traumatized disciples stand in the presence of the mysteriously risen Christ. Doubt is yet present along with faith, and probably is a necessary element in authentic faith; if "hope that is seen is not hope" (Rom 8:24), surely the same can be said of faith. Indeed, "we walk by faith, not by sight" (2 Cor 5:7). But it can still be jarring to imagine these disciples, even in the presence of the living Christ, experiencing doubt.

---

4. Placher, *Narratives of a Vulnerable God*, 91, 104.

Wisdom's Commission

To his wavering disciples, then and there and here and now, Jesus speaks his empowering word: "All authority in heaven and on earth has been given to me" (Matt 28:18). Jesus has already been described as a figure wielding authority—in his teaching (7:29), his forgiving of sins (9:6), his healing of others (8:9), his triumphal entry into Jerusalem and cleansing of the temple (21:23). But now, in the light of his having been raised from the dead by God, he is accorded the position of the heavenly Son of Man, receiving cosmic and universal authority from the One who raised him from death. It is not difficult to feel the power of "the night visions" of Daniel 7 behind this announcement of divine authority—

> I saw one like a human being [a Son of Man]
>   coming with the clouds of heaven.
> And he came to the Ancient One
>   and was presented before him.
> To him was given dominion
>   and glory and kingship,
> that all peoples, nations, and languages
>   should serve him.
> His dominion is an everlasting dominion
>   that shall not pass away,
> and his kingship is one
>   that shall never be destroyed.
> (Dan 7:13–14)

What sort of God is this, we might ask, who is so willing to give away "dominion and glory and kingship" to this human figure? We may recall the language of Psalm 8, where we read that the Holy One has made *adam* (indeed, *ben adam*, the "son of man") "a little lower than God [*Elohim*, the term translated as 'God,' most significantly, throughout Genesis 1], and crowned him with glory and honor," having given him "dominion over the works of your hands" (Ps 8:5), language clearly reminiscent of Genesis 1. What sort of God divests authority, entrusting it to *adam*? One might suggest that this is a God who is "gentle and humble in heart," pleased to share power with creatures created to 'image' or reflect God in creation. God is humble in outpouring, self-emptying love, seeking for creatures to receive, embody, and enact that love within the realm of creation. The Christian proclamation is that Jesus is the fulfillment of this divine project. He is the second Adam, the truly human one who, having been obediently responsive to God's desire even to the point of death on a Roman cross, has been crowned with glory and honor as God's unsurpassable representative.

"To him was given dominion and glory and kingship" (Dan 7:14), and Jesus correspondingly announces in Matthew that "all authority in heaven and on earth has been given to me." Again, he announces it on a mountaintop, just as on a mountaintop he was shown "all the kingdoms of the world and their splendor" and was promised by the tempter that it could all be his if only he would worship Satan. What was tempting about this? The temptation would lie in achieving dominion over the world in a way not coherent with the character of God; it would inevitably be the way of coercion and violence. It would be the easy way, certainly for one wielding divine power. Was Jesus tempted by this possibility? Apparently so. But he refused to pursue this course. In Placher's words quoted earlier, Jesus "turned away from the misuse of power" and thus, ironically, precisely as the crucified one received "all authority in heaven and on earth." Thankfully, this authority is wielded by one who is "gentle and humble in heart"—surely divine Wisdom would entrust it to no other—and so this authority does not become a crushing burden that squelches the life out of you or me or any other creature. Indeed, under Jesus's exercise of divine authority there is "rest for [our] souls" (Matt 11:29).

We see this already in the way in which Jesus exercises his authority in this well-known "great commission." "All authority in heaven and on earth is given to me"—at a first pass, that certainly sounds triumphal! We might feel moved to hum a few bars of "Onward Christian Soldiers, marching as to war"! But note that *the way in which this divine authority is exercised* is very far from coercive or militant. All authority is given to him; *therefore* he sends his fledgling community out among the many peoples of the world to make disciples, fellow learners, in Jesus's way, "teaching them to obey everything I have commanded you" (28:20). This is not the way the powers of this world generally exercise authority. Anthony Saldarini suggests that "the very high mountain where Jesus views all the kingdoms of the world and is tempted to gain control over them by demonic power is probably parallel to the mountain from which he sends his disciples forth to teach all nations at the end of the gospel."[5] Again in Placher's words, "the Jesus we encounter in these stories rejects coercive power," and this is no less true of the resurrected Christ to whom all power is given.

We may press this point further. Jesus commissions his disciples to teach the peoples of the world to obey "everything I have commanded you." Dale Allison has observed, "It is telling that the conclusion [of Matthew],

---

5. Saldarini, *Matthew's Christian-Jewish Community*, 76.

. . . in looking back upon the earthly ministry now completed, does not mention Jesus' miracles or sacrificial death or resurrection. The stress is rather upon 'all that I have commanded you.'"[6] Granted, there is much more to the gospel than teaching commandments of Jesus. But far too often Christianity has seemed to settle for much less. This very Jewish gospel will continually goad us back to a teacher, whom we confess to be Wisdom incarnate, beckoning us to come and learn from him. What we learn, I believe, is to become "gentle and humble in heart" and to live accordingly as Jesus's *ekklesia*. The church of tomorrow must recover a healthy sense of the ethical demands at the heart of Jesus's instruction. Christianity can never again espouse easy-believism or cheap grace. There is a yoke of teaching, which Jesus calls us to shoulder together with one another, and with him.

We note again the language of Daniel 7, "To him was given dominion and glory and kingship, that all peoples, nations, and languages should serve him" (Dan 7:14). Correspondingly, Daniel's vision is enacted in Jesus's commission to "make disciples of all nations [*ethne*]" or peoples of the world, i.e., all ethnicities. The term in Jewish writing nearly always entails the gentile peoples, and so it may be understood here. This need not imply that the Jewish people are not included as part of the mission. However, the more salient point is that these disciples ("the Eleven") represent all of Israel—the renewed Israel—in mission to the gentile peoples. If "dominion and glory and kingship" over all the peoples is given to Jesus by God, this does not occur with an apocalyptic, unilateral act of enforcing submission. It is enacted, instead, in the (noncoercive) *teaching* of Jesus's wisdom community, sent out from Galilee to all these peoples of the world. This is not a compulsory, let alone a military, enactment of God's reign—nor should it ever have been. We recall Matthew's citation of the prophet Isaiah, explored in chapter 5:

> He will not wrangle or cry aloud,
>   nor will anyone hear his voice in the streets.
> He will not break a bruised reed
>   or quench a smoldering wick
> until he brings justice to victory.
>   And in his name the Gentiles will hope.
> (Matt 12:19–21)

This is a gentle power, a quiet and even unassuming authority, a humble mission to all the peoples of God's good creation. Matthew understood

---

6. Allison, *The New Moses*, 315.

Jesus's community of disciples to function as the prophets envisioned the vocation of Israel would be fulfilled in the age to come, when the nations would be attracted to Israel and Israel's God by virtue of Israel's social embodiment of shalom. In this way, all the peoples of the world would be blessed by Abraham's offspring. "According to this divine pedagogy," writes Gerhard Lohfink, "the reign of God does not mean subjugation of the world but a call into freedom—a call, actually an alluring, according to the model of those called first."[7] In this great commission, Jesus is a Jew sending fellow Jews into the world to be a community that is the light of the world (5:14), like Jerusalem, a "city built on a hill," except that this city will turn out to be a mobile community, moving into and among the nations. We have already acknowledged Christianity's temptation toward triumphalism; Jesus resisted the temptation, but the church not so much. If we take his yoke upon ourselves, and learn from him, then as his wisdom community we will be faithful to his calling to "make disciples," learner-followers of Jesus, by the relatively humble act of teaching.

Relatedly, respecting the integrity of Matthew's Gospel, we surely must understand the phrase "everything that I have commanded you" first of all as everything that Jesus taught his disciples in this particular gospel. (That is presumably what Matthew had in mind!) "You are the light of the world," Jesus tells his circle of disciples, his *ekklesia*; thus, "let your light shine before others (*anthropon*, "people") so that they may see your good works and give glory to your Father in heaven" (5:16). *Teaching* the people of the nations, then, must first be a *living*, a communal embodying, of Jesus's words.

Wisdom's Commission and Other Religions

Let us pose this question: How might Matthew's model for mission here inform the church of tomorrow's understanding of, and encounter with, people of other religious traditions? They are certainly among those *ethne* to whom Jesus sends his disciples. How may the church exist in such a way as to embody God's "call into freedom" in relation to other religious, but non-Christian, communities? I offer the case of Islam for consideration. A common Islamic critique of Christianity is that the latter is a private, individualistic, and overly internalized faith, while Muslims understand themselves to be a people, the worldwide *umma*, and thus affirm that their religious tradition, unlike Christianity, espouses a particular political form

---

7. Lohfink, *Does God Need the Church?* 28.

of life. To the extent that Christianity can be legitimately criticized on this score, it only means that we have not paid sufficient attention to Jesus's good news about God's reign. Perhaps Muslims, in their life together as a people of God, may help us better to hear instructions of Jesus such as these: "You know that the rulers of the Gentiles lord it over them, and their great ones are tyrants over [their underlings]. *It will not be so among you*; but whoever wishes to be great among you must be your servant, and whoever wishes to be first among you must be your slave; just as the Son of Man came not to be served but to serve, and to give his life a ransom for many" (20:25–28). A form of social life is being both taught and exemplified by Jesus—a way of being in community that Matthew understands to be distinct from the power politics of the nations (the gentile "peoples," Rome in particular).

Indeed, as was discussed in chapter 1, Matthew expands this social critique of the gentile political powers to include first-century leaders of the Jewish community as well. "They love to have the place of honor at banquets and the best seats in the synagogues, and to be greeted with respect in the marketplaces, and to have people call them rabbi" (23:6). The trappings of power and prestige are alluring indeed. But Jesus repeats his earlier dictum, "The greatest among you will be your servant" (23:11). It should be clear to us that this community of disciples following Jesus is called to humility and is to be characterized by servanthood. Presumably this servant character is not to be expressed only within the community, among its own members; if it truly is shaped by the character of the one who is "gentle and humble in heart" (11:29), it will be a servant community in its relations and interactions with "strangers"—including religious "strangers," those outside of the social existence of the *ekklesia*—as well.

I mentioned in chapter 1 also that the Matthean Jesus, even as he criticizes leaders of the Jewish community, acknowledges that they "sit on Moses' seat," exercising the teaching authority of Moses handed down through the generations. Thus, Jesus teaches his disciples (along with "the [Jewish] crowds," 23:1) to "do whatever they teach you and follow it" (23:3). This instruction, unique (not surprisingly) to Matthew, may be shocking to us contemporary disciples—but certainly it is not to be dismissed on that account. We should at least acknowledge the implicit validation in Matthew of ongoing religious vitality within Jewish traditions. We grant that Matthew's Gospel was written in and for a very different world than the one we inhabit. But surely this surprising teaching of Matthew's Jesus—he who tells his disciples to teach the world's peoples "everything that I have commanded you," including, presumably, this very teaching about rabbinic authority—could be taken more seriously by us Christian disciples today. In some ways, it would demand of us some serious schooling in the traditions of Judaism, and at the very least an acknowledgement that those rich and stimulating traditions exist and continue to nourish Jewish communities. The fact that there are indications that some teachings of those Jewish traditions flowed orally through the experience of Muhammad in early seventh-century Arabia, and into the Qur'an, is fascinating as well as important.[8] I am convinced that a serious reading of Matthew nudges us disciples of Jesus toward a closer kinship with rabbinic Judaism, and thus also, *ipso facto*, with Islam.

If we who are Jesus's disciples were to see ourselves as a community among such other communities—which in historical fact we are—what kind of community would we, should we, be? What shall we be as the church of tomorrow? I think again of the Sermon on the Mount, up on a hill, where Jesus tells his disciples that they are like a city built upon a hill, where it cannot be hidden—a corporate, corporeal light shining among all peoples, actually inspiring at least some people among those peoples to "give glory to your Father in heaven" for the "good works" they see accomplished in and by this community (5:16).

Probably the most striking passage in the Sermon on the Mount directly addressing our present question occurs in Jesus's teaching on love of enemies. "You have heard that it was said, 'You shall love your neighbor and hate your enemy'" (5:43)—which is, we realize, a terribly natural way to behave. "But I say to you, Love your enemies and pray for those who persecute you, in order that you might be children of your Father in heaven" (5:44–45), i.e., so that you might be like God. Indeed, in a teaching that seems to connect well with Marjorie Hewitt Suchocki's suggestion that friendship become a new symbol of God's reign,[9] Jesus asks rhetorically, "[I]f you greet only your brothers and sisters [i.e., fellow members of the community of disciples], what more are you doing than others? Do not even the Gentiles do that much? Be perfect, therefore, as your heavenly Father is perfect" (5:47–48). Greeting the stranger as a sign, an expression, of the perfection of divine love! It is a mundane act indeed to offer greetings to those outside our community, simply to be friendly toward strangers as one would toward one's own brothers and sisters in the Messiah. It is

8. For abundant examples, see Lodahl, *Claiming Abraham*.
9. Suchocki, *Divinity and Diversity*, 81.

Wisdom's Commission

also risky; the greeting may be ignored, rejected, or belittled. The church of tomorrow ought to strive to become a community of such radical welcome that it risks recognizing the humanity of each and every "stranger," including and perhaps especially the religious "stranger." This speaks volumes to the profoundly sub-Christian attitudes toward Islam and Muslims found far too readily among Christians. Such attitudes, words, and deeds, Wisdom teaches us, are a horrid distortion of the indiscriminately lavish love of God.

For all of this radical openness and even potentially dangerous hospitality to which Jesus's wisdom community is called, it is not without boundaries. The church is a people with a collective identity and a distinctive ritual of initiation: "baptizing them in the name of the Father, and of the Son, and of the Holy Spirit" (28:19). "Using Trinitarian baptism as the initiation rite for all nations implicitly does away with circumcision as the key initiation rite introducing the convert into the people of God," Meier has written. "And once the convert enters the church, what is normative for his Christian life is not the Mosaic Law as such, but the commands of Jesus."[10] This Trinitarian baptismal formula is yet another reason why Matthew matters! We are not simply believers in God-in-general, some vague deity whose existence may be blandly acknowledged on U.S. coinage or in the pledge of allegiance to the American flag. We are baptized into a Trinitarian confession regarding who and what God is, and more importantly how God has acted within creation to bring about its regeneration (Matt 19:28). If this seems like the arbitrary insertion of a Trinitarian formula perhaps only developed at a later date, we should at least recall Jesus's language earlier in Matthew, "All things have been handed over to me by my Father; and no one knows the Son except the Father, and no one knows the Father except the Son and anyone to whom the Son chooses to reveal him" (11:27). As to the Spirit, we recall that Jesus had earlier acknowledged the Spirit's divine identity and power: "if it is by the Spirit of God that I cast out demons, then the kingdom of God has come to you" (12:28), warning that blasphemy against the Holy Spirit is the one unpardonable sin (12:32).

---

10. Meier, *The Vision of Matthew*, 213. Again, I would warn against too hasty a distinction between "the Mosaic Law as such" and "the commands of Jesus," given what Jesus says about the commands of love for God and neighbor in Matthew 22:34–40. (See chapter 2 of this book.) It certainly seems true that Matthew's Jesus offers a particular lens for interpreting and enacting the laws of Moses; indeed, Matthew seems to suggest that the real difference between Moses's laws and Jesus's teaching is that Jesus is more demanding! (Matt 5:17ff.).

We even find in Matthew Jesus's intriguing words to his disciples regarding their testimony before "governors and kings"—"it is not you who speak, but the Spirit of your Father speaking through you" (10:20).[11] It should be clear to us that "the Spirit of [our] Father" is none other than the Holy Spirit! The point is that the relations among Father, Son, and Spirit have already been adumbrated in Matthew's Gospel, though certainly not spelled out in any systematic fashion. For that matter, our baptism "in the name of the Father, the Son, and the Holy Spirit" is a clear echo of Jesus's own baptism: the Synoptic witness is that Jesus (and perhaps others) heard the heavenly voice announcing him as God's Son even as God's Spirit "descended" upon him, anointing and empowering him for his messianic role (cf. Acts 10:38). We need not be overly surprised at the apparently tight Trinitarian formula of Matthew 28.

After instructing his disciples to enact his cosmic authority through living faithfully according to everything he commanded, teaching all peoples to do the same, and baptizing them in the Trinitarian name, Jesus promises his presence. "And remember, I am with you always, to the end of the age" (28:20). This is the perfect ending to a story that begins with the proclamation of Jesus as "Emmanuel, which means 'God is with us'" (1:23), and in the middle of which Jesus promises that where two or three are gathered in his name, he is present in their midst (18:20). So now, as he commissions what amounts to little more than a motley crew, he is sure to be with them on the hard journey ahead. (I take this to be an essential aspect of Matthew 25:31–46, which we will explore in the following chapter, "Wisdom's Community.")

Let us appreciate that this is how the Gospel of Matthew ends. There is no ascension, no breathing of the Spirit, no disappearing act. What happens next? As far as Matthew is concerned, this is a non-question. For the final word is Jesus's word of assurance of his presence with his wisdom community, to the very end of the world as we know it. As the Son of Man of Daniel 7, Jesus has been "given dominion and glory and kingship," and he exercises that dominion by sending out his *ekklesia* to live, to teach, to baptize. Just as in Daniel "all peoples, nations, and languages should serve"

---

11. The parallel passages in the other Synoptics are noteworthy: Mark speaks of the Holy Spirit (13:11), as does Luke (12:12); Luke has essentially the same teaching again later, but in this case Jesus promises, "I will give you words and a wisdom that none of your opponents will be able to withstand or contradict" (Luke 21:15). This virtual interchangeability among "Spirit of your Father," "Holy Spirit," and "I" (Jesus) lends itself well to the later traditional theological notion of *perichoresis* among the trinitarian persons.

the glorified Son of Man, so his community is to "go and make disciples of all peoples." And just as Daniel's glorified Son of Man exercises "an everlasting dominion that shall not pass away," so Jesus is always with his people to the very end of the age.

While we will consider apocalyptic endings soon enough (in the following chapter), we note that this seems decidedly non-apocalyptic. History does not come crashing down in a dramatic denouement. The glory of Jesus the Son of Man is hardly obvious; the church's labors in the twenty intervening centuries have often been less than impressive; Jesus's "everlasting dominion" is far from wowing the world.

Wisdom's Ways, Whitehead, and Wesley

But should we expect anything other from a divine Wisdom that is "gentle and humble in heart"? Apparently God's way is not to wow the world, but to woo it. Why do our eschatologies so often anticipate a divine Warrior who will use all the divine force necessary to enact and enforce heavenly rule over the world? Is that not precisely the sort of coercion that Jesus refused? If it is, then why do we typically expect Jesus to return in such a way as to undo what Alfred North Whitehead called "the Galilean origin of Christianity . . . [which] does not emphasize the ruling Caesar, or the ruthless moralist, or the unmoved mover . . . [but instead] dwells upon the tender elements in the world, which slowly and in quietness operate by love"?[12] "Take my yoke upon you, and learn from me, for I am gentle and humble in heart, and you will find rest for your souls."

This question possesses a particular pertinence for Christians of the Wesleyan tradition. For while Wesley certainly held a high hope for the redeeming work of God in the world, such that one day "the earth will be full of the knowledge of the LORD as the waters cover the sea" (Isa 11:9), he also was willing to wonder in a sermon about how God intends to do such a thing. Will God, would God, finally resort to some great act of coercion to set things right? In "The General Spread of the Gospel," he acknowledged, for a moment, that if "the Almighty [were] to act *irresistibly*, [then] the thing is done; yea, with just the same ease as when 'God said, Let there be light; and there was light.'"[13] Something like this scenario seems to domi-

---

12. Whitehead, *Process and Reality*, 343.
13. Wesley, "The General Spread of the Gospel," in *Works*, Vol. 6, 280.

nate most eschatological expectations, whether among Christians or other traditions such as orthodox Judaism, Islam, and even certain strands of Buddhism and Hinduism. It is not surprising why this is the case; even a cursory glance at the world around us, with all of its attendant evils, suffering, sorrow, and sin, would lead easily to a terribly pessimistic prognosis. It would seem that our only hope would be for a power that is indeed "almighty" to act irresistibly to usher in justice and healing to our sad world.

I think Wesley understood this. Yet as soon as he raises the possibility of God acting in a unilateral, overwhelming way, he dismisses it. "But then man would be man no longer; his inmost nature would be changed. He would no longer be a moral agent, any more than the sun or the wind, as he would no longer be endued with liberty, a power of choosing or self-determination. Consequently he would no longer be capable or virtue or vice, of reward or punishment."[14] But if Wesley held such strong convictions regarding human agency and responsibility, why did he even bother to mention an eschatological scenario in which the human element is effectively silenced and nullified? Perhaps because of its enduring fascination, perhaps its widespread appeal among his presumed audience? Perhaps Wesley himself felt the attraction of this eschatological scenario, even while he judged it to be unacceptable. In any event, Wesley dismisses this possibility because he recognizes that, in it, the God who is "gentle and humble in heart," and who in that character calls humanity into covenantal partnership, would be undoing all the work that God has done. "Man would be man no longer," indeed—but perhaps also "God would be God no longer"? If it is the case that God is the ultimate in gentle, humble Love, "Love Divine, All Loves Excelling"—that "God is love," as Wesley loved to quote—then perhaps to act in such an ultimately violent (because violating creaturely integrity), coercive fashion is simply out of God's character. It would be uncharacteristic of God to do such a thing. Given the way I have interpreted divine Wisdom, it would truly be unwise. As contemporary United Methodist theologian Catherine Keller has asked, "If God ultimately overpowers the creation, even for the sake of the creatures' own 'restoration,' would this not violate the human creature's freedom to 'react upon' grace, either resisting or embracing it?"[15]

---

14. Wesley, "The General Spread of the Gospel," in *Works*, Vol. 6, 280.

15. Keller, "Salvation Flows: Eschatology for a Feminist Wesleyanism," 416. This brief quotation does not do justice to Keller's insightful, eminently creative reading of Wesley in this article. Her citation of the phrase "react upon" comes from Wesley's sermon "The Great Privilege of Those Who Are Born of God," where he describes grace as "a

Wesley was sensitive to this issue, though it seems to go unnoticed by most of his theological heirs. Love does not force its way; it invites and encourages and assists. He appeals to his audience's experience of grace:

> You know how God wrought in *your own* soul when he first enabled you to say, "The life I now live, I live by faith in the Son of God, who loved me, and gave himself for me." He did not take away your understanding, but enlightened and strengthened it. He did not destroy any of your affections; rather, they were more vigorous than before. Least of all did he take away your liberty, your power of choosing good or evil; [God] did not *force* you; but being *assisted* by his grace you, like Mary, *chose* the better part.[16]

All of this in the midst of a sermon in which he was trying to foresee how God would redeem all of creation! He believed that the power of this strengthening, enlightening, assisting grace was making its presence felt in the Methodist movement, that through it God was "already renewing the face of the earth."[17] He anticipated that a renewal in "experimental [i.e., *experiential*] knowledge and love of God, of inward and outward holiness" would recreate a Christian community like the Jerusalem church described early in Acts: "they will 'continue steadfast in the apostles' doctrine and in the fellowship, and in the breaking of bread, and in prayers,' . . . and 'none of them will say that [any] of the things which he possesses is his own, but they will have all things common.'"[18] In this renewed and radical community "there will be no partiality; no 'widows neglected in the daily ministration," no rancor or competitiveness—and thus Wesley envisions a kind of Methodist-infected, universal Christian community where "only love informs the whole."[19] And yet this would come about through "the work of God [that] is uniform in all ages," such that "considering how he *does* work *now,* and how he *has* [worked] in times past" provides the necessary insight to "conceive how he *will* work" in human lives "in times to come."[20] If Wesley is right about this, then it only need be added that the

---

continual action of God upon the soul" and the human response of gratitude, obedience, and prayer as "the re-action of the soul upon God."

16. Wesley, "The General Spread of the Gospel," in *Works*, Vol. 6, 280.
17. Wesley, "The General Spread of the Gospel," in *Works*, Vol. 6, 288.
18. Wesley, "The General Spread of the Gospel," in *Works*, Vol. 6, 284.
19. Wesley, "The General Spread of the Gospel," in *Works*, Vol. 6, 284.
20. Wesley, "The General Spread of the Gospel," in *Works*, Vol. 6, 280. Italics are Wesley's.

work of God "is uniform in all ages" precisely because the *character* of God "is uniform in all ages."

It is not difficult to suspect Wesley of an overbloated optimism about the future of our world, but at least he (and at least in this sermon!) was exploring an eschatology that cohered with his Arminian soteriology. And he was an optimist of grace! He anticipated the spread throughout the earth—among all of the world's peoples, we might recall—of these Christian communities where "only love informs the whole." Only then, he preached, would Muslims have any reason at all to "give attention to [Christians'] words" of proclamation.[21] Only when Christians actually live together as a distinct polity grounded in grace and love, sharing radically in life's material goods, will the worldwide Muslim community take serious note. *Let your light so shine* . . . . Wesley seems to have realized that only that kind of concrete, communal witness could bear weight among the *umma* or worldwide community of Islam. Muslims, experiencing themselves to be just such an alternative community around the world, would understandably give no serious heed to a disembodied, individualized, spiritualized gospel message. It would take a people, a *polis* "doing the will of God on earth as it is done in heaven," even to get the attention of the people of the house of Islam—and rightly so.

Writing out of this almost embarrassingly unbounded optimism of grace, then, Wesley predicted the spread of the gospel from one nation and people to another as God gradually "renews the face of the earth" (Ps 104:30) "until he hath put [an end] to sin, and misery, and infirmity, and death, and re-established universal holiness and happiness, and caused all the inhabitants of the earth to sing together, 'Hallelujah, the Lord God omnipotent reigneth!!'"[22]

Such an end as this may not have been exactly what Matthew anticipated as he wrote the final words of his gospel. He ends simply with Jesus's promise to be with his "small, minority, marginal community of disciples,"[23] with us today and tomorrow, his *ekklesia*, as we embody in our living and teach with our tongues "everything that I have commanded you." Wesley would warn us, and I think properly, that unless and until the church of tomorrow faithfully obeys Jesus's commands—particularly the Mosaic commands that he said were the two upon which all the law and

---

21. Wesley, "The General Spread of the Gospel," in *Works*, Vol. 6, 284.
22. Wesley, "The General Spread of the Gospel," in *Works*, Vol. 6, 288.
23. Carter, *Matthew and the Margins*, 549.

the prophets hang—then we have little reason to expect that the people, or peoples, of the world will feel compelled to listen.

10

Wisdom's Community

... just as you did it to one of the least of these who are members of my family ...

SURELY ONE OF THE very big reasons Matthew matters is that only Matthew features the so-called "Parable of the Sheep and the Goats." Whether it actually qualifies as a parable or not,[1] the story is the biblical passage probably most often cited or alluded to in sermonic or other hortatory appeals to encourage Christians to acts of mercy and justice in the world. Then there is that unforgettable criterion of judgment: "Inasmuch as you did it to one of the least of these my brothers and sisters, you did it to me." There is no question about the power of this imagery and its appeal, especially (though not exclusively!) to politically progressive Christians.

But in all of the voluminous references to this story in Christian writing and oration, have we typically misunderstood this passage? If we have, how ought we better to understand it? And what difference would a different interpretation make? These are the questions I intend to pursue in this final chapter.

Let us note the principal characters identified in this eschatological drama. There is first "the Son of Man [who] comes in his glory, and all the angels with him." The angels, however, play no further role in this passage;

---

1. Virtually all biblical scholars agree that it does not, and I am happy to accept their conclusion.

all attention stays on this Son of Man who will then "sit on the throne of his glory" (Matt 25:31) as judge. "All the nations [*ethne*]," that is, all of the different peoples or ethnicities of the world, are gathered before the Son of Man. We should recall that Matthew's Gospel concludes with Jesus sending his disciples ("the Twelve" minus the one) out into, and among, those very *ethne*, to make disciples. Further, just as the great commission text of Matthew 28 has rich resonances with Daniel 7 (as highlighted in the previous chapter), so also does Matthew 25's scene of the final judgment. For as the Son of Man comes with his angels, so in Daniel 7 "a thousand thousands stood attending" to the Ancient One while "the court sat in judgment, and the books were opened" (Dan 7:10). The judgment in Daniel includes God's "holy ones gain[ing] possession of the kingdom" (7:22), and there is no question that these "holy ones" signify God's people Israel (even if only as a holy remnant). Part of the point is that, if (and to the extent that) Matthew 25 echoes Daniel 7, then "all the nations" gathered in judgment before the Son of Man means all the gentile peoples of the world. I concur with Daniel Harrington that this is the most compelling interpretation of "the nations," given Matthew's usage of *ethne* elsewhere.[2] Further, as we will see, this correlates nicely not only with Daniel 7 but with other Jewish, and specifically rabbinic, stories of final judgment. "The nations" are all of those peoples generally understood as having been outside the pale of God's covenant with, and revelation to, the people of Israel.

What, then, of the people of Israel, the Jews, in this judgment scenario? Matthew has already offered something of an answer. When Peter wonders what reward awaits him and his friends for their willingness to give up their old lives and follow Jesus, the Master replies, "Truly I tell you, at the renewal of all things, when the Son of Man is seated on the throne of his glory [cf. 25:31], you who have followed me will also sit on twelve thrones, judging the twelve tribes of Israel" (19:28). Matthew seems to have no difficulty imagining two distinct judgments, one for God's people Israel and one for "the nations." In Harrington's words, "Whereas the twelve apostles have a special role in the judgment of Israel, no such role is attributed to them in the judgment of the Gentiles. That is the task of the Son of Man."[3]

While no particular list of criteria for judgment of Israel is offered in Matthew 19, it does not seem far afield to suggest that, for Matthew, the leading (and perhaps sole) criterion would be, in Jesus's phrase, "do[ing]

---

2. See Harrington, *The Gospel of Matthew*, 358ff.
3. Harrington, *The Gospel of Matthew*, 359.

the will of my Father in heaven" (7:21) as described in the Sermon on the Mount. At the end of that astounding (and very often stumbling) block of teaching, Jesus identifies two groups of people: the wise who hear his words and act accordingly, and the foolish who hear his words but do not obey (7:24–26).[4] Since his audience in this context is essentially a Jewish one, we should not be surprised to encounter an essentially Jewish criterion of judgment: faithful obedience to the teachings of this new Moses, who teaches God's word and God's will from this mount that re-signifies Sinai. Further, Matthew mentions that "the crowds"—quite clearly a Jewish designation—"were astounded at his teaching, for he taught them as one having authority, and not as their scribes" (7:28–29). Of course, being astounded at teachings is not at all the same thing as living in accordance with them; hence, the necessity of judgment. While we may not have the capacity to imagine what such a judgment would actually look like—and while Matthew seems not to have been overly bothered by the fact that, by the end of his story, there are only the Eleven instead of the Twelve to judge the twelve tribes of Israel—it seems arguably safe to assume that Matthew anticipated a judgment for Israel distinct from that of "the nations." It may be helpful to recall that in the same context of the ending of the Sermon on the Mount, Jesus enjoins his (originally Jewish) listeners to "enter through the narrow gate; for the gate is wide and the road is easy that leads to destruction, and there are many who take it. For the gate is narrow and the road is hard that leads to life, and there are few who find it" (7:13–14). The point here, perhaps, is that the narrow path of following Jesus's teachings "just naturally" leads to life, i.e., the fullness of social existence as the people of God, *shalom*—while pursuing one's own "broad way" naturally and inevitably leads to the erosion of life and well-being. Jesus's concluding parable about the wise and foolish home-builders might well point in this direction.

Who Are "the Least"?

There is just one other group of principal characters in the story of the sheep and goats: those whom the Son of Man (or "the king," 25:40) identifies as "the least of my brothers and sisters," or, in the unforgettable KJV, "the least of my brethren" (25:40). It is true that verse 45 uses simply "the least of these" without the sibling reference, but it seems unavoidable that the same group of people is being specified. Thus we have the Son of Man,

---

4. See chapter 5 of this book, "Wisdom and Foolishness."

"the nations," and whoever are "the least of these [Jesus's] brothers and sisters."

Is there any good and convincing way around the idea that the phrase "the least of my brothers and sisters" signifies Jesus's family of followers? We remember the story shared by the Synoptic Gospels, that one day the press of the listening crowd was so great that his own family members could not get to Jesus. When informed that his mother and brothers were outside, desiring to speak to him, "Jesus replied, 'Who is my mother, and who are my brothers?' And pointing to his disciples, he said, 'Here are my mother and my brothers! For whoever does the will of my Father in heaven is my brother and sister and mother'" (Matt 12:46–50; the addition of "sister" is in the Greek!). Here Jesus identifies his family by the precise phrase used at the end of the Sermon on the Mount to describe those who will enter the kingdom of heaven: "those who do the will of my Father in heaven" (7:21). Further, the resurrected Jesus commissioned "Mary Magdalene and the other Mary" to "go and tell my brothers to go to Galilee, where they will see me" (28:10). If such texts as these inform our understanding of who counts as Jesus's siblings, is there any reason to assume that in Matthew 25 a different understanding is in play?

But what of "the least"? One of the reasons Matthew matters is that this gospel expresses a particular concern for those who are identified as "little ones." We find in 10:40–42 a listing of representatives of God's reign that moves in a descending order, even if Matthew's overall intent is to disrupt such hierarchy. Jesus, speaking to his "Twelve" before sending them out in mission to "the lost sheep of the house of Israel" (10:6), teaches that "whoever welcomes you welcomes me, and whoever welcomes me welcomes the One who sent me." Then, "Whoever welcomes a prophet in the name of a prophet will receive a prophet's reward; and whoever welcomes a righteous person in the name of a righteous person will receive the reward of the righteous; and whoever gives even a cup of cold water to one of these little ones in the name of a disciple—truly I tell you, none of these will lose their reward" (10:40–42). But who *are* "these little ones"? Notice the apparent parallel: welcoming a prophet in the name of a prophet; welcoming a righteous person in the name of a righteous person; welcoming "one of these little ones" *in the name of a disciple.* Do "these little ones" bear some relation to "these the least of my brothers and sisters" of Matthew 25? If whoever welcomes one of Jesus's disciples is welcoming Jesus, and in so doing also welcomes the God who sent Jesus, what of this cup of cold water for a little one? Is that not also a cup of cold water given to Jesus? It seems we are not far from the ideas of Matthew 25.

This particular concern in Matthew for "these little ones" focuses on those most vulnerable, least important, and perhaps youngest among Jesus's community of disciples. In Matthew 18 it becomes clear that actual, literal children are at least a part of what is meant. In response to his disciples arguing unwisely over who is greatest in God's reign, Jesus beckons a child into the mix: "Whoever becomes humble like this child is the greatest in the kingdom of heaven" (18:4). Biblical scholars are right, I believe, to discourage romanticizations about children and what it is about them that makes them great in God's reign. This is not about childlike wonder, or a child's innocent trust, or some other quality associated with a child's nature. Rather, it is about the humility, or lowly standing, of the child's place in the social pecking order of first-century cultures—"no social status or political significance."[5] Becoming humble like a child requires an intentionally chosen downward mobility. Allow me to say once more that only one who is "gentle and humble in heart" can legitimately make such a demand as this. Humility is the nature of this God's reign because humility is the nature of *God*. To become humble like a child is to find oneself in divine company. We are being called upon to become like this sort of God, this One who is revealed in Wisdom incarnate to be "gentle and humble in heart." Thus Jesus repeats, "Whoever welcomes one such child in my name welcomes me" (18:5). Welcome of the little child is emblematic of his wisdom community.

It is precisely because these "little ones" are vulnerable that they receive particular attention and care in the Matthean community. "If any of you put a stumbling block before one of these little ones who believe in me, it would be better for you if a great millstone were fastened around your neck and you were drowned in the depth of the sea" (18:6). The element of judgment here is strong; the young, the weak, and the vulnerable are given special consideration by God. "Take care that you do not despise one of these little ones," Jesus warns—and then continues, in one of these uniquely Matthean phrases that likely reflects Jewish lore but whose meaning may ultimately escape us—"for I tell you, in heaven their angels continually see the face of my Father in heaven" (18:11). (Is it not reasonable to suppose that, at least for Matthew, these angels would be among those who accompany the Son of Man "when he comes in his glory"?) The little ones, the weak, the socially awkward and outcast, the nobodies—the church of

---

5. Harrington, *The Gospel of Matthew*, 264.

tomorrow must, if it takes up the yoke of Jesus, be a place of welcome for all of these readily excluded ones. It will become a haven of safety for the vulnerable, the thirsty, the homeless, the stranger. But we should note too that Jesus's concern seems particularly focused on "these little ones who believe in me" (18:6). These "little ones" are a part, or at least always potentially a part, of the *ekklesia*. Matthew matters because it woos us toward becoming a wisdom community such as this, where the little ones are welcomed, treasured, and protected. "So it is not the will of your Father in heaven that one of these little ones should be lost" (18:14).

Intratextual connections within the Gospel of Matthew itself, then, strongly suggest that "the least of my brothers and sisters" are these very disciples of Jesus—particularly the youngest, the weakest, the most vulnerable—sent out into the world to make disciples among all the *ethne* of the world. It is these ones who will stand beside (or at least somewhere near!) the Son of Man. They stand beside him ("these," *touton*) precisely because he has been with them always, to the very end of the present age (Matt 28:20). Since they have been sent out in gentleness and humility, they are themselves humble, poor, vulnerable, and dependent upon the good graces of those among the *ethne* who welcome them. Thus, "I was hungry and you fed me" would mean, essentially, "When my brothers and sisters came as my emissaries to you, you welcomed them with food for their hungry stomachs." This of course also coheres nicely with the resurrected Jesus's question to Paul, "Why do you persecute *me*?" In turn, this interpretation also has the benefit of corresponding well with Paul's imagery of the church as the body of Christ, and the Pauline claim that "in my flesh I am completing what is lacking in Christ's afflictions for the sake of his body, that is, the church" (Col 1:24).[6] Jesus identifies himself fully with his *ekklesia*. "Whoever welcomes one such child in my name welcomes me."

In his exhaustive study of the history of interpretation of this passage, *The Least of My Brothers*, Sherman W. Gray shows that an unrestricted (as opposed to an ecclesial) interpretation of "the least of these my brothers [and sisters]" was relatively rare until the twentieth century. Not that it didn't exist at all! Irenaeus seems to have understood Matthew 25 as indicating our need to give to God "who has no need of anything" and the way we can do this is through "good works" associated with "compassion on the poor,"[7] with no obvious connotation that the poor in question need

---

6. See John A. T. Robinson's classic study, *The Body: A Study in Pauline Theology*.
7. Gray, *The Least of My Brothers*, 13. For a compelling counter-argument in favor

be Christians. But Irenaeus was unusual in this regard. Among the leading early to medieval Christian theologians, Origen, Athanasius, Basil of Caesarea, Gregory of Nazianzus, Jerome, Augustine, and Aquinas all tended strongly to interpret "the least of these" as Christian disciples; besides Irenaeus, those who tended toward a more universal interpretation, i.e., anyone at all who is ill, hungry, homeless, etc., were Gregory of Nyssa and John Chrysostom.

Of course, a question like this is not settled by vote; we will not determine Matthew's meaning simply by piling up names for or against an ecclesial interpretation of "the least of these my brothers and sisters." But in his conclusion Gray submits that the "most common exegetical failing with regard to these verses . . . is the inability of many commentators to realize that 'the least' form a distinct category and are not to be included among the sheep or the goats. This, I believe, is clearly indicated by the demonstrative *touton* ['these']."[8] Since "these brothers and sisters" are distinct from the sheep and the goats who are "the nations," i.e., gentile peoples, and since Jesus has already identified in Matthew who are his family members, it seems quite unavoidable that "the least of these" actually are—or at least are among—those disciples that Jesus sent out into the nations in Matthew 28 to "teach them to obey everything I commanded you" (28:20). Indeed, the resurrected Jesus makes it quite clear where he is to be found: "I am with you [all] always, to the end of the age" (28:20). It is precisely because of his promised presence with his Jewish disciples as they go forth to the world's gentile *ethne* that Jesus can experience (and can be experienced in) their hunger, thirst, nakedness, imprisonment, illness, and loneliness.

Further, from within the world of Matthew's Gospel, those who are celebrated for having performed good deeds for the Son of Man are quite unaware of having done so. They don't know this story! "When did we see you . . . ?" These "sheep" among the *ethne* apparently had never received the memo about the sheep and the goats. Thus, they are not within Matthew's community; they really are the *ethne* who apparently are unaware of Matthew's Gospel. They are entirely clueless about the Son of Man having been present through the vulnerable presence of "the least of his brothers and sisters." Correspondingly, these surprised *ethne* cannot really include us as we read and preach this passage, for we do know the story. Thus, it would

---

of the unrestricted interpretation of "the least of these," see McMahon, "Christology, the Poor, and Surpassing Righteousness."

8. Gray, *The Least of My Brothers*, 354.

seem difficult for Matthew to imagine that anyone among the nations would have an "inside track" on the Son of Man's criteria for judgment. Only his "least of these," his disciples sent out into those nations to proclaim, teach, and perform the good news, would already be privy to this story of final judgment. Thus the Christians in this scenario, those who know about the presence of the Son of Man—which is to say, "the Eleven" and all of their missionary company, representing Jesus's renewed Israel—can only be "the least of these." Accordingly, Warren Carter cites a barrage of Hebrew canonical and apocryphal texts (Joel 3:1–3; Dan 7:9–27; 1 En. 62–63; 4 Ezra 7:31–44; 2 Bar. 72–74) that evoke great judgment scenes, adding, "The scenes are usually presented from the perspective of the underdog."[9] But it is not simply that of the underdog; it is that of those under God, that is, the people of God, Israel. Let the Joel passage suffice to illustrate this point: "in those days and at that time, when I restore the fortunes of Judah and Jerusalem, I will gather all the nations and bring them down to the valley of Jehoshaphat, and I will enter into judgment with them there, on account of my people and my heritage Israel, because they have scattered them among the nations" (3:1–2). To be sure, in Matthew 25 the scattering of Israel among the nations is the expression of God's will, but the criterion of judgment still involves the nations' treatment of God's people, God's wisdom community. As Stanton notes, "If this 'particularist' interpretation is adopted, the pericope has the same general purpose as many apocalyptic writings: to offer consolation and encouragement to minority communities who are hard-pressed by the dominant society which surrounds them and ... is perceived to be threatening."[10]

Scenarios of Final Judgment: The Talmud

Such judgment scenarios are not limited to the apocalyptic era. Consider the following rabbinic embellishment on judgment-scene literature, found in the Talmudic document *Avodah Zarah* ("strange worship"), in a story attributed to teachers who lived in the third century of the Christian era. In this judgment scenario, God will step forth, embracing a scroll of the Torah scroll, and announce, "Let him who has occupied himself with the Torah come and receive his reward!" The heavenly scene is riddled with chaos, great numbers of people milling around uncertainly, for "all the nations

9. Carter, *Matthew and the Margins*, 491.
10. Stanton, *A Gospel for a New People*, 208.

[i.e., gentile ethnicities] will crowd together in confusion."[11] This seems comparable to "the nations" in Matthew 25 who, even divided into sheep and goats, all express at least a measure of confusion: "Lord, when . . . ?" In *Avodah Zara* 2b, the Holy One responds to the madding crowd: "Do not come before Me in confusion, but let each nation come in with its scribes."

The first nation to enter is Rome. "Why them? Because they are the most important." In true rabbinic style, the counter-question is asked, "How do we know they are so important?" and is answered by scriptural appeal. "Because it is written, 'And he shall devour the whole earth and shall tread it down and break it in pieces' (Dan. 7:23) and Rabbi Johanan says that this refers to Rome, whose power is known to the whole world."

So the Holy One, Torah scroll cradled in his arm, interrogates Rome: "'What have you been doing with yourselves?' They will reply: 'O Lord of the Universe, we have established many marketplaces, we have built many baths, we have accumulated much gold and silver, and all this we did only for the sake of Israel, that they might [have leisure] for occupying themselves with the study of the Torah.'" Unimpeded by their sizable lie, God unveils the truth: "'You foolish ones among the peoples, all that you have done has been done only to satisfy your own desires. You have established marketplaces to place courtesans therein; baths, to revel in them; [as to the distribution of] silver and gold, that is mine'"—and like a good rabbinic scholar, God establishes divine ownership by citing Scripture: "As it is written: 'Mine is the silver and mine is the gold,' says the Lord of Hosts" (Hag 2:8). Referring to this text from Haggai (and, by extension, to all of Jewish Scripture), God then asks the Romans, "Are there any among you who have been declaring *this*?" At this, the rabbis speculated, "The Romans will then depart crushed in spirit." Similarly, the goats of Matthew 25 are commanded by the Son of Man to "depart from me" (25:41).

In *Avodah Zara* another gentile people, the Persians, step up next, "Why Persia next? Because they are next in importance. And how do we know this?" ask the rabbis. "Because it is written, 'And behold another beast, a second like unto a bear'" (Dan 7:5), and "Rabbi Joseph learned that this refers to the Persians" because, in Rabbi Joseph's estimation, they "eat and drink greedily like a bear." But one rabbi asks the logical question: "Why would the Persians, having seen Rome humiliated, even step forward

---

11. All citations of this Talmudic tale are from https://www.sefaria.org/Avodah_Zarah?lang=bi.

at all?" But there is an answer! "They will say to themselves: 'The Romans have destroyed the Temple, whereas we have built it.'"

So the Holy One interrogates the Persians. "What have you been doing with yourselves?" Persia will reply, "Sovereign of the Universe, we have built many bridges, we have captured many cities, we have waged many wars, and all this for the sake of Israel, that they might engage in the study of the Torah." God, however, is no more fooled by the Persians than he was by the Romans, and answers in kind: "You foolish ones among the peoples, you have built bridges in order to extract toll, you have subdued cities, so as to impose forced labor; as to waging war, I am the Lord of battles, as it is said: 'The Lord is a man of war' (Ex. 15:3). Are there any amongst you who have been declaring *this*?" This scribal God who quotes Scripture to the nations puts them in their proper place. "The Persians, too, will then depart crushed in spirit."

The rabbis imagine that every nation, every gentile people, will fare equally poorly in the presence of the God of the Torah. Why would they even dare to step up before God? "They will say to themselves: 'The others have oppressed Israel, but we have not.'" But none of these peoples has engaged with God's Torah. Note the stunning contrast in the criteria of judgment against the nations: in the Talmud it is the question of what the gentile peoples have done with the Torah; in Matthew it is the question of what they have done with "the least of these my brothers and sisters." In one scenario, the Judge stands as the Torah scribe, impervious; in the other, the Judge stands as one who has been radically vulnerable: hungry, thirsty, alienated, naked, sick, imprisoned. In one scenario, none of the people of the *ethne* are rewarded; in the other, there are sheep among the peoples who are welcomed into "the kingdom prepared for you from the foundation of the world" (Matt 25:34).

In *Avodah Zara*'s often humorously imaginative judgment scene, the criterion invariably is faithfulness to the Torah. God is imagined as a great rabbinic figure, a Torah scroll tucked under his arm, loaded with biblical citations and superior arguments. For all of the ingenious legal arguments and loopholes that the scribes of each nation can muster, finally the rabbis imagine that all of the gentile peoples are put to shame. The nations even lobby for another chance at obeying the Torah, and God relents, commanding them simply to build *sukkot* or little huts for an eschatological Festival of Booths. They do so, but then God sends the burning heat of the midday sun to practically cook them in their huts. They storm out, hot and bothered, and trample their huts underfoot. Even with such a simple command, the nations prove themselves unworthy. The rabbinic argument is that there are years when Israel's Festival of Booths occurred during hot seasons, so surely the gentiles should be able to handle it. When one scribe observes that there is an earlier rabbinic ruling that exempted the Jews from staying in their *sukkot* if the weather got too hot, he is met with the reply, "Yes, but would the children of Israel stamp upon their huts contemptuously?" No further questions; the prosecution rests.

It is difficult to date precisely when a story like this might have developed, though the Talmud itself, as mentioned earlier, places it in the early third century. It undoubtedly had precedents. There may even have been earlier versions of it contemporary with Matthew or even earlier, in Jesus's time and before. The point is not to try to trace some particular influence of one story on another; it is to indicate that such stories of final judgment, in which God's justice is properly levelled against the world's *ethne*, were part of a common literary and theological atmosphere in the centuries surrounding Jesus's time of ministry. Such stories are a form of theodicy, offering a future scenario that will compensate for the past and present injustices suffered by God's chosen. For the rabbis, the ultimate criterion for this judgment was the Torah and its community; for Matthew, that criterion is the lowly-but-glorified Son of Man and his community, "the least of these my brothers and sisters." This is the Wisdom community that has built itself upon the rock of practicing the words that Jesus has spoken.

Interpreting Matthew 25 Today

We can grant with John P. Meier that "this point is hotly disputed."[12] Indeed, Meier champions the alternative interpretation, i.e., that "the criterion for the [judgment] is not constituted by church membership"—an odd way to put the matter—"but by the deeds of love and mercy shown to the poor and outcast of mankind," and thus "in terms of what we do to the Son of Man in everyman."[13] But where in the world, we might ask, does he get this notion of "the Son of Man in everyman"? To make that argument is to ignore all of the Matthean texts, cited above, about Jesus's brothers and sisters and especially "the little ones" among them. Further, while "the Son of Man" in Daniel, as well as in the Synoptic Gospels, does often carry a

12. Meier, *The Vision of Matthew*, 178, n. 206.
13. Meier, *The Vision of Matthew*, 178.

social connotation, it is never associated with some universally shared human essence but instead with the community of Israel. That is, the Son of Man is identified with, and can be identified by, association with a particular representative people. Nonetheless, Meier is not alone. I recall the first time, during my seminary days, that I heard this more restricted, ecclesial interpretation of "the least of these." Having been schooled in a liberationist hermeneutic, I did not like it at all. We may prefer to imagine Jesus more romantically dwelling among and within all the hungry, the thirsty, the homeless, the imprisoned, the naked, the displaced and marginalized throughout the world. For example, Anna Case-Winters writes in this vein to fellow Christian believers, "Christ is already in our midst now and comes to us again and again—unexpectedly—in the form of the person in need. Our response to 'the least of these' is our response to the judge of all the nations."[14] This is a more inclusive and universalist Jesus, and we may be happier to love and serve this somewhat anonymous Jesus who dwells among and within the poor and oppressed. Further, if indeed Matthew is describing the judgment of the world's *ethne* by the standard of how and to what extent they welcomed Jesus's disciples, we may be troubled by what seems to be the self-serving nature of this standard: someday the gentile peoples of the world will be judged by how they treated us Christians?

Two considerations suggest themselves. First, rather than rejecting this more particularist interpretation of Matthew 25, we might ask about what happened historically such that most Christians today do not readily identify themselves as "the least" of Jesus's brothers and sisters. How is it that, over the generations since Jesus told the story, Christians increasingly became the comfortable and wealthy people with the resources to feed the hungry, clothe the naked, visit the imprisoned, etc.—rather than being the people in need of food, clothes, and a roof over our head? Why have so few of us (there are some!) sacrificed our resources and energies such that we have become, even metaphorically, the naked, the homeless, the hungry, the imprisoned? Granted, we live in a very different social world than did Jesus and his Matthean disciples near the end of the first century. We—I speak as a North American to a British audience in the comfortable confines of an academic institution—tend not today to be the vulnerable, the hungry, the imprisoned, the endangered. But why not? This may be a more serious word of judgment than most of us want to acknowledge, let alone

---

14. Case-Winters, *Matthew*, 281.

consider. How have we come to be so comfortable with our comfortable lives? (I speak to myself here.)

Let me put it another, but similar, way. If this reading of the passage is on target, then "the least of these my brothers and sisters" were Jewish disciples of Jesus, having been sent out into the gentile world of *ethne*. In their mission they experienced hardships like hunger, thirst, illness, imprisonment, alienation, and homelessness. In this eschatological scenario, the *ethne* are judged by their responses to these weak and vulnerable siblings of Jesus. In one sense, then, this scenario describes the historical situation of nearly two thousand years ago. We in this room and on this campus, these many generations later, are the spiritual descendants and heirs of *ethne* who, at least to some significant extent, welcomed those Jewish messengers and so welcomed the Son of Man who sent them—and who were transformed by this encounter. We are descendants of the "sheep," the gentile people(s) who, to one extent or another, said "yes" to this Jewish figure who, as Matthew cites Isaiah, would be one in whom the gentiles would hope. If this be true, then it certainly raises a question regarding how we might properly interpret this eschatological scenario in Matthew 25 today, in our time.

The second consideration may in fact hold something of an answer to this question. In chapter 3 we explored Augustine's rule of biblical interpretation, based on words unique to Matthew: "On these two commands [love for God and love for neighbor] hang all the Law—and the Prophets." Augustine argued, accordingly, that the entirety of Scripture "hangs" on these two commands, such that the purpose of the Bible in every passage and place, ultimately, is to nurture greater love for God and all people. He brilliantly acknowledged that it is impossible for any reader to know the mind of the biblical author, and in any case there is a surplus of meaning in any text that might well exceed what the author imagined as he or she wrote. Thus, while attempting to approximate as best we can what it seems to us that Matthew's Gospel "means" when it speaks of "the nations" and "the least of these" is a worthy undertaking, if we follow Augustine's lead we cannot be content with this. There can be many meanings, wrote Augustine, "all of which [may be] true"—but the *truest*, he insisted, is the reading that, in our judgment, is most generative of greater love for God and all neighbors. "You should take pains to turn over and over in your mind what you read, until your interpretation of it is led right through to the kingdom of love"[15]—and of course Matthew 25 would be no exception

---

15. Augustine, *De Doctrina Christiana*, 179. Hill's translation actually employs the

to this hermeneutic. Which reading, at least among first-world, generally well-off Christians of Western Europe and North America, actually nurtures greater and deeper love for God and all neighbors: the ecclesial one that I have argued is Matthew's meaning, or the more inclusive one that has become typical in the past century? Just as Augustine wrote of Moses's intent in writing the opening of Genesis, perhaps we could acknowledge that Matthew did not have in mind all of the meanings we might find in the story of the sheep and the goats—but that these meanings are nonetheless true, because they nurture a greater and deeper love for all people.

If we require any further encouragement in this direction, we in the Wesleyan tradition may draw upon our theological guide John Wesley, who in Sermon IV of his series "Upon Our Lord's Sermon on the Mount" proclaimed: "[W]hether [the hungry and naked] will finally be lost or saved, you are expressly commanded to feed the hungry and clothe the naked. If you can and do not, whatever becomes of them, you shall go away into everlasting fire."[16] Those are some serious words. At this point, nearing the end both of this chapter and of this book, I will not try to reconcile the judgment of "everlasting fire" with the overarching theme of these lectures, that divine Wisdom is "gentle and humble in heart." But we can surmise that if indeed the Creator and Sustainer of all things *is* "gentle and humble in heart," then that is, ultimately, the grain of the universe. The proud, the hoarding, the boastful, the hard-hearted are finally and deeply out of step with the way things truly are. Perhaps the fiery judgment of the eschaton consists in their experiencing, directly, all the hunger, thirst, alienation, nakedness and suffering of "the little ones" that they mistreated, persistently ignored, or further belittled during their earthly lives. Perhaps the experience will be enough to destroy them. In at least some cases, that would probably be a mercy.

I turn to the rabbis one final time for a little help on this matter. Later in the same passage as we have explored above, Rabbi Simeon ben Lakish says of that bright sun of judgment upon the nations:

> There is no Gehenna in the Future World, but the Holy One, blessed be He, brings the sun out of its sheath, so that it is fierce: the wicked are punished by it, the righteous are healed by it. The wicked are punished by it, as it is said: "For, behold, the day is coming when the sun burns like a furnace; and all the proud, and

---

word "charity" rather than "love."

16. Outler and Heitzenrater, eds., *John Wesley's Sermons*, 204.

all who work wickedness, shall be stubble; and that coming day will set them ablaze," saith the Lord of Hosts, "that it shall leave them neither root nor branch." It shall leave them neither root—in this world, nor branch—in the world to come. [Meanwhile,] the righteous are healed by it, as it is said, "But unto you that fear My name, shall the sun of righteousness arise with healing in its wings." (*Avodah Zarah* 3b)

May we, as those who venture to consider ourselves members of the community of divine Wisdom incarnate, be willing to live in such a way as to be among the least of Jesus's brothers and sisters. May the bright shining of God's love heal us rather than burn us to stubble. It is Wisdom divine, after all, who beckons us: *Come unto me . . . take my yoke upon you, and learn from me, for I am gentle and humble in heart."* May it be so, both now and in the collective living of the church of tomorrow.

Bibliography

Akhtar, Shabbir. *The New Testament in Muslim Eyes: Paul's Letter to the Galatians*. London: Routledge, 2018.
Allison, Dale C. *The New Moses: A Matthean Typology*. Edinburgh: T. & T. Clark, 1993.
Andersen, Francis I., and David Noel Freedman. *Hosea: A New Translation with Introduction and Commentary*. Anchor Bible 24. Garden City, NY: Doubleday, 1980.
Armstrong, Karen. *The Great Transformation: The World in the Time of Buddha, Socrates, Confucius and Jeremiah*. New York: Knopf, 2006.
Augustine. *Confessions*. Translated and edited by Philip Burton. London: Everyman, 2001.
———. *De Doctrina Christiana*, or *Teaching Christianity*. In *The Works of Saint Augustine: A Translation for the 21st Century*, I/11, introduction, translation, and notes by Edmund Hill, O.P. Hyde Park, NY: New City, 1996.
Borg, Marcus. *Jesus: A New Vision*. San Francisco: Harper & Row, 1987.
Borowitz, Eugene. *Contemporary Christologies: A Jewish Response*. Mahwah, NJ: Paulist, 1980.
Buber, Martin. *Between Man and Man*. Translated by Ronald Gregor Smith. 3rd ed. London: Collins, 1947.
Carter, Warren. *Matthew and the Margins: A Sociopolitical and Religious Reading*. Maryknoll, NY: Orbis, 2000.
Case-Winters, Anna. *Matthew*. Belief: A Theological Commentary on the Bible. Louisville, KY: Westminster John Knox, 2015.
Coakley, Sarah. *God, Sexuality, and the Self: An Essay 'On the Trinity'*. Cambridge: Cambridge University Press, 2013.
Cullmann, Oscar. *Peter: Disciple, Apostle, Martyr*. Philadelphia: Westminster, 1953.
Davies, Brian, and G. R. Evans, eds. *Anselm of Canterbury: The Major Works*. Oxford University Press, 1998.
Davies, W. D., and Dale Allison. *A Critical and Exegetical Commentary on The Gospel according to Saint Matthew*, Vol. II. ICC. Edinburgh: T. & T. Clark, 1991.
Denny, Frederick M. *Islam and the Muslim Community*. Prospect Heights, IL: Waveland, 1987.
Firestone, Reuven. "Sakina." In *The Encyclopedia of the Qur'an*, Vol. 4, edited by Jane Dammens McAuliffe, 589–91. Leiden: Brill Academic, 2004.

Bibliography

Ford, David F., and C. C. Pecknold, eds. *The Promise of Scriptural Reasoning.* Oxford: Wiley-Blackwell, 2007.

Frymer-Kensy, Tivka. "Deuteronomy." In *The Women's Bible Commentary*, edited by Carol A. Newsom and Sharon H. Ringe, 52–62. Louisville: Westminster John Knox, 1992.

Gray, Sherman W. *The Least of My Brothers: Matthew 25:31–46, a History of Interpretation.* SBLDS. Atlanta: Scholars, 1989.

Gregory of Nazianzus. *On God and Christ: The Five Theological Orations and Two Letters to Cledonius.* Yonkers, NY: St. Vladimir's Seminary, 2002.

Griffin, David Ray, ed. *Deep Religious Pluralism.* Louisville, KY: Westminster John Knox, 2005.

Harrington, Daniel J., S.J. *The Gospel of Matthew.* Sacra Pagina Series. Collegeville, MN: Liturgical, 1991.

Hartman, David. *A Living Covenant: The Innovative Spirit in Traditional Judaism.* New York: Free, 1985.

Hill, David. *The Gospel of Matthew.* The New Century Bible Commentary. Grand Rapids: Eerdmans, 1972.

Heschel, Abraham Joshua. *The Prophets.* New York: Harper & Row, 1962.

Jantzen, Grace. *Becoming Divine: Towards a Feminist Philosophy of Religion.* Bloomington, IN: Indiana University Press, 1999.

———. *Power, Gender and Christian Mysticism.* Cambridge: Cambridge University Press, 1996.

Johnson, Elizabeth. *Consider Jesus: Waves of Renewal in Christology.* New York: Herder & Herder, 1992.

———. "Wisdom Was Made Flesh and Pitched Her Tent among Us." In *Reconstructing the Christ Symbol: Essays in Feminist Christology*, edited by Maryanne Stevens, 95–117. Eugene, OR: Wipf & Stock, 2001.

Justin the Martyr. *The First Apology*, in *Library of Christian Classics, Vol. I: Early Christian Fathers.* Translated and edited by Cyril C. Richardson. Philadelphia: Westminster, 1953.

Kasemann, Ernst. *Jesus Means Freedom.* Philadelphia: Fortress, 1968.

Keller, Catherine. "Salvation Flows: Eschatology for a Feminist Wesleyanism." *Quarterly Review* 23.4 (2003) 412–24.

Kierkegaard, Søren. *Practice in Christianity.* Edited and translated by Howard V. Hong and Edna H. Hong. Princeton, NJ: Princeton University Press, 1991.

Kingsbury, Jack Dean. *Matthew.* 3rd ed. Nappanee, IN: Evangel, 1998.

Kupp, David D. *Matthew's Emmanuel: Divine Presence and God's People in the First Gospel.* Cambridge: Cambridge University Press, 2005.

Lee, Bernard. *Conversations on the Road Not Taken*, Vol. 1, *The Galilean Jewishness of Jesus: Retrieving the Jewish Origins of Christianity.* Mahwah, NJ: Paulist, 1988.

———. *Conversations on the Road Not Taken*, Vol. 2, *Jesus and the Metaphors of God: The Christs of the New Testament.* Mahwah, NJ: Paulist, 1993.

Lodahl, Michael E. "'And He Felt Compassion: Holiness beyond the Bounds of Community." In *Embodied Holiness: Toward a Corporate Theology of Spiritual Growth*, edited by Samuel M. Powell and Michael E. Lodahl, 145–65. Downers Grove, IL: InterVarsity, 1999.

———. *Claiming Abraham: Reading the Bible and the Qur'an Side-by-Side.* Grand Rapids: Brazos, 2010.

Bibliography

———. *Shekhinah/Spirit: Divine Presence in Jewish and Christian Religion*. Mahwah, NJ: Paulist, 1992.

———. "To Whom Belong the Covenants? Whitehead, Wesley, and Wildly Diverse Religious Traditions." In *Deep Religious Pluralism*, edited by David Ray Griffin, 193–209. Louisville, KY: Westminster John Knox, 2005.

Lohfink, Gerhard. *Does God Need the Church? Toward a Theology of the People of God*. Collegeville, MN: Liturgical, 1999.

———. *Jesus and Community*. Philadelphia: Fortress, 1984.

Luz, Ulrich. *The Theology of the Gospel of Matthew*. Cambridge: Cambridge University Press, 1993.

McMahon, Christopher. "Christology, the Poor, and Surpassing Righteousness: Reading Matthew 25:31–46 with 26:6–13." *Revue Biblique* 123.4 (2016) 554–66.

Meier, John P. *The Vision of Matthew: Christ, Church and Morality in the First Gospel*. New York: Paulist, 1979.

Mitchell, Matthew W. "The Yoke Is Easy, but What of Its Meaning? A Methodological Reflection Masquerading as a Philological Discussion of Matthew 11:30." *Journal of Biblical Literature* 135.2 (2016), 321–40.

Montague, George T. *Companion God: A Cross-Cultural Commentary on the Gospel of Matthew*. Mahwah, NJ: Paulist, 2010.

Murphree, Mark A. "'Pure Religion and Undefiled': A Wesleyan Analysis of Ibn Tufail's *The Improvement of Human Reason*." *Wesleyan Theological Journal* 48.1 (2013) 106–16.

Ochs, Peter. *Another Reformation: Postliberal Christianity and the Jews*. Grand Rapids: Baker Academic, 2011.

Ochs, Peter, and Nancy Levene, eds. *Textual Reasonings: Jewish Philosophy and Text Study at the End of the Twentieth Century*. Grand Rapids: Eerdmans, 2003.

Outler, Albert C., and Richard P. Heitzenrater, eds. *John Wesley's Sermons: An Anthology*. Nashville: Abingdon, 1991.

Overman, J. Andrew. *Church and Community in Crisis: The Gospel according to Matthew*. The New Testament in Context Commentaries. Valley Forge, PA: Trinity, 1996.

Placher, William C. *Narratives of a Vulnerable God: Christ, Theology, and Scripture*. Louisville: Westminster John Knox, 1994.

Pregeant, Russell. *Christology beyond Dogma: Matthew's Christ in Process Hermeneutic*. Philadelphia: Fortress, 1987.

Rambo, Shelley. *Resurrecting Wounds: Living in the Afterlife of Trauma*. Waco, TX: Baylor University Press, 2018.

Robinson, John A. T. *The Body: A Study in Pauline Theology*. Philadelphia: Westminster, 1977.

Saldarini, Anthony J. *Matthew's Christian-Jewish Community*. Chicago: The University of Chicago Press, 1994.

Samely, Alexander. *Rabbinic Interpretation of Scripture in the Mishnah*. Oxford: Oxford University Press, 2002.

Schafer, Peter. *Jesus in the Talmud*. Princeton, NJ: Princeton University Press, 2000.

Schnackenburg, Rudolph. *The Gospel of Matthew*. Grand Rapids: Eerdmans, 2002.

Sievers, Joseph. "'Where Two or Three . . .': The Rabbinic Concept of *Shekhinah* and Matthew 18:20." In *Standing before God: Studies on Prayer in Scriptures and in Tradition with Essays, in Honor of John M. Oesterreicher*, edited by Asher Finkel and Lawrence Frizzell, 171–82. New York: Ktav, 1981.

BIBLIOGRAPHY

Sim, David C. *The Gospel of Matthew and Christian Judaism: The History and Social Setting of the Matthean Community.* Edinburgh: T. & T. Clark, 1998.

Stanton, Graham M. *A Gospel for a New People: Studies in Matthew.* Louisville: Westminster John Knox, 1992.

Stevens, Maryanne, ed. *Reconstructing the Christ Symbol: Essays in Feminist Christology.* Eugene, OR: Wipf & Stock, 2001.

Suchocki, Marjorie Hewitt. *Divinity and Diversity: A Christian Affirmation of Religious Pluralism.* Nashville: Abingdon, 2003.

———. *In God's Presence: Theological Reflections on Prayer.* St. Louis: Chalice, 1996.

Suggs, M. J. *Wisdom, Christology and Law in Matthew's Gospel.* Cambridge: Harvard University Press, 1970.

van Buren, Paul. *A Theology of the Jewish-Christian Reality,* vol. 1, *Discerning the Way*; vol. 2, *A Christian Theology of the People Israel*; vol. 3, *Christ in Context.* San Francisco: Harper & Row, 1980, 1984, and 1988.

Wesley, John. *A Plain Account of Christian Perfection.* Kansas City, MO: Beacon Hill, 1966.

———. *Works.* London: Wesleyan Conference Office, 1872.

Whitehead, Alfred North. *Process and Reality.* Edited by David Ray Griffin and Donald W. Sherburne. New York: Free, 1978.

Yates, Kelly Diehl. "The Wesleyan Trilateral: Prevenient Grace, Catholic Spirit, and Religious Tolerance." *Wesleyan Theological Journal* 48.1 (2013) 54–61.

Name/Subject Index

Akhtar, Shabbir, xivn1, xivn2, 36n4
Allison, Dale, 134–35
Andersen, Francis I., 20n7
Anselm, 29–32
Arminius, Jacob, 73, 144
Armstrong, Karen, 73n14
Athanasius, 151
atonement, doctrine of, 27–32
Augustine, 42–49, 152, 158–59
Augustus, 84
ayat in the Qur'an, 59–60

bat kol (heavenly voice), 3
binding and loosing, 89–96
Basil of Caesarea, 152
Bonhoeffer, Dietrich, 55
Borg, Marcus, 20
Borowitz, Eugene, 79–80
Brueggemann, Walter, 118
Buber, Martin, 36, 41, 46, 76

Carter, Warren, 12–13, 24, 29, 36n5,
    66n1, 67, 68, 70, 84–85, 105,
    115, 118, 121n7, 126, 129–30,
    144n23, 153
Case-Winters, Anna, 129, 157
'cheap grace,' 55
Christology, low, 84
Christos (anointed one), 83–84
Coakley, Sarah, 10n16
Crowther, Daniel J., xiv1, xiv2
Cullmann, Oscar, 85n8

Cunningham Leclerc, Diane, 47n29

Davies, W.D., 102, 103, 104, 106
Denny, Frederick, 107, 108

Elijah, 82
eschatology, 65, 69, 141–44, 146–60
    as theodicy, 156
eunuchs, 126–27
evangelism, 56, 62–65, 79–80, 135–36

Firestone, Reuven, 107–8
flesh, 118–19
Freedman, David Noel, 20n7
Frymer-Kensy, Tivka, 117

Glaser, Ida, xiv1, xiv2
Golden Rule, 69–77
Gray, Sherman W., 151–52
Gregory of Nazianzus, 95, 152
Gregory of Nyssa, 152

Harrington, Daniel, 6, 18, 24, 82, 84,
    87–88, 98n2, 99, 147, 150n5
Hartman, David, 92
Heschel, Abraham, 23n8, 24
hesed, 21–23, 62
Heim, Mark, 57n16
Heitzenrater, Richard, 159n16
Herod, 84
Hill, David, 70n9, 86, 89n14
Hillel, 39–40, 48, 76, 115

Name/Subject Index

Hutcheson, Francis, 73

Ibn Tufail, 111n30
incarnation, 60, 95, 119
Irenaeus, 151

Jantzen, Grace, 10n16
Jaspers, Karl, 73n14
Jeremiah, 82-83
Jerome, 152
Johanan, 154
John the Baptist, 2-6, 58n17
John Chrysostom, 152
Johnson, Elizabeth A., 11, 28, 82
Johnson, M.D., 10n15
Justin Martyr, 123, 125

Kasemann, Ernst, 29
Keller, Catherine, 142
Kierkegaard, Søren, 1-2, 16
Kingsbury, Jack Dean, 42
Kupp, David D., 102-3, 104, 106

Lee, Bernard, 15n25
Levinas, Emmanuel, 76
little ones, 149-51
Lohfink, Gerhard, 7, 13-14, 62, 136
Luther, Martin, 93
Luz, Ulrich, 53n7, 68, 92, 93

Madigan, Daniel, S.J., xivn2
McMahon, Christopher, 151-52n7
Meier, John P., 28, 42, 49n34, 67, 85n7, 139, 156-57
mishpat, 64-65
Mitchell, Matthew W., 16n26
Montague, George, 18-19
Mormon, Book of, 51n2, 54n9
Murphree, Mark A., 111n30

Ochs, Peter, 107n20
Oord, Thomas Jay, xivn1
oral Torah, 104
Origen, 127, 152
Outler, Albert, 159n16
Overman, J. Andrew, 51, 72

patriarchy, 10, 117-18

Paul, 88-89, 106
Peter, 85-90, 92-94
Pharisees, 11, 14-15, 18-26, 113-16
Philo, 34n1
Placher, William, 132, 134
Plato, 46
Pregeant, Russell, 60, 70n12
prevenient grace, 73-80, 110-11

qadosh, 54

Rambo, Shelley, 128n1
Rashi, 43
religious pluralism, 56-60, 136-39
resurrection, 128-32
revelation, 94-96, 109
Robinson, John A.T., 151n6

Sabbath, 23-26
Sabeans (in the Qur'an), 58n17
Sadducees, 123-24
sakina, 107-11
Saldarini, Anthony, 134
Samely, Alexander, 121n8
Schafer, Peter, 19n5
Schnackenburg, Rudolph, 34n1, 59n19, 68
Schweizer, Eduard, 54n8, 55n10, 56n13, 61, 62
Scriptural Reasoning, 107
Senior, Donald, 51
Shafaie, Shirin, xivn1, xivn2
Shammai, 39-40, 115
Shekhinah, 100-111
Sievers, Joseph, 100, 102, 104
Sim, David, 39
Simeon ben Lakish, 159-60
social grace, 110-11
Stanton, Graham, 8-12, 153
Stendahl, Krister, 70
Suchocki, Marjorie Hewitt, 56, 123, 138
Suggs, Jack, 5, 8

teleios, 54-55
Thomas Aquinas, 152
Tillich, Paul, 38
Trible, Phyllis, 118

Name/Subject Index

Trinity, God as, 84, 139–40

van Buren, Paul, 15n25, 90
Vulcan mind-meld, 47

Welch, Reuben, 46
Wenham, David, 52n5
Wesley, Charles, 39n6
Wesley, John, 38, 55–56, 59n18, 72–80, 100, 106, 110–11, 129, 141–45, 159

Whitehead, Alfred North, 141
Wisdom (divine), 4–16, 22–26, 60–65, 66–67, 89, 94–96, 98–99, 105, 109–12, 122–25, 135, 142, 150, 160
wisdom tradition, 59–60, 66–70
witness of the Spirit, 106

Yates, Kelly, 111n30

Scripture Index

OLD TESTAMENT

Genesis
1:1	43
1:3	43n16
9:9–17	118

Exodus
3:1—4:17	123–25
19:6	19, 69
19:18	34
24:3–8	29, 52

Leviticus
19:2	35, 54
19:17	35
19:18	35–36, 53, 121
19:33–34	35–37, 57
21:20	126

Deuteronomy
6:4–6	34, 37, 38, 40–41
7:1–6	53
19:15	103
20:1–18	53, 120–22
23:1	126
23:25	24
24:1–4	115, 117, 120
28	19
30:12–14	90, 91, 94

1 Samuel
15:2–22	21
15:22–23	20

2 Chronicles
32:8	118–19

Psalms
8:5	133
51:16–17	20, 27
77:16–19	84
82:1	101
104:30	144
139:19–22	53

Proverbs
8:27–31	6
9:1–4	67
9:4–6	6

Isaiah
11:9	141
40:6	118
42:1–7	63–65
56:3–5	126–27
58:6, 7	119

Scripture Index

Jeremiah

7:3–7	82
17:5	118–19
18:19	46

Ezekiel

36:26	119

Daniel

7:5	154
7:10	147
7:13–14	133–35, 140
7:22	147
7:23	154

Hosea

4:1–3	21
4:4–9	22
5:6	21
6:6	17, 22, 26, 27, 31, 61
11:8	22

Joel

3:1–2	153

Micah

6:5–8	75, 76

Haggai

2:8	154

Zechariah

9:9–11	28

Wisdom of Solomon

8:4	6
8:7–8	6

Sirach

14:20–25	67
20:4	126

24:1	8
24:5	7
24:7–8	7, 97
24:19	7
24:22–25	7–8
31:15	70n8
40:1	12
51:23–27	7–8

Tobit

4:15	70n8

NEW TESTAMENT

Matthew

1:21–23	69, 140
1:24	97
2:17	82
3:2	3
3:10–12	3
3:14	2
3:16–17	2
4:8	129
4:17	3
5–7	50
5:1	52, 129
5:14–16	52–53, 59, 69, 79, 129, 136, 138
5:17–19	50–51, 69, 120
5:20	50, 51
5:21–38	53, 60
5:23–24	60–62
5:32	115
5:43	53
5:43–48	37, 51, 53–56, 70, 72, 73, 122, 138
5:44	22
5:46	59
6:15	78
7:12	40, 69, 120
7:13–14	57, 71, 148
7:15–23	82
7:21–28	57, 147–48

Scripture Index

Matthew (continued)

7:21	52n6, 67, 72, 82, 149
7:22	67
7:24–26	66, 67, 72, 77–78, 86
7:28	67
7:29	133, 148
8:1	129
8:9	133
8:11–12	79
9:6	133
9:9	18
9:11	17
9:12–13	20
9:36	12
10:5–6	63, 149
10:20	140
10:40–42	149
11:2	2, 3, 10
11:5–6	4
11:11	4
11:14	4
11:15	4n3
11:18–19	4, 11
11:25–27	6, 9, 11, 84, 139
11:28–30	1–2, 7, 9, 11–16, 63, 68, 72, 134, 137, 141, 159, 160
12:1	17, 23
12:2	24
12:7	17, 24
12:9	25
12:14	27, 31
12:15–16	62
12:18–21	63, 135
12:19	9
12:21	65
12:28	139
12:32	139
12:46–50	149
13:52	103, 123
14:23	129
14:27–33	84
15:29	129
16:13–20	81–90
16:16–27	77
16:17–19	85, 86, 89, 93, 94
16:21–23	94
17:1	129
18:4–6	98, 150–51
18:11	150
18:14	151
18:16–17	98, 103
18:17–18	92–93, 98
18:19	93, 98
18:20	93, 99, 101–11, 125, 140
19:3–9	113–22
19:10	115
19:11–12	125, 127
19:28	139, 147
20:25–28	13, 137
21:23	133
21:33–41	27–28
21:45	27
22:15–22	33–34
22:23–33	33–34
22:31	123
22:34–40	33–34, 39–49, 51, 120, 158
22:40	50, 69
22:41–46	34
23:2–3	14, 125n13, 137
23:3–7	15, 137
23:8–10	93
23:11	137
23:12	15
23:34–36	5–6, 28
23:37	10, 25, 28, 82
24:3	129
25:31–46	140, 146–53, 155–60
26:27–28	28, 52, 78
27:9	82
28:1–10	129
28:10	149
28:2–4	130
28:16–20	64, 65, 69
28:17	130
28:18	133
28:19	139
28:20	67, 80, 97, 134, 140, 152

Scripture Index

Mark

2:17	26
3:5	26
8:27–30	81n1, 83
10:2–12	113–122
12:1–12	27–28
12:28–34	34
13:11	140n11

Luke

6:27–36	37, 71
6:46	67
7:26	4n3
7:31–35	4
7:35	5
9:18–21	81n1, 83
10:25–37	34–37
11:49–51	5–6
12:12	140n11
12:48	78
20:9–19	27–28
20:37	123
21:15	140n11
24:16–35	131

John

1:1–14	44
1:18	37
1:42	86n9
5:10	47
6:31	79
6:56–68	81n1
14:6	46
19:30	50
20:15–18	131
20:19–29	128
20:23	93
21:12	131

Acts

10:34–35	79
10:38	83–84, 140
10:40–41	131
17:26–27	75, 79
17:28	73

Romans

2:14–15	77
3:29	22
5:19	30
8:24	132
10:5–10	90n16
10:9	68
13:8–10	32, 40n8

1 Corinthians

1:12	88
1:18–25	128
3:4	88
3:10–11	88
3:15–17	88
3:21	88
4:6	47, 88
13:12	46, 47

2 Corinthians

5:7	132

Galatians

2:6	88
2:11–14	88
6:17	45

Colossians

1:24	151

1 Timothy

1:5	43
1:5–8	45

2 Timothy

2:14	43

Hebrews

5:8–9	16

1 John

4:12	37

Scripture Index

Talmud

Pirkei Avot 3	100
Mishnah Avot 3	101n7
Baba Mesia 59b	91–92
Shabbat 31a	40
Yoma 8:6	24
Avodah Zara 2b	153–56
Avodah Zara 3b	159–60

Qur'an

2:248	108
5:48	58
13:3	59
29:46	57
48:26	109
49:13	56–57

www.ingramcontent.com/pod-product-compliance
Lightning Source LLC
Chambersburg PA
CBHW020850160426
43192CB00007B/859